Cupcakes, Pinterest, and Ladyporn

CUPCAKES, PINTEREST, and LADYPORN

Feminized Popular Culture in the Early Twenty-First Century

edited by
ELANA LEVINE

UNIVERSITY OF ILLINOIS PRESS
Urbana, Chicago, and Springfield

Manufactured in the United States of America
1 2 3 4 5 C P 5 4 3 2
∞ This book is printed on acid-free paper.

Library of Congress Cataloging-in-Publication Data
Cupcakes, pinterest, and ladyporn : feminized popular
culture in the early twenty-first century / edited by Elana
Levine.
    pages   cm. — (Feminist media studies)
Includes bibliographical references and index.
ISBN 978-0-252-03957-7 (cloth : alk. paper)
ISBN 978-0-252-08108-8 (pbk. : alk. paper)
ISBN 978-0-252-09766-9 (e-book)
1. Sex role. 2. Popular culture. 3. Feminism. 4. Women in
popular culture. 5. Women and mass media.
I. Levine, Elana, 1970–
HQ1075.C86   2015
305.3—dc23   2015004609

Contents

Acknowledgments

My greatest appreciation goes to this volume's contributors, who were not only willing to share their impressive research but were prompt, responsive, and always pleasurable to work with. Thanks also to Ron Becker and Michael Z. Newman, important sounding boards for me as I developed this project, and to Rick Popp, for his engaged inquiries about its progress. Carol Stabile was such an enthusiastic supporter; I'm honored to be included in the Feminist Media Studies series she edits. I am grateful to the anonymous manuscript readers who advised the contributors and me in making this book as strong as possible. Larin McLaughlin, Dawn Durante, and Amanda Wicks were helpful and supportive in their editorial duties at the press. Thanks to all of the above for helping to make my vision of this project such an exciting reality.

Cupcakes, Pinterest, and Ladyporn

Introduction

Feminized Popular Culture
in the Early Twenty-first Century

ELANA LEVINE

Picking up a gossip magazine to read the latest on that reality celebrity divorce, entering pregnancy symptoms into a smartphone app, searching social media for recipes and fashion blogs for clothing inspiration while downloading best-selling erotic romance fiction to an e-reader. The cultural products targeted to and experienced primarily by women have proliferated in the early twenty-first century. With the expansion of media into digital realms and the ever-further segregation of media users into specialized niches, the early twenty-first century has offered up a broad array of popular spaces identified culturally as feminine. That such sites are often denigrated by the culture at large further signifies their feminization. Whether by dismissive naming—*chick flicks*, *mommy blogs*, *ladyporn*—or by the general derision with which they are treated, feminized popular culture is often constructed as lightweight, frivolous, and excessively emotional. Yet a serious consideration of feminized popular culture—of that which is so readily disregarded as fluff or so eagerly co-opted as a commercial gold mine—offers compelling insights into our culture's most passionately consumed products. It also helps us to understand the ways such products speak to, and about, the broad category of beings identified by the terms *feminine*, *female*, and *woman*. *Cupcakes, Pinterest, and Ladyporn* is centrally concerned with forms of early-twenty-first-century popular culture that are strongly associated with femininity—the social and economic forces that create such culture, the ways these cultural products speak to and about feminine identity, and the ways that audiences, readers, and users engage with and experience this culture.

In the United States and much of the western world throughout most of the twentieth century, a small number of sites were commonly understood as feminine cultural spaces—women's magazines, women's films and chick flicks, television soap operas, romance novels. These forms were not important to all women, nor were women their only audiences, but in a culture oriented largely around mass-targeted products and narrow conceptions of appropriate gender roles, these sites helped to define what identities such as feminine, female, and woman meant. The interventions of feminism, multiculturalism, and lesbian, gay, bisexual, and transgender rights in the late-twentieth-century United States shook up expectations about gender in numerous respects, leading some popular culture to expand or shift the ways it spoke to and about gendered identities, a process that continued into the new century. Meanwhile, the technological innovations of digital media have altered the ways in which people engage with and experience popular forms, and the economic imperatives of the culture industries have driven the proliferation of products around which demographically specific groups congregate. Socially, politically, technologically, and economically, the early twenty-first century has seen marked changes from earlier eras, even as long-standing forces such as patriarchy and capitalism have persisted.

These contextual developments have led to changes in popular media, as some of the earlier media so central to feminized popular culture have declined in prominence, popularity, and profitability and new forms have emerged. While print magazines have taken multiple hits to their economic viability, websites and blogs often speak to similar concerns, whether those of celebrity gossip or of fashion and beauty culture. The number of daytime soap operas airing in the United States has been drastically reduced, but the interpersonal dramas playing out in social media and "docu-soap" reality programs have generated some of the same kinds of narrative and affective appeals. Acknowledging such shifts is important to understanding early-twenty-first-century culture, but *Cupcakes, Pinterest, and Ladyporn* is concerned with much more than documenting the proliferation of new feminized cultural products. In the pages to follow, the contributors examine the logics of feminized popular culture in the early twenty-first century, seeking to understand the economic, technological, representational, and experiential dimensions of some of the cultural products and phenomena that speak most overtly to and about the feminine.[1] What makes the feminized popular culture of the early twenty-first century distinctive? How does it differ from earlier forms and how might it speak to audiences' needs, interests, and desires? Through their engagement with feminized cultural forms, the chapters in this book explore what femininity has come to mean in the early twenty-first century.

Studying Feminized Popular Culture

Feminized popular culture was once a key object of analysis for media and cultural studies, and especially for the feminist scholars whose work propelled the establishment of these academic fields. In foundational scholarship such as Tania Modleski's *Loving with a Vengeance: Mass-produced Fantasies for Women*, Ien Ang's *Watching* Dallas: *Soap Opera and the Melodramatic Imagination*, and Angela McRobbie's *Feminism and Youth Culture: From* Jackie *to* Just Seventeen, the pioneers of these fields sought to understand the pleasures and the problems of such cultural products as romance novels, soap operas, and teen girl magazines for their feminized readership.[2] Instead of wholly condemning these popular forms as duping women and girls into patriarchal passivity, these scholars identified what made these cultural experiences pleasurable and compelling. They sought to understand the social and political contexts within which feminized audiences gravitated to such texts, and sometimes turned to those audiences themselves to give voice to this brand of feminine cultural experience. Alongside such trailblazers as Janice Radway's *Reading the Romance: Women, Patriarchy, and Popular Culture* and Jacqueline Bobo's *Black Women as Cultural Readers*, this earlier generation of work understood feminized cultural forms as sites of hegemonic negotiation between the demands of patriarchy and the needs and desires of women.[3] Such work validated the significance of frequently delegitimated cultural products while seeking to understand how they may have at once reinforced patriarchy and opened the door to feminist empowerment. In the contradictory nature of feminized popular culture, such work discovered, was a crystallization of that which makes all popular culture a site of struggle over power.

This impressive tradition of feminist scholarship on feminized cultural forms had a robust intellectual life from the late 1970s through the mid-1990s, when these key works were published. Since that time, however, feminist approaches to media and culture have turned in new directions, with only sporadic attention to feminized culture from these nuanced perspectives.[4] More recent feminist scholarship has tended to focus on an expanded arena of inquiry, attending to masculinized cultural realms, to alternative and/or explicitly feminist cultural spheres, and to the ways in which gender matters in cultural spaces not necessarily gendered in and of themselves. Similarly, not all attention to feminized cultural products foregrounds their gender politics, as industrial and production-oriented analyses, for example, have been applied to these sites.[5]

The turn away from examinations of feminized popular culture has multiple causes, some of which are a welcome broadening of the field. Yet these developments can suggest that scholarship on gender and feminized forms is an interest belonging in the past, rather than an ongoing concern. In part, the assumption that we know all we need to about the gender politics of feminized forms is a product of shifting conceptions of femininity and of women. The influence of poststructuralist thought and the interventions of third-world feminists, feminists of color, queer theorists, and transgender theorists have fundamentally challenged our ability to talk about "woman" in any unified way. Queer and transgender theories in particular have made both femininity and masculinity categories that can be transgressive rather than normative. If feminist scholars once conceptualized femininity as a construction of a male-dominated society and popular culture as a space wherein women are trained to take on that construction—and sometimes to challenge it, queer and transgender theorists understand the feminine and the masculine as having much more disruptive potential, and as being but two iterations of many gendered (and transgendered) identities.[6] As a result, the differences among women and the range of potential conceptions of femininity loom larger than any universal definition can contain, sometimes paralyzing our ability to talk about—or to advocate for—women in any coherent way. Poststructuralist and queer feminists, however, point us to the utility of focusing on the *categories* of woman and of femininity (and masculinity), on unearthing the ways in which the criteria and rules through which these categories get defined take shape, as well as the ways these categories work to delimit and exclude.[7] Keeping our focus on femininity as one form of gender expression—a trait that a range of sexed bodies may possess, or perform—also allows for the recognition of and respect for the differences between real human beings and their experiences of gender. *Cupcakes, Pinterest, and Ladyporn* is focused upon the ways that the category of woman gets defined, shaped, and experienced through that labeled as feminine. Because early-twenty-first-century U.S.-centric popular culture still tends to construct femininity as a cis-gendered set of traits, many of these analyses center on that particular construction. Still, moments of queer disruption can be found even in the relatively mainstream spaces the contributors examine, testifying to the multiple meanings of femininity across cultural sites.

The influences of poststructuralism, multiculturalism, and queer and transgender theory have been progressive shifts in intellectual life. But much more troubling developments in the social, political, and cultural mainstream have appeared alongside such shifts, developments that also may help to explain the limited attention to feminized popular culture in recent scholarship. The cultural formation typically identified as postfeminism has garnered an increasingly prominent and entrenched status, one akin to a hegemonic common sense of early-twenty-first-century western societies. Postfeminist culture is one in which feminism is painted as passé, as an historically specific outlook that once made an important intervention, but is now no longer necessary. Postfeminist logic sees gender equality as having been accomplished, freeing up women to choose for themselves that which they most desire, both professionally and personally. That the "empowerment" of "choice" so heralded in postfeminist culture is in fact limited to a narrow range of privileged women is ignored; these postfeminist traits are naturalized as universal, which in part accounts for their power. The postfeminist context, paired as it often is with a similarly constructed postracial perspective which sees racial inequality as likewise in the past, is crucial to understanding many forms of feminized popular culture in the early twenty-first century, as chapters in this volume examine.

However, postfeminist culture has arguably also had an impact on feminist cultural scholarship. Postfeminist thinking suggests that attending to gender-specificity amounts to a sort of grudge holding, a refusal to let go of "old" categories of discrimination that are no longer relevant. Indeed, in a postfeminist culture, paying attention to the specificity of gendered experience is sometimes seen as *reproducing*, rather than challenging, old-fashioned sexism, as seen, for example, in cultural debates over whether it is sexist to identify the social bookmarking site, Pinterest, as feminine.[8] This cultural sensibility has left some feminist scholars, particularly those of younger generations who have come of age in a postfeminist context, disinclined to consider cultural products and experiences as distinctly gendered. Analyzing representations of gender in popular culture remains a valued project, but conceiving of the ways in which gender is implicated in the production and reception of cultural forms is a less comfortable endeavor. Because the postfeminist context that encourages such perspectives arises alongside poststructuralist challenges to the notion of "woman" as a unified category and queer reimaginings of gender normativity, it is understandably confusing to try to talk about something like "women's popular culture" or feminized cultural spaces in ways that reject dismissive characterizations of these forms while still engaging critically with their limitations and pleasures.

Yet *Cupcakes, Pinterest, and Ladyporn* takes up this challenge by engaging with feminized forms in just these ways, offering an injection of energy into a lapsed area of inquiry, reviving a tradition foundational to feminist media and cultural studies but updating it for the early twenty-first century. This updating takes place with attention to early twenty-first century cases and with an understanding of the attendant social, political, and cultural contexts within which we experience feminized popular culture. Delimiting the cultural products and experiences classified as feminine and popular in an age of audience fragmentation and user-generated content is something of a challenge, as our media culture is premised upon the sort of individual tailoring that threatens to make the very notion of a collective social experience moot. Yet the contributors to this volume identify many sites of early-twenty-first-century culture that remain distinctly feminized and meaningfully popular, from celebrity culture to prime-time TV dramas. These sites do not necessarily match up with those examined in earlier generations of scholarship—they do not reach as large an audience, for example—but they are all patronized by significant enough gatherings of people as to be identifiable as more mainstream, more "mass," than as alternative or fringe. And they all remain culturally articulated to feminine interests, concerns, and traits, including those of personal appearance, romantic and familial relationships, and caretaking labor.

This volume also updates past inquiries by examining feminized popular culture with new questions and issues in mind. Earlier generations of scholarship often sought to understand the ways feminized popular culture allowed women fulfilling conventionally feminine roles to negotiate their place within patriarchy and thereby offered an example of the kinds of hegemonic struggles audiences engaged in through their pursuit of popular pleasures. The practice of hegemonic struggle has not changed, but the terms audiences and users struggle within and between have. Long-standing forms of patriarchy, masculinism, and sexism persist, but fewer women fulfill, or seek to fulfill, traditionally feminine roles, such as "housewife." Instead, the influence of postfeminist culture adds a new layer of complication, as expectations for conventional femininity have expanded beyond those of physical appearance and nurturance to include career-oriented success and sexual self-possession.[9]

How do feminized popular culture and the people who engage with it negotiate a world of such demands? How do they grapple with the postfeminist assumption that there is no more inequality at the level of gender, even while many experience such inequalities on a regular basis? How do accompanying pushes toward neoliberal entrepreneurialism and self-help shape the ways femininity is constructed and addressed? How does femininity intersect with other axes of identity, such as race, particularly in a postrace context, when racial inequality—much as gender inequality—is presented by dominant discourses as a relic of the past? While the contributors find many instances of dominant conceptions of gender and race bearing down upon audiences and users, at the same time they have discovered some pushback against the postfeminist and postrace notions that have pervaded the early twenty-first century. In multiple instances, these chapters discover audience and user pleasures in women's connections to other women and in culturally specific representations that indicate cracks in the hegemonic veneer of popular culture. In all cases, the convergence of media-specific shifts toward niche-oriented digital cultures and the broader social and political developments of post–civil rights, postfeminist, and neoliberal environments make for a complex backdrop for exploring the pleasures and perils of feminized popular culture in the early twenty-first century.

What IS Early-Twenty-first-Century Feminized Popular Culture?

Just as feminized cultural products and the outlets through which we access them have proliferated in the early twenty-first century, so too have the ways these products speak to and about femininity. Women of different social positions have long experienced popular culture in distinctive ways, but difference, rather than the unifying sameness of gender, has become all the more prominent an organizing concept in an increasingly niche-ified world. Still, the persistence of gender as a cultural category means that the kinds of popular culture that are typically feminized are no less identifiable than in the past. Sometimes this classification is a product of naming—there is no doubt with whom chick lit or mommy blogs are associated; other times it is a result of cultural assumptions. While celebrity gossip or serialized prime-time TV dramas need not be gendered phenomena, when those cultural sites focus largely upon female figures or display the kinds of circuitous interpersonal conflicts identified as "soapy" they are also classified as feminine. Meanwhile, many sites of masculinized popular culture (such as professional football or "quality" TV dramas) escape gendered labeling. Classification as feminine may denigrate such spheres in the eyes of some, but it can also be an invitation to audiences who take pleasure in feminized traits to find something for themselves therein.

Feminized popular culture in the early twenty-first century has continued to value and foreground those areas of feminized concern that are simultaneously required of women and culturally dismissed as trifling. Whether matters of personal appearance—fashion or nail polish, for example—or of maintaining interpersonal relationships, from the romantic to the maternal, conventionally feminized subjects remain as central to the feminized popular culture of the early twenty-first century as they were to that of the twentieth. Yet the more recent incarnations of such concerns do take on new dimensions. Because the advice and ideas about fashion, or beauty, or personal relationships are as likely to be mediated in horizontal, peer-to-peer versions like the blogs and social media pages of "regular" people as they are to be transmitted in more typically mass-mediated forms, they also have the potential to embrace a wider range of experience and to resist some of the normative assumptions of a strictly top-down media culture. Thus, in her chapter, Michele White explores the ways in which nail polish bloggers interrogate the meanings of femininity when it comes to nail art, negotiating among themselves the fit—or lack thereof—between their own uses of beauty products and the dominant meanings of such practices. Even in the reception of mass-mediated fare, online communities allow for the expression of perspectives once hidden from view. For example, the ways that audiences respond to fictional, "soapy" TV dramas in online communities can reveal how viewers negotiate with media representations in ways specific to their gendered, raced, and classed identities, as Jillian Báez and Kristen J. Warner both examine.

But the feminized popular culture of the early twenty-first century is also identifiable according to newer terms and concerns associated with the feminine, conceptions of what it means to occupy this gendered space in a world altered by feminism. In some such cultural realms, the multitude of pressures placed upon women encouraged to "have it all"—a formulation typically referring to the successful combination of career, personal and family life, and convention-ally attractive physical appearance—has led to a focus on just how to manage such voluminous responsibilities and occasionally to critiques of this very logic. Thus, feminized popular culture of the early twenty-first century has become extraordinarily focused upon labor, upon the multiple forms of work that women in particular are expected to do. Sometimes popular culture can assist with these labors. As Barbara L. Ley examines in her chapter, a growing culture of smart phone apps have been designed to lead expectant women and their male part-ners through the figurative and literal labors of pregnancy, childbirth, and early parenting, promising a means of managing digitally the self- and other-directed care of reproduction. Other times, early-twenty-first-century feminized popular culture tells stories of women struggling to manage these multiple demands, as the docu-soap programming of reality TV foregrounds. Suzanne Leonard and Diane Negra examine the ways that Bethenny Frankel's celebrity brand offers lessons and cautions for feminized labor, while Alice Leppert explores the ways the Kardashians' insistence on the importance of sisterhood serves as both a counterweight and an aid to their brand's example of feminine productivity.

While the threads of conventionally feminine interests and concerns and newer preoccupations like feminine productivity run across many forms of early-twenty-first-century feminized popular culture, *Cupcakes, Pinterest, and Ladyporn* is structured around three broad themes that are especially prominent. The first of these is "Passions." In this section, the contributors analyze a range of cultural spaces in which feminized interests and desires are expressed, explored, and even shaped, often in ways considered extreme or excessive by a dominant culture eager to marginalize the explicitly feminized or the overly associated with emotion, from Melissa A. Click's study of *Fifty Shades of Grey* readership to Erin A. Meyers's take on the draw of celebrity gossip. As a result, here are studies of multiple kinds of fandom and their particular engagements with feminized entertainment. These authors consider the intense feelings of actual audiences, but many also frame those reception practices within the motivations and strategies of the commercial media industries, as in Jillian Báez's exploration of the cable channel, Lifetime, and its changing strategies in figuring itself as "television for women." How do audiences, readers, and users find ways to make mediated content their own, to speak to their most deeply held pleasures and concerns, within a commercialized sphere that is most interested in them as consumers?

Some of these same questions carry over to the second section, structured thematically around "Bodies." While still addressing feminized spheres within which audiences and users are deeply invested, these particular analyses focus on the multiple ways in which the body—its appearance, its health, its expressions of spirituality—is a site of labor and pleasure. Women's bodies have long been understood as central to their very beings, although only those bodies that meet very stringent ideals of femininity are valued in the broader culture. While early-twenty-first-century modes of digital culture perpetuate some of the same limited requirements for femininity, they also demonstrate ways in which users can challenge those limitations. For example, Kyra Hunting examines the world of fashion blogs and focuses on a strain of such blogs that allow users to embrace nonnormative gender presentations. Even in user engagements with mass-mediated culture, however, we can find modes of embodiment that push against dominant strictures of femininity. As Beretta Smith-Shomade explores, black women's somatic engagement with spirituality in key moments of televised gospel and R&B performances allows for a culturally specific, feminized experience of media.

The third thematic section focuses on "Labors." While feminized forms of labor have long been both demanding and dismissed, in the early twenty-first century, new pressures of work and productivity have been especially prominent. This section focuses on cultural products and practices that highlight feminized labor, sometimes offering lessons on how best to "have it all," sometimes presenting cautionary tales, sometimes questioning and challenging the post-feminist and neoliberal imperative to produce a branded, individualized self that has beset women in the early twenty-first century. Suzanne Ferris points out that chick lit offers an inherent critique of women's economic precarity, while Julie Wilson and Emily Chivers Yochim theorize the labors of happiness promised in the feminized, classed, and racialized spheres of Pinterest and mommy blogs. In these five chapters, we see the most dramatic shift from earlier incarnations of feminized popular culture. While women's magazines have long offered how-to content, and fictional narratives have long dramatized the challenges of feminine care work, the early twenty-first century is distinct in its overt attention to negotiating the multiple realms of feminized productivity. Such cultural forms strive to reconcile the ideals of conventional femininity (such as physical appearance and nurturance) with the more conventionally masculinized traits of career ambition and public prominence, all amid a shaky economic climate. As Elizabeth Nathanson's exploration of the popularity of cupcakes illustrates, early-twenty-first-century narratives of feminine success depend upon a tenuous blend of feminized and masculinized characteristics, appealing to audiences not only with this sort of modeling but also with reminders about the ongoing bonds between women. *Cupcakes, Pinterest, and Ladyporn* traces such early-twenty-first-century tensions and the ways they circulate within and alongside more expected popular pleasures. The "labor"-themed chapters are important reminders of the ways popular culture can speak to real needs, even while reinforcing hegemonic ideals.

What follows is an exciting investigation of a feminized popular culture both continuous with and diverging from earlier forms. While the chapters take on a range of popular texts and practices, the diversity of femininity makes it impossible for one volume to consider all dimensions of its popular circulation. Because *Cupcakes, Pinterest, and Ladyporn* is specifically focused on cultural spaces that are feminized in the culture at large, there are many aspects of women's cultural pleasures, and of cultural pleasures that speak to traits of femininity, that are not explored, such as women's participation in masculinized cultural spaces such as video gaming, or feminist DIY cultures, or male fandoms of feminized TV dramas. But interrogating that which is broadly identified as feminine allows for a focus upon the power and appeal of feminized forms in a historical period in which conceptions of femininity, not to mention means of experiencing popular culture, are in a state of flux. By looking closely at that which culture so often denigrates and dismisses, *Cupcakes, Pinterest, and Ladyporn* tells us a great deal about a cultural sphere in which passionate investments impact our senses of ourselves and others, shaping conceptions of the feminine in ways that affect all gendered beings.

Notes

1. While not exclusively focused on American culture, most of the contributors write from within the United States and focus on phenomena originally created in English. Because the culture of Hollywood and the United States more generally is so globally influential, the contributors' perspectives often apply beyond U.S. borders. Yet the volume offers a necessarily partial picture of early-twenty-first-century feminized popular culture in being U.S.–centric.

2. Tania Modleski, *Loving with a Vengeance: Mass Produced Fantasies for Women*, 2nd edition (New York: Routledge, 2007). Ien Ang, *Watching Dallas: Soap Opera and the Melodramatic Imagination* (New York: Routledge, 1985). Angela McRobbie, *Feminism and Youth Culture: From Jackie to Just Seventeen*, 2nd edition (New York: Routledge, 2000).

3. Janice A. Radway, *Reading the Romance: Women, Patriarchy, and Popular Literature*, 2nd edition (Chapel Hill: University of North Carolina Press, 1991). Jacqueline Bobo, *Black Women as Cultural Readers* (New York: Columbia University Press, 1995).

4. This is not to deny that some such scholarship is still being produced, including Stacey Abbott and Deborah Jermyn, eds., *Falling in Love Again: Romantic Comedy in Contemporary Cinema* (London: I. B. Tauris, 2009); Melissa A. Click, Jennifer Stevens Aubrey, and Elizabeth Behm-Morawitz, eds., *Bitten by Twilight: Youth Culture, Media, and the Vampire Franchise* (New York: Peter Lang, 2010); Suzanne Ferriss and Mallory Young, eds., *Chick Lit: The New Women's Fiction* (New York: Routledge, 2005); Stephanie Harzewski, *Chick Lit and Postfeminism* (Charlottesville: University of Virginia Press, 2010); Hilary Radner, *Neo-Feminist Cinema: Girly Films, Chick Flicks, and Consumer Culture* (New York: Routledge, 2010). Perhaps most prominent has been scholarship focused on the popular culture of girls, such as Anita Harris, ed., *All about the Girl: Culture, Power and Identity* (London: Routledge, 2004).

5. For example, see Elana Levine, "Toward a Paradigm for Media Production Research: Behind the Scenes at *General Hospital*," *Critical Studies in Media Communication* 18 (March 2001): 66–82; Brooke Erin Duffy, *Remake Remodel: Women's Magazines in the Digital Age* (Urbana: University of Illinois Press, 2013); Erin A. Meyers, *Dishing Dirt in the Digital Age: Celebrity Gossip Blogs and Participatory Media Culture* (New York: Peter Lang, 2013).

6. On the intersection of gender and transgender studies, see Anne Enke, ed., *Transfeminist Perspectives: In and beyond Transgender and Gender Studies* (Philadelphia: Temple University Press, 2012). On the relationship of femininity to transgender identity, see Julia Serrano, "Reclaiming Femininity," in *Transfeminist Perspectives*, 170–183.

7. See, for example, Judith P. Butler, *Gender Trouble: Feminism and the Subversion of Identity* (New York: Routledge, 1990) and Denise Riley, *Am I That Name?: Feminism and the Category of Women in History* (Minneapolis: University of Minnesota Press, 2003).

8. See, for example, Mary Elizabeth Williams, "Pinterest's Gender Trouble," *Salon*, May 2, 2012, http://www.salon.com/2012/05/02/pinterests_gender_trouble/ (accessed December 22, 2014).

9. For a useful overview of postfeminist culture, see Rosalind Gill, "Postfeminist Media Culture: Elements of a Sensibility," *European Journal of Cultural Studies* 10 (2007): 147–166.

PART I

Passions

CHAPTER 1

Fifty Shades of Postfeminism

Contextualizing Readers' Reflections on the Erotic Romance Series

MELISSA A. CLICK

The *Fifty Shades of Grey* (*Fifty Shades*) book series has dominated best-seller lists and sold more than 70 million copies worldwide since Vintage Books, a division of Random House, published the series in April 2012.[1] Written by Erika Leonard, a British, middle-aged television executive using the pseudonym E. L. James, the three-book series began as *Twilight* fan fiction (a fan's rewritten version of the popular young adult vampire romance series by Stephenie Meyer). Initially called *Master of the Universe*, the series was released in August 2009 on fanfiction.net. *Master of the Universe* was so popular that the author removed the story's most obvious ties to *Twilight* and reworked the story; this new version was published in May 2011 by the Australian Writer's Coffee Shop, a print-on-demand company.[2] The series received many positive reviews from online sites like goodreads.com, which drew the attention of Hollywood executives interested in buying the series' film rights. Leonard quickly found an agent, who helped negotiate the sale of her story to Universal/Focus Features for a rumored $5 million and to Vintage Books for worldwide distribution.[3] The series' unusual path to print and the bestseller list has raised questions about possible new models for the ailing publishing industry—but it is the series' content that has drawn the most attention.

Fifty Shades chronicles the love affair between inexperienced and naive virgin Anastasia ("Ana") Steele, a 21-year-old college student, and Christian Grey, a wealthy entrepreneur in his late twenties whose BDSM (bondage, discipline, sadism, and masochism) practice is tied to a dark past. The erotic romance's popularity with adult women, and the series' graphic descriptions of Christian and Ana's sexual encounters, has led to its frequent description as ladyporn and mommyporn. Although these flip labels trivialize women's interests in the series, they point to one of the series' major controversies: the appeal of the unequal sexual relationship to female audiences. Writing about the series in a contentious cover story in *Newsweek*, New York University professor Katie Roiphe argues that the series' popularity suggests that contemporary women, who experience more power and freedom than their mothers and grandmothers, have a secret wish to be spanked: "It may be that, for some, the more theatrical fantasies of sexual surrender offer a release, a vacation, an escape from the dreariness and hard work of equality."[4] Roiphe's titillating suggestion that *Fifty Shades'* representation of a dominant-submissive sexual relationship has become "the modern woman's bedroom fantasy" may have sold copies of *Newsweek*, but it fails to consider what feminist cultural studies research has already shown about the blending of patriarchal domination and love in women's romance reading, precisely that, "The romance's preoccupation with male brutality is an attempt to understand the meaning of an event that has become almost unavoidable in the real world. The romance may express misogynistic attitudes not because women share them but because they increasingly need to know how to deal with them."[5]

In response to Roiphe's suggestions, I argue that to understand *Fifty Shades'* popularity, it is necessary to understand the postfeminist environment in which early-twenty-first-century western women live. Angela McRobbie describes postfeminism as "a process by which feminist gains of the 1970s and 1980s are actively and relentlessly undermined."[6] Rosalind Gill asserts the importance of understanding contemporary media culture, which she argues has a "postfeminist sensibility" composed of a complex mixture of feminist and antifeminist themes. Among the features of a postfeminist sensibility is the increasing sexualization of culture, or "the extraordinary proliferation of discourses about sex and sexuality across all media forms . . . as well as to the increasingly frequent erotic presentation of girls,' women's, and (to a lesser extent) men's bodies in public spaces."[7] Susan Douglas also explores the sexualization of media culture and suggests that media texts like *Cosmopolitan* and *Sex and the City*, and music videos produced by sexualized celebrities like Britney Spears, teach

> that it is precisely through women's calculated deployment of their faces, bodies, attire, and sexuality that they gain and enjoy true power—power that is fun, that men will not resent, and indeed will embrace. True power

here has nothing to do with economic independence or professional achievement (that's a given): it has to do with getting men to lust after you and other women to envy you.[8]

The impact of this postfeminist sexualized media culture on everyday attitudes and behaviors has also been chronicled in more mainstream venues, like Kathleen Bogle's *Hooking Up* and Carmine Sarracino and Kevin Scott's *The Porning of America*.[9] Bogle suggests that "hooking up" or casual, nondating sex, changes the previously normative pattern of dating before having sex, "With hooking up, the sexual interaction comes first; going on a date comes later, or not at all for those who never make it to the point of 'going out' or at least 'hanging out.'"[10] Sarracino and Scott argue that porn has become so absorbed into daily life that it impacts sexual practice: "Simple male-female couplings begin to seem old-fashioned, quaint, like holding hands on a porch swing. . . . [T]hreesomes of various combinations, bondage and domination, sadomasochism, group sex, public sex, and so on, become the new standards of sexual excitement."[11] Both demonstrate that the sexual environment has been changing in the late twentieth and early twenty-first centuries, and that women have had to adjust to new sexual standards and expectations.

It is in the context of this postfeminist sexualized culture that I examine the meaning of *Fifty Shades of Grey* to the women who read it. Like the *Twilight* series upon which it is based, *Fifty Shades* has resonated deeply with readers around the world, and although the popular press has endlessly ruminated about the meaning of the series' popularity, no study has yet explored what *Fifty Shades* means to readers. To investigate *Fifty Shades'* appeal, I interviewed 36 readers and grounded their reflections with feminist media research that explores women's use of romance reading. In the process, I explore the series' messages about gender roles, romance, and sexuality, bringing crucial attention to the cultural and social aspects of the *Fifty Shades* phenomenon. Overall, I argue *Fifty Shades'* appeal is rooted in women's use of the series' recurrent themes of fantasy, romance, and sex to make sense of the sexualized cultural environment in which they are immersed.

Understanding Romance Reading

Although more has been written on the content of romance novels than on the people who read them, scholarship on romance readers has been a foundational component of feminist cultural studies.[12] Such scholarship has critically engaged with feminist debates over romance reading, female sexuality, and pornography,[13] and offered compelling responses to Carole S. Vance's insistence that to better understand the relationships between pleasure and danger, we need to ask, "[H]ow does the audience perceive sexual representations?"[14] Janice A. Radway's *Reading the Romance* is the most influential example. Using ethnographic methods, Radway explored why women in the suburbs of the pseudonymous midwestern city, Smithton, read romances and the kinds of romances they preferred. The Smithton readers described that their favorite novels contain an emphasis on the development of a loving relationship between an intelligent heroine and strong hero who comes to realize his need for and dependence upon the heroine. They preferred to read stories about heroes who are both gentle and tender and to imagine the details (rather than read a thorough accounting) of the couple's sexual encounters. Radway argues that what women most want out of romance reading is "the opportunity to project themselves into the story, to become the heroine, and thus to share her surprise and slowly awakening pleasure at being so closely watched by someone who finds her valuable and worthy of love."[15] Radway's study also demonstrated that women enjoy reading romances because the act of reading allowed them a quiet time and space away from their families to relax, escape, and recuperate from the demands of their daily lives.

Although Radway's work on romance readers has been critiqued, her study usefully complicated previous feminist work that, primarily through textual analysis, disdained romance reading for its assumedly negative impact on the women who enjoyed it.[16] Radway refuses to offer a decisive conclusion about the role of romance reading in women's lives; instead, she suggests that there are competing forces at play in the meaning of the act of reading romances (which she understands to be somewhat resistive of patriarchy) and the meaning of the texts (which she asserts uphold patriarchal values).

In her work on readers of erotic romances, *The Romance Revolution*, Carol Thurston is more celebratory of the impact of women's romance reading. Thurston's work, which traces the emergence of the erotic romance genre in the United States between 1972 and 1982, is based upon a content analysis of more than 100 romance novels and 600 surveys with erotic romance readers in 1982 and 1985.[17] Grounding her arguments about erotic romances in the impact of feminist politics and scholarship on the changing sexual norms of the 1970s and early 1980s, Thurston argues: "[T]he huge increase in romance reading over the past decade and more took place coincidentally with changing lifestyles, which have put increasing pressures and stress on women. . . . [T]his increase occurred during a time when women have been exploring and learning about themselves as sexual beings."[18] Thus, Thurston sees erotic romance reading as a feminist-influenced, if not fully feminist, practice that engages messages about women's sexual freedom and packages them into a romantic story.

Although the sexual nature of erotic romance is at the forefront of Thurston's analysis, her work on erotic romance aligns in many ways with Radway's work on romance readers. For example, like Radway, Thurston found that erotic romance readers primarily read for entertainment. Thurston also found that erotic romance readers consciously used the novels' female heroines to "[try] out their own ideas about interacting with the hero and [resolve] conflict, free of the constraints of dangers of the real world."[19] Thus, erotic romances, like romances generally, allow readers to imagine how they would navigate the situations in which the novels' heroines find themselves.

In contrast to Radway's insistence that the practice and the content of romance reading are at odds with each other, Thurston emphasizes the significant cultural contributions of the empowering messages about sexuality in erotic romances. In particular, Thurston demonstrates the importance of the novels' impact on readers' sexual practices by highlighting readers' reports of using erotic romances "for sexual information and ideas, to create a receptive-to-sex frame of mind, and even to achieve arousal."[20] Such findings ground Thurston's insistence that erotic romances are "one of the most effective channels for communicating feminist ideas to the broad base of women who must be reached if the women's movement is to continue to effect significant social change."[21] Although Thurston is more celebratory of romance reading than Radway, her insistence that erotic romances can have positive impact on readers' lives is an assertion that, in conjunction with Radway's findings, can offer support to the present examination of *Fifty Shades* readers, which endeavors to examine how and why readers enjoyed the series.

There are few other sustained analyses of adult women's romance reading in the feminist cultural studies literature, in part because subsequent feminist scholarship on female audiences continued with a focus on a range of different feminized media texts, like women's magazines and televised soap operas.[22] Additionally, new subgenres of women's fiction, such as chick lit, which became popular in the 1990s, became hot topics for scholarly exploration because of their reworkings of familiar romantic frameworks. Although there are no published studies of chick-lit readers, the genre is worth mentioning in relation to *Fifty Shades of Grey* because chick lit has "transformed the dominant romantic formula of the Harlequin," reworking it for a postfeminist context.[23] This is not to argue that *Fifty Shades* is a chick-lit series—it is not—but it does contain many of the postfeminist themes present in the genre. In fact, *Fifty Shades*, as a rewritten version of Stephenie Meyer's *Twilight*, is a descendant of what

Stephanie Harzewski calls "paranormal chick lit," a lucrative offshoot of the chick-lit genre.[24]

Chick lit is characterized as a semiautobiographical, confessional, humorous style of writing that, while romance-focused, emphasizes the ironic culture of single life for urban, working women in their twenties and thirties. Shaped by two of its most famous titles, Helen Fielding's *Bridget Jones's Diary* and Candace Bushnell's *Sex and the City*, Stephanie Harzewski suggests chick lit is "a postfeminist alternative to the Harlequin."[25] Chick lit is recognized for its assumedly "realistic" portrayal of dating norms in the early twenty-first century, and for its portrayal of female protagonists as sexual agents with "a number of sexual partners and experiences."[26] As one of the first genres to be labeled "postfeminist," chick lit is characterized by a complex and contradictory relationship with feminist values. Harzewski concludes that the genre ultimately positions itself against feminism, painting feminism as "an outdated style and misread as a bilious monolith, its strident tendencies embarrassing and not fully compatible with chick lit's ties to the values of romance fiction and its embrace of commodities, especially beauty and fashion culture."[27]

Although both sales and best-seller lists demonstrate that romance overall remains an incredibly popular genre,[28] market saturation and the increasing popularity of other genres have led to changes in the chick-lit genre, resulting in the production of romantic stories that lack the irony and self-reflexivity of its earlier work.[29] These recent transformations in the popular romance genre demonstrate that some romance narratives have changed significantly since Radway's and Thurston's explorations, and *Fifty Shades* exemplifies the ways contemporary novels blend familiar romantic formulas with postfeminist elements. Given this shifting context, it is especially important to evaluate how the postfeminist sensibility that has altered some instances of the romance genre, as well as the cultural milieu of the early twenty-first century, has impacted readers' uses of erotic romance.

To explore how *Fifty Shades of Grey*, written and read in a postfeminist context, resonates with readers' lives, I conducted 8 group interviews in April and May of 2013 with 36 *Fifty Shades* readers recruited from a midsize, midwestern college town. The interviewees were female, White (29), and heterosexual (33). Their ages ranged from 18 to 55, with an average age of 27. The majority of participants were single (28), had no children (26), and did not identify as feminist (20). All had read the series' three books; many considered themselves to be fans of the series (23), although a majority stated that they would not like to have a relationship like Ana and Christian's (23). To preserve the participants' confidentiality, all names have been changed.

The group interviews lasted from 90 to 120 minutes. Each interview typically began with participants' discussions of when, why, and how they read the books. Following this, participants were asked to describe and evaluate the series, its characters, and Ana and Christian's relationship. Finally, the participants were asked to discuss how the book series impacted their relationships with friends, family, and romantic partners and the series' larger impact on American culture. In what follows, I discuss the major themes that emerged from the focus group conversations I had with *Fifty Shades* readers.

Reading *Fifty Shades of Grey*

The conversations I had with *Fifty Shades* readers give necessary perspective to the series' popularity. In line with Radway's and Thurston's scholarship, *Fifty Shades* readers suggest that their interest in the series has less to do with wanting to be in dominating sexual relationships, and more to do with wanting to reflect on their perspectives on sex and their experiences in romantic relationships with men. In other words, the series gives readers the opportunity to make sense of the sexualized postfeminist environment in which they live. In this section, I discuss why the interview participants read *Fifty Shades*, how they felt about its portrayals of sex, and how reading the series impacted their sexual attitudes and behaviors.

As I write in November 2013, *Fifty Shades of Grey* is number three on the *New York Times* Paperback Trade Fiction Best Sellers list, and has spent 85 weeks total on the list (the second and third books in the series are at numbers 6 and 7, and have spent 82 and 81 weeks on the list respectively). From *Saturday Night Live* and off-Broadway parodies, to entertainment news about the *Fifty Shades* movie and licensed lingerie and sex toy collections, the series has demonstrated an overwhelming and enduring popularity. The majority of the *Fifty Shades* readers with whom I spoke reported that the buzz around the series enticed them to read the books. Avery (24, White, single), for instance, who had been travelling for work when *Fifty Shades* first became popular, recounted, "Every plane I was on, which was like four or five a week, women everywhere had *Fifty Shades of Grey* . . . so I decided to read the first one." Lily (22, White, single) was drawn to the series by some of the blogs she regularly reads, "My feminist blogs had been talking about it over and over again and I didn't even know what it was, so I bought the first book." Grace was persuaded to read the series after getting an unusual recommendation from a friend, "I started reading them because my best friend who does not read anything longer than a paragraph started reading it . . . so if she is reading it, it has to be good."

In line with *Fifty Shades'* overwhelming popularity, the interview participants reported a strong pull to the books. Lauren (23, White, single) shared, "Every free minute that I had I was reading: on lunch break, after work, before work, sometimes I would read it when I was driving." Sheila's (51, White, married) friend loaded the books on her phone, and after that she recounted, "I couldn't put my phone down . . . I read them every chance I could . . . my phone was on all the time, I had to carry my charger around." Chloe (18, White, single), who was initially convinced the books would not appeal to her, bought only the first book despite insistence from others that she ought to buy all three. She reported, "I finished the first one and I've never driven so fast to the bookstore in my life."

The strong reactions readers have had to *Fifty Shades* have led many to ponder the series' appeal—numerous stories in popular press outlets from the *Christian Science Monitor* to CNN and Roiphe's *Newsweek* cover story speculate about the answer to this question. Despite popular insistence that the series' depictions of sex are the foundation of *Fifty Shades'* appeal, the readers with whom I spoke suggested the sex was only the initial draw to the books. Thus, readers like Kaylee (19, White, single), who were not frequent erotic romance readers, picked the books up to read the sex. She remarked, "I think I liked it for the shock value, the sex just kept shocking me because I never read anything like that before, so I just wanted to keep seeing what was going to happen." But many of the readers shared that other elements of the book were more appealing; Chloe asserted, for instance, "I think the scandalous stuff got people to pick it up, but the rest of it is what made people keep reading."

The interview participants asserted that one of the series' most engaging elements involves the development of Ana and Christian's relationship. This finding is in line with the preferences of the Smithton women Radway interviewed, who "placed heavy emphasis on the importance of development in the romance's portrayal of love."[30] Thus, for the readers with whom I spoke, the series would not have been as appealing without its romantic development. Bailey (38, White, married), insisted that "[The sex] pulls you in but if you didn't have [love] it wouldn't be as interesting." Deemphasizing the erotic elements of the books, Brooklyn (20, Black, single) described *Fifty Shades* as, "Different . . . but at the end of the day it's a love story."

The story line these *Fifty Shades* readers found most compelling involved Christian Grey, who initiated a sexual relationship with Ana Steele through a contract outlining the BDSM relationship he would like to have with her. Shocked by Christian's interest in having such a formalized sexual relationship without romantic aims, these readers were driven to discover if and how

Christian would change from a character who is, in Faith's (55, White, single) words, "broken," to a loving, reciprocating, romantic partner. Kennedy (36, White, married) shared, "Just seeing him change so much, and he seemed to get more tender . . . that's what kept me going was seeing his change." Audrey (24, White, single) emphasized that this story line was more compelling than the sex, "Yeah it's hot . . . but I could also see a lot of women liked the books because Ana was able to . . . turn [Christian] into more of a loving individual."

Underscoring the fact that the sexual encounters in *Fifty Shades* were not what sustained their interest in the series, many readers described that the sex became boring as the story progressed. Kaylee recounted, "It started to be to the point where the sex scenes didn't have that much effect on me anymore and I was just like 'OK, can I have more plot with the characters?'" Such comments about *Fifty Shades'* depictions of sex are driven by the readers' desire to know how Ana and Christian's relationship would evolve. Carrie's (20, Black, single) statement illustrates this: "There were points where I was like, 'Oh my god, seriously, another sex scene? I just wanna know how you guys are gonna work this out.'"

While these comments demonstrate that readers enthusiastically consumed the *Fifty Shades* series in large part to follow the development of Ana and Christian's romantic relationship, the interview participants' emphasis on romance obscures their feelings about Ana and Christian's sexual relationship. Thurston emphasizes that romance and sex are interwoven in erotic romance and stresses that the development of romantic relationships frequently heightens readers' sexual pleasure, "This time factor . . . speaks to what many women believe to be a fundamental difference between pornography and erotica—the encounter versus the relationship—and ultimately to why one is sexually stimulating to most women while the other is usually not."[31] In the next section I explore more fully how the interview participants responded to Ana and Christian's sexual relationship.

Vanilla Sex and the Red Room of Pain

When Radway asked the Smithton readers to describe the qualities they like least in romances, their most common answers suggested a dislike of violent sexual relations, specifically rape and physical brutality. Radway argues that readers disliked these characteristics because they impede the development of the romantic relationship between the two main characters: "They cannot understand how a heroine finds it within herself to ignore such an event, forgive the man who violated her, and then grow to love him."[32] Thurston's research with erotica readers prompted her to critique the popular assumption that readers' interests in historical erotica, or "bodice rippers," meant that they had rape fantasies. She argued that, "To describe the bodice rippers as purveyors of the myth that women (heroines) wish to be raped, as some critics have done, is evidence of the yawning gap between two realities—that of readers contrasted with most critics."[33] Understanding readers' motivations for reading and preferences for specific kinds of stories is particularly important in the context of the *Fifty Shades* series because a number of critiques of the novels express concern about the book's portrayal of emotional and sexual violence.[34] Although these criticisms raise important questions about the series' romantic and sexual messages, it is necessary to ground concerns about impact with audience studies because, as Radway's and Thurston's studies demonstrate, readers' interest in depictions of aggressive sexuality are often quite complex.

The *Fifty Shades* readers I interviewed made distinctions about the kinds of sex they enjoyed reading in the series. They separated the sex that took place in Christian's "red room of pain" (described as "fucking"), where he practiced BDSM, from the sex in Christian's bedroom (described as "lovemaking" or "vanilla"), a space he initially designated as off limits to Ana. Isabella's (23, White, single) description is exemplary, "I feel like the red room of pain is the f-word and his bedroom was lovemaking . . . his personality just changed when he walked in the red room, his dominant side was on." The majority of these *Fifty Shades* readers indicated that they preferred the scenarios involving lovemaking to those involving fucking. Melanie (33, White, married) asserted, "I didn't like any of the sex stuff that was in the red room of pain . . . but the parts when they were laying in bed together and [were] all of sudden passionate or something, that's what I liked." Mia agreed, "My favorite sex scenes were the vanilla ones." Violet (31, White, married) shared that her favorite sexual moments in the book involved very little sex at all, "My favorite sex moment of the entire series is when she has him on the couch and she tells him they're just gonna make out and he's like 'I don't know what making out is' and she's like, 'we're just gonna kiss and . . . that's all we're gonna do' and he's like, 'no sex? I don't understand why we're doing this then.'"

In opposition to Roiphe's suggestion that *Fifty Shades* readers are interested in the series for its "fantasies of submission," the readers with whom I spoke expressed anxiety over the aggressive moments in the series, particularly the sexual encounters that readers felt were motivated by Christian's desire to punish or discipline Ana. Reagan (23, White, single), describing her reaction to some of these scenes, shared, "I was more worried for [Ana], not excited for her, more like, 'oh god, is she gonna be ok?'" Like many readers, Avery made distinctions between arousing sex and disturbing sex: "I think there were some scenes, and even some scenes in the red room of pain, that were enticing to read, or exciting, but it was when things got—again, it's like that level of too far, that level of controlling and punishment—that I was like, 'I don't want to read this anymore.'"

This discomfort, and a particular unease with Christian's domineering personality, influenced many readers' disinterest in having a sexual relationship like Ana and Christian's. Amelia (21, White, single) offered, "Yeah, when I was reading the punishment parts I just kept thinking I could never imagine myself letting someone treat me that way." Jasmine (22, Black, single) insisted, "I definitely would not let a guy try to have all the control." Isabella shared, "As soon as I saw that [BDSM] contract and the red room of pain I would've been out the door." Far from being passive readers of *Fifty Shades*' troubling scenes, these readers revealed that they used the series to consider how they would react if put in similar situations.

In opposition to their negative reactions to the more worrisome aspects of Ana and Christian's sexual relationship, readers shared that they would be interested in the adventurousness in Ana and Christian's sexual relationship. Madison (21, Biracial, single) explained, "That sexual relationship I might try just because obviously that was one of the things that appealed to every reader." Lily emphasized, "I don't want my whole sex life to be like theirs, [but] mixing it up once in a while, the variety they have, new ideas, things you can try." But these women resisted the suggestion that they wanted to be "dominated" in the bedroom and emphasized instead their desire for a sexual partner with confidence and knowledge. Abigail (22, White, single) asserted, "'Dominated' is the wrong word . . . it's just being taken care of, it's just like having him know what he's doing for you and wanting to please you but not dominating." Madison similarly insisted, "It's not 'dominated' but it's like you as the man use your knowledge to guide the way for us to get to the pleasure that we want."

Readers with spouses and children were more likely to express interest in having a dominant partner in the bedroom but stressed that they would not be interested in being submissive in any other area of their lives. Jocelyn indicated, "In the bedroom, I could give up control completely and it would never bother me . . . now you step outside the bedroom and you start messing with my schedules, we might have some issues." More frequently, readers who expressed this position connected it to their abundance of responsibilities and resulting exhaustion. Emma (43, White, divorced) joked that giving up control in the bedroom would allow her to relax, "If you're tied up then you don't have to do anything."

The interview participants' discussions about their preferences for loving sex, and their discomfort with Christian's controlling and punishing behaviors, suggest that far from having a wish to be dominated sexually, *Fifty Shades* readers are interested in sex that accompanies the development of a romantic relationship. Further, these readers' interests in wanting a partner to take the lead sexually are tied to their confident assertions of their desires and to wanting a skilled partner who will fulfill their most intimate wishes. Underneath these readers' comments is the suggestion that they use sex to unwind from their numerous tasks and responsibilities and rely upon their partner to take the lead in helping them relax. This finding reiterates Radway's conclusion that the Smithton readers used romance to fantasize about "a man who is capable of the same attentive observation and intuitive 'understanding' that they believe women regularly accord to men."[35]

Additionally, *Fifty Shades* readers' interests in being pleased sexually suggest that they may not have embraced fully the postfeminist messages about female sexuality that Douglas argues tell women, "The true path to power comes from being an object of desire."[36] Nor do these readers embody, for example, the "phallic girl" that McRobbie describes as "emulate[ing] the assertive and hedonistic styles of sexuality associated with young men."[37] Although it is difficult to tell if these readers' attitudes are examples of a failed postfeminist hegemony or a form of resistance to postfeminism, it is clear that reading *Fifty Shades* had a productive and affirming rather than a regressive impact on the interview participants' sexual attitudes and behaviors. I discuss these changes below.

Talking about Sex

While reading *Fifty Shades* is not an indication of readers' interests in having a dominant-submissive sexual relationship, it has had an impact on readers' sexual talk, feelings, and behaviors. In fact, the experiences of the readers I interviewed suggest that *Fifty Shades'* popularity, like other popular texts before it (e.g., *The Joy of Sex*, *Sex and the City*) has altered cultural perceptions about women's sexuality and encouraged readers to talk more openly about sex with others. This finding echoes Thurston's assertion that, "[T]he erotic romance has been an important voice in the social dialogue responsible for raising the consciousness of millions of women."[38]

When I asked readers to reflect on *Fifty Shades'* cultural impact, the most frequent answer I received involved perceptions of women's interest in sex. For example, Emily shared that *Fifty Shades*, "Allowed women to be open about their sexual-ness . . . there's such a stigma . . . men watch porn, women don't . . . we can be sexual too, maybe we're not as open about it, but this kind of allowed us to be that way." Allison (20, White, single) echoed, "It definitely empowers women to like come out of the closet and be like, 'I am a sexual being, it's OK.'"

Spurred by the validation of women's sexual feelings that readers argue *Fifty Shades* brought to mainstream culture, many interview participants reported having more open and honest conversations because of the series. Kaylee disclosed, "It definitely made me more open to talking about sex, because I used to be afraid to discuss it . . . it just made it easier and more comfortable talking about that kind of thing." Chloe agreed, "It opens a door to talk about it. I wouldn't just go up to my friends, like, 'Hey let's talk about sex now,' but I'd be like 'Hey, have you read this?' [It] kind of gives you a way to bring it up."

Fifty Shades also impacted readers' talk with their sexual partners. Emily described conversations with her boyfriend initiated while reading *Fifty Shades*, "I'd read it to my boyfriend over the phone . . . it definitely opens new doors for relationships if you're both comfortable and willing." Emma attributed part of her satisfaction with her current partner to the conversations *Fifty Shades* encouraged, "When me and [my boyfriend] started dating, it was a struggle, we didn't connect for a long time, I was like, 'Boy are we ever gonna have sex?' . . . the books kind of brought out us to be able to talk about that."

Many readers disclosed that reading the *Fifty Shades* series also made them more sexually adventurous. Brooklyn offered that reading the books, "Did make me want to try different things, not all of the stuff that they talk about, but a couple things I was like, 'Well, hmm, that might be interesting to try.'" Allison maintained that the books, "Definitely gave me ideas . . . I would like to try certain things once—probably not the whole tied up to the cross type of deal—but something similar, yeah." Thus, in line with Thurston's finding that, "Many readers have been spurred by the stories they read to seek change in their own lives," *Fifty Shades* readers similarly use the series to rework their sexual attitudes and practices.[39]

Aligned with the readers' interest in becoming more sexually adventurous, many interview participants reported increased sexual activity while reading the *Fifty Shades* series. Grace shared, "It made me wanna have sex with [my partner] a lot . . . not necessarily anything they're doing in the book, but it was like, 'Let's go have sex now.'" Melanie reflected, "It does make you think about sex a lot, you know? A lot of husbands of friends that read it, they were like, 'Yeah, you know, it was a great two weeks [when their wives were reading the books],' and I'm thinking 'Yeah, you know, it really was.'"

Although Thurston's assertions that erotic romances are important tools for raising readers' consciousness about women's sexuality may initially have seemed overstated, especially in the context of Radway's conflicting conclusions about the value of romance reading in women's lives, the increased comfort and openness with their sexuality that these *Fifty Shades* readers expressed speaks to the series' individual and cultural impact.[40] Juxtaposed with Roiphe's assertions that *Fifty Shades*' popularity is due to readers' interest in "The incandescent fantasy of being dominated or overcome by a man," the comments made by the women I interviewed align with cultural commentators' arguments that the popular series has empowered readers to speak more openly and honestly with partners and friends about their sexual desires and experiences.[41] This assertion is underscored by numerous reports from sex shops of the increased sales of the sex toys used by the main characters in the book.[42] That *Fifty Shades* has the potential to open readers' pathways to being more comfortable talking about sex with friends and asking for what they want from partners is perhaps one of the most important reasons to ground its cultural meanings with the actual experiences of readers.

Conclusion

These readers' comments demonstrate that it would be a mistake to see *Fifty Shades of Grey*'s popularity as an indication of women's desires to be sexually dominated. Quite the contrary, I reassert Radway's and Thurston's arguments that readers use romantic narratives to think through how they would act if they were the heroine in the story. Through *Fifty Shades*, readers can, for example, imagine how romance—even marriage—could develop from a sexual contract, and how a skilled partner could fulfill their sexual needs. Thus, I suggest that the *Fifty Shades* readers I interviewed use the series to negotiate a cultural environment that is marked by a postfeminist sensibility in which "notions of autonomy, choice and self-improvement sit side-by-side with surveillance, discipline and the vilification of those who make the 'wrong' 'choices.'"[43] The increasing sexualization of culture, marked in part by the practice of hooking up and the mainstreaming of pornography, is a fundamental component of post-feminist culture. The cultural insistence that women simultaneously emulate men's sexual attitudes and behaviors and use their sexual knowledge to please men can be difficult to navigate.

Many of *Fifty Shades*' messages about romance and sex reflect and contribute to the postfeminist messages constitutive of the early twenty-first century, a point that was regularly made by the interview participants who were critical about many of the series' themes. However, the interviews I conducted demonstrate that the series allows readers to safely explore their positions on romance and sexuality through the development of Ana and Christian's romantic relationship. Such explorations echo Thurston's contention that erotic romances serve as "a means of exploring new ideas about the changing role and status of women in society—a kind of test run or sounding board for a variety of ideas, attitudes, and behavior—at the same time that it provides the security of the familiar."[44] Demonstrating this, these *Fifty Shades* readers suggested that the series' portrayal of risqué sexuality encouraged them to pick up the books, but the romantic story lines captivated them. Similarly, they found the sexual activity in the books to be titillating, but disliked sexual encounters that were framed with violence or punishment. Finally, the series offered readers a validation of their sexual interests and gave them an entry point for discussing their curiosities and desires with friends and partners.

Situated in the postfeminist sexualized media culture of the early twenty-first century, these readers demonstrate how erotic romances like the *Fifty Shades* series can help them traverse the push and pull of feminist and antifeminist cultural sentiments that mark this culture. In line with Radway's refusal to draw a neat conclusion from her work with romance readers, I argue that the experiences of these *Fifty Shades* readers complicate arguments about the impact of sexualized media culture. Although the series is structured by the conflicting messages about women's sexuality that are constitutive of postfeminism, readers used the series to nurture their romantic desires and explore their sexual agency. *Fifty Shades'* enduring popularity is by no means a sign of the real cultural change needed to challenge the media's postfeminist sensibility, but neither is it the dire sign that Roiphe fears is indicative of women's submission to our sexualized culture. Instead, *Fifty Shades'* popularity demonstrates that most women's lives are framed in shades of grey.

Notes

1. "Bestselling novelist Barbara Taylor Bradford calls 'Fifty Shades of Grey' 'Not Even Sexy.'" *International Business Times*, June 19, 2013.

2. Rachel Deahl, "E. L. James," *Publisher's Weekly*, December 3, 2012.

3. Lisa Schwarzbaum, "Tie Me Up! Tie Me Down!" *Entertainment Weekly*, April 6, 2012.

4. Katie Roiphe, "At the End of the Day, She Wants to Be . . . Spanked?" *Newsweek*, April 23, 2012.

5. Janice A. Radway, *Reading the Romance: Women, Patriarchy, and Popular Literature* (Chapel Hill: University of North Carolina Press, 1991), 72.

6. Angela McRobbie, *The Aftermath of Feminism: Gender, Culture, and Social Change* (Thousand Oaks, Calif.: Sage Publications, 2008), 11.

7. Rosalind Gill, "Postfeminist Media Culture: Elements of a Sensibility," *European Journal of Cultural Studies* 10 (2007): 150.

8. Susan J. Douglas, *The Rise of Enlightened Sexism* (New York: St. Martin's Press, 2010), 10.

9. Kathleen A. Bogle, *Hooking Up: Sex, Dating, and Relationships on Campus* (New York: New York University Press, 2008); Carmine Sarracino and Kevin M. Scott, *The Porning of America: The Rise of Porn Culture, What It Means, and Where We Go from Here* (Boston: Beacon Press, 2009).

10. Bogle, 159.

11. Sarracino and Scott, 202.

12. See Rachel M. Brownstein, *Becoming a Heroine: Reading about Women in Novels* (New York: Viking Press, 1982); Clare Hanson, *Hysterical Fictions: The "Woman's Novel" in the Twentieth Century* (New York: St. Martin's Press, 2000); Tania Modleski, *Loving with a Vengeance: Mass-produced Fantasies for Women* (Hamden, Conn.: Archon Books, 1982); and Deborah Phillips, *Women's Fiction: 1945–2005* (New York: Continuum, 2006).

13. See Ann Douglas, "Soft-porn Culture," *New Republic* 183.9 (August 30, 1980): 25–29; and Ann Barr Snitow, "Mass Market Romance: Pornography for Women Is Different," *Radical History Review* 20 (Spring/Summer 1979): 141–161.

14. Carole S. Vance, "Pleasure and Danger: Toward a Politics of Sexuality," in *Pleasure and Danger: Exploring Female Sexuality*, ed. Carole S. Vance (Boston: Routledge and Kegan Paul, 1984), 15.

15. Radway, 67–68.

16. See Ien Ang, "Feminist Desire and Female Pleasure: On Janice Radway's *Reading the Romance*," *Camera Obscura* 16 (1988): 178–191; and Tania Modleski, Introduction, in *Studies in Entertainment*, ed. Tania Modleski (Bloomington: Indiana University Press, 1986).

17. Carol Thurston, *The Romance Revolution: Erotic Novels and the Quest for a New Sexual Identity* (Urbana: University of Illinois Press, 1987), 12.

18. Ibid., 134.

19. Ibid., 132.

20. Ibid., 10.

21. Ibid., 163.

22. Dawn H. Currie, *Girl Talk: Adolescent Magazines and Their Readers* (Toronto: University of Toronto Press, 1999); Ellen McCracken, *Decoding Women's Magazines: From Mademoiselle to Ms.* (London: Macmillan, 1993); Nancy K. Baym, *Tune In, Log On: Soaps, Fandom, and Online Community* (Thousand Oaks, Calif.: Sage, 2000); Mary Ellen Brown, *Soap Opera and Women's Talk: The Pleasure of Resistance* (Thousand Oaks, Calif.: Sage, 1984); and Charlotte Brunsdon, *The Feminist, the Housewife and the Soap Opera* (Oxford: Clarendon Press, 2000).

23. Stephanie Harzewski, *Chick Lit and Postfeminism* (Charlottesville: University of Virginia Press, 2011), 195.

24. Ibid., 190.

25. Helen Fielding, *Bridget Jones's Diary: A Novel* (New York: Viking Penguin, 1996); Candace Bushnell, *Sex and the City* (New York: Grand Central Publishing, 1996); and Harzewski, 15.

26. Suzanne Ferris and Mallory Young, Introduction, in *Chick Lit: The New Woman's Fiction*, eds. Suzanne Ferris and Mallory Young (New York: Routledge, 2006), 10.

27. Harzewski, 16.

28. See, for example, the statistics from the 2013 report of the Business of Consumer Book Publishing, available in part at the Romance Writers of America website, http://www.rwa.org/p/cm/ld/fid=580 (accessed July 29, 2014).

29. Harzewski, 190, 192.

30. Radway, 65.

31. Thurston, 154.

32. Radway, 75.

33. Thurston, 218.

34. Amy E. Bonomi, Lauren E. Alternburger, and Nicole L. Walton, "'Double Crap!' Abuse and Harmed Identity in *Fifty Shades of Grey*," *Journal of Women's Health* 22.9 (2013): 733–744.

35. Radway, 83.

36. Douglas, 156.

37. McRobbie, 84.

38. Thurston, 65.

39. Ibid., 217.

40. Ibid., 65.

41. Sharon Jayson, "'Shades' of a Kinky Sex Revolution?" *USA Today*, May 10, 2012.

42. David Sax, "The 'Fifty Shades of Grey' Stimulus," *BusinessWeek.com*, May 25, 2012.

43. Gill, 163.

44. Thurston, 131–132.

CHAPTER 2

ABC's *Scandal*
and Black Women's Fandom

KRISTEN J. WARNER

On November 20, 2013, ABC's hit prime-time series *Scandal* aired "Vermont Is for Lovers Too." The third season episode sparked a full day of social media fodder ahead of its airing as fans tweeted their excitement about the potential story lines that could unfold. The following day, Black television bloggers like Awesomely Luvvie recapped the episode. Luvvie's popularity stems from her ability to humorously code-switch linguistically between standard English and African American Vernacular English (AAVE) in her episode summaries as well as through her use of gifs[1] that operate as visual metaphors of her feelings and moods. For example, in reaction to unhappily married but lovesick President of the United States Fitzgerald (Fitz) Grant's admission to the object of his affection and *Scandal*'s central figure, Olivia Pope, that after a moment of hope about their future, he built her a house in Vermont, Luvvie responded: "GAHTDAMBIT! I was SO READY to be off Team Olitz.[2] SO READY! And just like that, they pulled me back. Shit. You build me a house you want me to make jam in and we might could go together. OWWWWW!"[3]

Luvvie's switch to AAVE becomes the only way she can express her feelings about one of the major story lines in the episode between Olivia and Fitz. Her inability to stop loving the couple she loves, as well as the way she demonstrates that love (in fandom called "feels") for Olitz through her wording and yelling, also illustrates classic "fan girl" behavior. Moreover, it is not just Luvvie who joyously participates in the episode's afterglow.[4] Her comments section peaked with more than 200 responses to her recap. Many of the posters, primarily Black women, utilized the same AAVE speech patterns as their Luvvie. Responding to the Olitz story line, a conversation between fans addressed not only the relationship but also named a very culturally specific racial moment that *Scandal* elided:

> [Fan 1] Do y'all remember when Senator Pudding Pop[5] told Liv he wanted to marry her, and live a normal life with a house in Vermont, where she could make jam and have a couple babies? [Fan 2] She also said that to Fitz, too. I think it was the episode where she went and got in her bed and stayed for a couple of days (with no head scarf and her hair stayed in place the entire time) and she talked to him on the phone. [Fan 3] Forget Olivia's coat. I need the name of her hairdresser. A long night of lovin' and the hair was still laid like a burden. Even Fitz's back looked good!! Isn't he like 50 years old? [Fan 4] LOL to the hair. That is what I thought—and with no headscarf? How did she manage that? That is civilized loving! [Fan 5] This episode was everything, I just wish they would have given Liv post-hot sweaty, you built me a house, sex hair. No edges were sweated out, curls were still bouncing. Naw girl, you need a ponytail holder after that type of on the floor, wrapped up in the blankets session.[6]

Just pulling a few comments from the thread illustrates the excitement some fans felt about the Olitz scene as well as the manner by which the show elided the reality of how a Black woman's textured hair will behave after the vigorous love scene depicted in the episode (the answer: not the way it looked afterward). The ways these fans focus on small details that help them connect and identify with their protagonist is key to Black women's *Scandal* fandom, and to my claims in this chapter.

Conversations like these are rarely made visible outside of the safe fandom spaces where Black women perform their fan love. What's more, few people even realize that Black women take part in fandom at all. The stark reality is that the only people who are allowed to be visible within fandom and imagined to be fans by the media industries are White men and women. John Fiske acknowledges the dearth of scholarship on race and fandom as justification for why he is not discussing that frame in his fandom scholarship: "I regret being unable to devote the attention to race which it deserves, but I have not found studies of non-white fandom. Most of the studies so far undertaken highlight class, gender and age as the key axes of discrimination."[7] Decades later, fan studies still has not arrived at the place to consider how fandoms erase Others from the notion of fandom altogether. This chapter cannot attempt to take on all of that heavy lifting, but it is my goal to shine some light on fan studies' erasure of racialized bodies from the canonical primary texts as well as point to ways that fans of color turn their exclusion into a means of creating safe, productive spaces.

While the stereotype of women in fandom generally precludes women of color as participants and producers of content, it is nevertheless true that Black and Brown female bodies do exist in fan communities. Producing content is a necessary act of agency for women of color, who strive for visibility in a landscape that favors a more normative (read: White) fan identity and that often dismisses and diminishes the desires of its diverse body to see themselves equally represented not only on screen but in the fan community at large. While fan studies functions at nearly every level of identity *except* for the intersections of race and gender, Black female fandom continues to thrive. In fact, part of what may strengthen these pluralist communities is the fact that they are left alone to create safe spaces for interaction and creative labor. One of the main ways that Black female fandom makes Black femininity visible is by consciously moving mediated women of color, who often occupy supporting roles, to the center, transforming them into leads in fan-produced discourse. The objective of this sort of subversive act is to create imagined moments of identification and representation for an audience that rarely, if ever, gets the opportunity to see an actress of color in a leading role—until *Scandal.*

Why have Black women's fandoms been so ignored before this point? The answer emerges through an exploration into how fandom and fan studies consider fandom a set of practices only peripherally informed by issues of identity. While fan studies traditionally understood fandom as a space that negotiates the subordinated tastes of particularly disempowered bodies, critical and industrial perspectives on fandom in the early twenty-first century have distanced fan practices from this origin point, reinventing fandom as a non-identity-specific-yet-common-interests phenomenon.[8] The liminal space between these two conceptions of fandom underpins the Black female fan community.

In this chapter I analyze the ways Black women fans have reacted to not being visible in the dominant spaces of fandom. As a primary example of the ways Black women fan communities work toward reinscription, I offer the fandom of ABC's *Scandal*—a program with Black women in central positions both behind and in front of the camera. Premiering on ABC in April 2012, the prime-time dramatic series produced by *Grey's Anatomy* showrunner Shonda Rhimes and starring African American actress Kerry Washington became a literal embodiment of the type of labor Black women practice in fan spaces. In this case, Black female fans have transformed the central Black lead, canonically

drawn as normative and racially neutral, into a culturally specific Black character. This is commonplace labor for non-White fans—particularly in the early-
twenty-first-century's so-called postrace moment.

Based on the life of famous crisis management "fixer" Judy Smith, *Scandal*
focuses on the work and love life of the statuesque, fierce, and extremely beautiful Olivia Pope. Largely written in what I have coined as the "spirit of color-
blindness," the series avoids race talk and stereotypical assumptions about Black
femininity in favor of a more neutrally raced, woman first, Blackness-as-flavor
discourse. Against this context, I will demonstrate how Black female fan communities work to fill in those racially specific gaps to make Olivia Pope a more
culturally specific Black woman. This work ranges from discussions of Olivia's
hair, to reinterpretations of her dialogue to "Black lady"–speak, to negotiating
and speculating on Washington's real life. In sum, my chapter argues that while
Black women's fandom utilizes the same creative labor as normative fandom-at-
large, its unique striving for visibility charges those fan activities with a political
agency that ruptures our contemporary understanding of the experiences and
desires embedded within Black femininity.

Re-situating Black Women in Fan Studies

Before discussing the types of fan practices Black women participate in, it is
first important to restate that part of the reason Black female fandom exists as
its own niche area of fandom is because these women choose to exist despite
their invisibility and exclusion from mainstream fan spaces. Further, exclusion
pushed them to develop spaces where their own interests, agendas, and perspectives could be foregrounded. Thus, briefly exploring how fandom is viewed
through the lens of fan studies is a useful start to unpacking how this group
had become so marginalized. In the early twenty-first century, fan studies set
its interests in understanding the ways that fans interact with their love objects
and articulating its legibility and its intelligence as a means of normalizing
these individuals considered outsiders by the mainstream. In their introduction to their anthology on fandom, Jonathan Gray, Cornel Sandvoss, and C.
Lee Harrington recount three "waves" of fan studies.[9] For brevity, this chapter
primarily focuses on the first wave of research from scholars who were fans
themselves seeking to rehabilitate the image of fans as pathological. Described
by Gray, Sandvoss, and Harrington as the "Fandom Is Beautiful" period, in the
late twentieth century, fandom was first considered an object worthy of consideration. The editors' synopsis of the ways fan studies became a tool to recoup
and rehabilitate the image of fans as not socially awkward, deviant "weirdos"

is important because it foregrounds the significance of identity to fandom. Further, they describe how fandom functions for those outside of it through a strategy of Othering.

However true this might be, when considering fans as a deviant subculture, I am troubled by the notion that fandom wholesale operates as Other—especially when considering the fact that many fans are part of dominant identity groups—White, cis-gendered, and heterosexual. I recognize that Gray, Sandvoss, and Harrington (not to mention other fan studies scholars) reappropriate "Other" as a description of how fandom is perceived from the outside. Still, I contend that the very act of reappropriation without consideration of the fact that racialized Others exist within the scope of fandom demonstrates the necessity of reclaiming racialized and gendered fan identities.

Let me be clear: Much of the work of contemporary fan studies assumes fans are a homogeneously normative band of Othered outsiders who devote time and allegiance to their love objects not underpinned by a politic or a desire to rupture the notion of normative fandom. Interestingly enough, scholars did not arrive at this conclusion without the help of fandom-at-large, whose imagined community is not altogether that different. Mel Stanfill articulates the naturalized logic implicit in fandom's imaginary:

> In examining the discourse of fandom circulating in contemporary culture, it quickly becomes apparent that, in addition to being constructed as losers, as other scholars have noted, fans are culturally understood to be white people, particularly white men.[10]

This assumption becomes problematic with regard to discussions of racialization when much of the scholarship focuses on unshackling the early formations of fan studies work concerned with understanding subordinate, marginalized groups in favor of research that treats all consumers (who in this global capitalist moment are all marked as fans in some respect) as agents of fandom. By distancing from Fiske's early characterization of fandom as "associated with the cultural tastes of subordinated formations of the people, particularly with those disempowered by any combination of gender, age, class and race,"[11] all potential fandom clusters could constitute as Other.

As a tag to this section, I want to clarify that fandom-as-a-whole is not necessarily made up of scholars with an investment in diversity or checking their privilege or even an interest in seeing their own selves as racialized bodies in a system designed to benefit some and disadvantage Others. Thus, the gap between beginning a conversation on intersectionality and concluding with real, viable solutions is a long and weary journey many fans are not interested in taking. Moreover, the culture industry that produces the texts that cultivate fandom is often ill prepared to discuss and negotiate bodies unlike their imagined demographic joining the conversation. This is the predicament in which Black female fans find themselves and the rationale for why they have created their own communal spaces.

A Home of Our Own: Women of Color Fan Communities

A fan community is created not only out of a shared interest in a love object but also out of similar approaches to demonstrating that love. Carving out a space for individuals who share common agendas and perspectives can be a lucrative incentive for building such a community. Digging deeper, Darlene Hampton paraphrases Cornel Sandvoss for a more specific description of what fans gain from consuming their media texts:

> Sandvoss views fannish consumption as a process through which individual fans use media texts as mirrors to reflect their own concerns, values, and ideological subject positions back to themselves. Seeing the relationship between fans and media texts as essentially narcissistic, he insists that fans are not only emotionally and financially invested in their objects of fandom, but that it becomes "intrinsically interwoven with our sense of self, with who we are, would like to be, and think we are."[12]

Neither Sandvoss nor Hampton considers the "narcissistic" approach of fans to their texts as pathological. Instead, the act of a fan seeing him- or herself in a text provokes the narcissistic cue. This mirror moment is doubly necessary for Black women fans. The dearth of media representations of women of color means that when one such representation appears, however marginal to the media text, fans instantly transform it into an identifiable, relatable body that reflects or refracts their own value systems. Seeing oneself on screen is a privilege that not all bodies are allowed, thus the "make do" culture that women of color—and, specific to this essay, Black women   participate in to make those identities recognizable is worthy of consideration. The ways Black women reappropriate themselves into the text through characters who look (and potentially act) like them is inherently narcissistic; yet, it serves a greater purpose of identification and visibility.

While not specifically engaging Black women and fandom, in her seminal work (and, for the record, still the only book that specifically examines Black women's reception to media) Jacqueline Bobo argues that Black women who operate as cultural readers do so not only for identification but also as individual acts of resistance: "[Black women] have opposed cultural as well as social domination and have contested detrimental images in a specific text, either as audience members or as cultural producers who created alternative and more viable images. Although their opposition is not always so pronounced, black women are continually involved in patterns of resistance."[13] If one can consider the narcissistic act of seeing themselves as a kind of resistance, then Black women in fandom are doing this work. Moreover, Bobo borrows the notion of an "interpretive community" from Stanley Fish to illustrate how Black women make sense and make do with the representations that they are allowed. She explains:

> [Patricia Hill] Collins states that black women's individual acts of resistance can be seen in the context of a culture of resistance, where there is a supportive black female community. Consequently, their collective actions are part of a sustained movement. Black women within an interpretive community are also part of this movement. As cultural producers, critics, and members of an audience the women are positioned to intervene strategically in the imaginative construction, critical interpretation, and social condition of black women.[14]

These three interventions of imaginative construction, critical interpretation, and Black women's social condition also speak to some of the labor done in Black women's fan communities. Bobo's strategies create useful frames for illustrating specific examples of Black women's fan labor. For example, imagining a peripheral Black female character as the lead, or writing "meta"[15] about the ways the series depicts the woman of color, or even discussing within the group how the dearth of roles is emblematic of Black women's place in society are all part of what make an interpretive as well as a fan community.

As an example, the manner by which largely Black female fandom transformed supporting character Bonnie Bennett of CW's *The Vampire Diaries* (*TVD*) from peripheral to lead character, to discussing among themselves how the character's never-acknowledged racialization impacts what happens to her, to fighting it out with anti-Bonnie fans when they assert that her character's trajectory is intentionally maligned because of her Blackness, this community found a common interest in serving as Bonnie's champion—even becoming so boisterous as to take on *TVD*'s cocreator and showrunner, Julie Plec. The strategies of Bonnie Bennett fans are but a few of those Black women fans employ to produce and interpret their objects.

Another way that online fan communities attempt to reinscribe Black women into central roles that previously rendered them invisible is "racebending." A word with many definitions and contexts,[16] for the purposes of this essay, *race-bending* is deployed through fan-generated work such as fan fiction, when writers change the race and cultural specificity of central characters or pull a secondary character of color from the margins, transforming her into the central protagonist. Race bending allows for a negotiation between the original actor's performance and the audience's acceptance of the performance.

Diana Taylor argues that performances "function as vital acts of transfer, transmitting social knowledge, memory and a sense of identity through reiterated, or what Richard Schechner has called 'twice-behaved' behavior."[17] I like Taylor's translation of performance as an act of transfer because it literally creates a link between the performer and the audience member. Both the actor and the audience member understand that what is occurring is a performance, and they jointly engage in a multifaceted process of meaning-making. As an example of racebending on a different level from that of fandom but which still utilizes a similar approach, in 2005, Denzel Washington portrayed Julius Caesar in a revival of Shakespeare's play. The act of transfer involved between actor and audience would have included the acknowledgment that Caesar was probably not a Black man and the understanding that Washington merely inhabited the "essence" of the character. In this instance, racebending functioned as an industrial practice more commonly known as *color-blind casting*. However, as the character is based on a real person who likely was not African American, the audience member has to accept Washington subsuming into the role and suspend their disbelief—this is the heart of racebending. Alternatively, some audience members may have resisted the concept of a universal or common essence that Washington could embody. Either way, it is clear that racebending as an act of performance carries a complex web of potential meanings, incarnations, and identifications in which the audience takes part.

Similar to Washington racebending to become Julius Caesar for an official production, fans racebend to reinsert versions of themselves into texts within which they have long been ignored. In one online community for women fan fiction writers of color called The Chamber,[18] the writers are allowed to write whatever they want, provided that the main character is a woman of color. This opens up a world of possibilities, because they can transform Jane Austen's *Pride and Prejudice* by making its lead, Elizabeth Bennett, a Black woman. Adjusting the story world to accommodate the reality of a Black Elizabeth Bennett, the narrative can be molded to adapt to the needs of a Black lead. For example, changing the lead's race meant shifting the time and space of the novel, relocating it in present-day New York City. In addition, the backstory of the character shifted to accommodate Elizabeth's family structure as well as make her coupling with her love interest, Will Darcy, bound by real-world hardships: He's wealthy and White while she comes from a middle-class Black family. The place of race is underscored by the difficulty required for Darcy and her to get together. Thus, unlike the original, where class difference is the primary barrier, the combination of race and class difference make this new version more complex, and more attuned to the women of color who write and read it.[19]

One last way Black women fan communities reinscribe themselves into these texts is by making background women of color characters the primary leads. The Chamber's primary audience is Black women who want to create redemptive narratives for women of color characters who were not given the proper, multidimensional characterizations offered to others. Thus, transforming Star Trek's Uhura from a peripheral character to one in a leading role, with her choice of love options, becomes possible in this community. Uhura in a love triangle may seem simplistic but is actually a key strategy of visibility. A major strain of fandom is the act of coupling, otherwise known as "shipping." In many ways, establishing the legitimacy of a character can be easily crafted by placing her in a relationship with a lead. Pulling a Black supporting character from the margins and placing her in a heterosexual courtship is again a way to offer the possibility of multidimensional characterization. What I find most fascinating about shipping these relationships is that if there is enough of a fandom built around them, it can actually become incorporated into the "canonical" text, as when story lines are designed to please fans who are clamoring for the pairings they desire to happen. For example, Uhura's relationship with Spock in the J. J. Abrams reboot of the Star Trek franchise may have seemed an original pairing for Abrams, but it has long been the stuff of fan fiction.

Similarly, the quasi-coupling of characters Joss Carter (a Black woman) and White costar John Reese in the third season's 2013 winter finale of CBS's Person of Interest (POI) is largely due to the "Careese" fandom's vigorous efforts to argue that these two characters could be together. This is significant because while Carter, portrayed by Taraji P. Henson, is technically a lead in the series, her character is often relegated to the periphery in publicity for the show, with the most egregious example being TV Guide opting not to include her on the cover of the magazine featuring POI as the main story.[20] After some back and forth between Henson and the magazine, they ultimately decided to drop POI as the cover story, replacing it with Charlie's Angels. Nevertheless, fans shipping Careese finally saw their couple go from a nonofficial pairing to an extremely short-lived canonical one when they kissed just before Carter was gunned down while protecting Reese. An ambivalent win for the Black female fans that long believed in their ship becoming official, yet likely felt duped by how safe the coupling was for the writers. Blogger and fan An Nicholson interviewed the *POI* cast and producers about Careese. She wrote:

> Considering the ongoing "CaReese" development, I wondered if the produc-
> ers read any of the on-line fan fiction. Most "POI" fan fiction surrounds John
> in Joss' apartment, a Zeese/Careese weekend away, an all hot girls sting op-
> eration and/or a tearful declaration by Joss/John for each other. Considering
> that covers Season Two's "Bad Code," "The High Road," "2 Pi R," "Prisoner's
> Dilemma" as well as season three's "Lady Killer," I wondered if he or his staff
> ever read fanfiction.net. While he confessed to reading the on-line boards,
> he believes recent episodes coincide with fanfic because that's what he and
> his writing staff want to see as fans of the characters.[21]

Thus, for the *POI* writers, the desires of the fans lined up with their own story lines for the characters, moving the Black woman from the peripheral third lead to the love interest of the main protagonist. However, fans generating visibility can also work for media texts with Black women already in leading roles. In these instances, the predominately Black female fandom not only maintains the visibility through common fan labor practices, but also works to fill in the gaps to add dimension and specificity. To illustrate how this functions, I return to the case of ABC's *Scandal* and its lead star, Kerry Washington. Not only have these fans been partly responsible for the series' initial survival and the way it became known as "water cooler television" but they can also be credited with the rise of Washington to A-list talent.

Scandalistas: Black Women Fans and *Scandal*

Creator and Executive Producer of *Scandal* Shonda Rhimes has cornered the market on improving diversity casting on network television. Prior to *Scandal*, Rhimes became respected around the television industry for reintroducing color-blind casting to television. Her first television series, ABC's *Grey's Anatomy*, proved that color-blind casting could be a successful strategy of increasing diversity on television without alienating the mainstream [White] audience with unidentifiable characters. But with *Scandal*, based on real-life fixer Judy Smith, Rhimes opted against the blind casting model. In an interview, she describes the casting process for the lead role, Olivia Pope: "We auditioned every actress of color in town, every one, and I wanted everyone to have a chance. . . . So it was really difficult because we saw a ton of actresses. [But the decision] was really simple because when Kerry came in and sat down and started to read, I thought, well, there she is. So you know it when you see it."[22] That Rhimes was intentionally casting a woman of color for the lead role in *Scandal* is wholly different from the way she cast most of *Grey's* or *Private Practice*. Still, although *Scandal* is loosely based on the life of a real Black female fixer who lives and works in Washington, D.C., Rhimes makes no explicit points toward racial specificity within the series.

Thus, while the casting for Pope was about intentionally auditioning women of color, the actual part required the actress to transcend the fixed reality of her race so she could become the (color-blind) character Rhimes (and a White-dominated mainstream culture) needed her to be. Here's the point: Fixed racial identities operate at the level of skin color, thus Rhimes builds characters that occupy a more universally normative appeal. This is the way the spirit of color-blindness functions in *Scandal*, with Rhimes even going as far as placing Pope in a relationship with Fitzgerald Grant, the married, White, Republican president of the United States, without directly acknowledging the racial structures that make interracial relationships a complicated enterprise. Applying Rhimes's logic to their relationship, because both Fitz's and Olivia's racializations are fixed and immutable, their race is what it is; what is more important is what comes after the racial moment, as if race is something that can be pushed aside or beyond.

That said, Rhimes did a few small pivots toward racial recognition during season two. In a flashback episode, Pope, feeling guilt about her feelings for Fitz, argues in a flight of fancy that their relationship is the equivalent of that between Thomas Jefferson and his slave, Sally Hemmings. A second moment occurs when Fitz decides he will divorce his wife Mellie and marry Olivia. He enlists the fixer's help in creating a public relations campaign that serves a dual purpose: Make America fall in love with her and forgive Fitz's infidelity with a woman [of color particularly] so that he can be reelected for a second term in office. Telling Mellie and his Chief of Staff Cyrus Beene Olivia's plan, he stresses, "My relationship with Olivia is going to spark a real dialogue about race in this country and is going to blow the Republican party wide open."[23] Yet, Fitz is never allowed to spark that dialogue because his relationship with Olivia is thwarted at every turn. When asked about how she felt about the intricacies of power dynamics intersecting with racial dynamics in that relationship, Rhimes asserted, "I don't think that we have to have a discussion about race when you're watching a Black woman who is having an affair with the white president of the United States. . . . The discussion is right in front of your face."[24] Ultimately, Rhimes leaves it to the audience to fill in those cognitive gaps, to have that "discussion about race" in their own minds if nowhere else. This becomes the primary strategy of the series, allowing it to appeal to mainstream (White) audiences who do not want to "see" race and to those audiences who want to read Olivia and Fitz as distinctly raced characters. To do this, Rhimes not only forgoes much explicit discussion of race, but also keeps Olivia from demonstrating any visible signs of Blackness. As one reviewer listed:

> Olivia Pope established her skill set, her power, her uncompromising commitment to her work, her character, her grace under fire and it was stunning! Stunning! There was no finger waving, no back and forth head motion, no pulling of weaves; it was pure and uncompromising intelligence. She wasn't anyone's (basketball) wife, she was in complete possession of herself. And dressed to the nines while doing it![25]

The spirit of color-blindness renders Pope normatively neutral, which allows a variety of audience members to identify in the ways that they can. Even in a case of a Black female lead character, then, Black female audiences have to work to find ways of seeing Olivia and her actions as resonating with their experience. If stereotypical signs of Blackness are not deployed in service of showing us a Black woman, how have Black female audiences filled in the gaps?

With Pope's position as Black woman extraordinaire, Black female fans quickly took to their online communities—primarily social media platforms such as Twitter and Tumblr—to express their love for the show, for Pope, and for its biggest super couple: "Olitz." Creating gifsets reanimating shots of the couple engaging in banter and sexual rendezvous, discussing the motivations of the couple, defending their couple against naysayers, and writing fan fiction about Olitz moments the series did not capture are but a few of the activities in which these women of color online communities have participated.

Scandal has shattered numerous records for social media, particularly for Twitter. In 2013, *Scandal* episodes reportedly drew around 2200 tweets per minute, culminating in an average of 351,000 tweets per episode and a unique audience measurement of 2.214 million.[26] What happens on Twitter when *Scandal* airs is a mixture of plot analysis, emotional reactions, and cultural observations about the characters. On Tumblr, a social media platform that operates as a visual microblogging site, scenes are uploaded into gifsets in order to relive the best moments of that week's episode or to closely analyze a sequence. In addition, on both platforms, communities build memes that speak to the absurdity of the fandom or the characters. For example, in the season three premiere, Pope finds herself in a pickle as reports of her affair with Fitz are leaked. Her father Rowan (also referred to as Elijah) Pope, the leader of a high-powered, covert governmental organization, tries to put her on a plane to vanish while the story dies down. In one of the series' most interesting moments, Rowan lambastes Olivia for her poor life choices and tells her, *"Did I not raise you for better? How many times have I told you? You have to be what?"* Olivia responds,

"Twice as good," to which Rowan says, *"You have to be twice as good as them to get half of what they have."*[27] To the mainstream eye, it was just a father admonishing his wayward adult daughter. But to Black fandom, this moment took on greater significance that demanded gap filling. Instantly, the common expression that in order for Black folks to become successful, they had to "be twice as good to get half as much" as their White counterparts virally spread throughout Twitter. Then, on Tumblr, users grabbed the scene and translated the conversation (or code-switched it) into culturally specific AAVE: "Didn't I tell you not to embarrass me in front of these white people? Can't take your ass nowhere,"[28] became the text of the gifs made to humorously illustrate the racial specificity of that moment between the Black father and daughter (see Figure 2.1).

Black female fandom also has to fill in the cognitive gaps that the spirit of color-blindness leaves open for mass identification. Gifsets dedicated to Olivia's hair and sartorial choices as well as discussions around Olivia's hairstyles are part of the fandom, as they add layers of cultural specificity to the character for Black female fans. Hair culture is a major part of the Black community and conversations about natural versus relaxed hair textures, hairstyles, weaves, and wigs are commonplace. So when Olivia wears her hair in sophisticated, yet impossible-to-create-based-on-her-very-tight-timeframes styles, conversations about her "magical" hair emerge. As an example, *Glamour*'s Phoebe Robinson (a Black woman) recaps a moment from season two: "We open with Olivia swimming in a pool with a swimming cap on, to which I say, 'Good for you, girl,' because I'm tired of seeing all these black women in music videos splash around in water without covering their hair like they don't know that the

FIGURE 2.1. Tumblr user scandalouscastleanatomy's culturally specific interpretation of Rowan Pope's admonishment of his daughter, Olivia, October 4, 2013.

SECOND they get out of the water, they will look like Frederick Douglass on a Black History Month stamp."[29] Later in the same recap Robinson continues:

> Returning to Olitz, they are in the shower looking at each other all lovey-dovey, and Liv doesn't have her hair covered! Y'all, Olivia does not care if she looks like Frederick Douglass, Sallie Mae Douglass, or Lucas Douglass (Note: the last two people aren't real), she is bathing with her man without a shower cap on. LAWD, FITZ, DO NOT F—K THIS UP! BLACK WOMEN DO NOT GET THEIR WEAVE WET FOR MEN UNLESS THEY'RE TRYING TO GO HALF ON A MORTGAGE AND HULU PLUS ACCOUNT.[30]

Robinson's jokes concerning the way Black women protect their hair from water by any means necessary have little play within the canonical narrative but resonate with other Black women. While they realize that movie magic is how we can understand Olivia's hair miraculously withstanding water, the gap filling is a necessary function for Black women who in their everyday lives have little access to Liv's miracles. Black women's hair and the discourses around it are not pathological but a set of rituals that, just as easily as any fan text, can invoke communal relations among Black ladies.

Olivia's hair is not the only big topic up for discussion within the Black female *Scandal* community. The one area where fandom shows up in great number is around the love triangle of Fitz, Olivia, and Jake Ballard. Ballard (played by White actor Scott Foley), joined the cast in season two, helping to protect Olivia at Fitz's request, unintentionally falling for her, and competing for her heart. Closely analyzing love scenes by frequently rewinding the episode as well as studying the gifsets that are made and turned in every direction to try to reveal pieces that may have been overlooked in the editing suite serve a key function within the fandom (see Figures 2.2a and 2.2b). Olivia's sexuality allows

FIGURES 2.2a and 2.2b. These images from *Scandal* fan scandamonium's gifset, "Olitz +Stare off," emphasize the intense looks between Olivia and Fitz, February 3, 2013.

Black female fans an opportunity to make visible their own desires—something not often seen or allowed for Black women. Ogling over Fitz's and Jake's bodies and even naming parts of their anatomy (The Cobra, for example)—and then tweeting at the actors about it—are, again, mainstream fan activities that gain double meaning with Black female bodies attached to the actions. Indeed, when the only time Black women are discussed in the news is when they are being told they are less likely to get married than any other racialized group—or that they are the least attractive racialized group—the opportunity for the expression of Black female desire, and desirability, is scarce. Enter Olivia Pope, whose sexuality and ability to make two very attractive, very assertive, very determined-to-win-the-subject-of-their-desire White men nearly lose their minds to possess her, makes her a major point of identification. For a fandom eager to feel desired and in control of their own romantic fates, this particular love triangle is especially exciting.

Yet, maintaining Pope's centrality to the series is an ongoing activity for Black female fandom. Although canonically, the narrative will always make Olivia the center, popular journalistic discourses have drifted away from that notion and in some instances even have suggested that decentering the lead in favor of other costars could produce more favorable story lines. In season three, a story line around Fitz's wife Mellie brought the character to a place where she could have dethroned Olivia:

> *Scandal* was Kerry Washington's show. Until last Thursday night, when supporting player Bellamy Young, who plays First Lady Mellie Grant, hijacked the series away from her. In a stunning flashback that won Mellie the kind of sympathy Olivia Pope—Washington's hard-charging man-eater—will never attain, we learned that 15 years ago Mellie's drunken father-in-law Senator Jerry "Big Jerry" Grant raped her.[31]

Articles like these ironically accomplished their own gap filling—in this instance reading Pope as a hypersexual, angry Black woman. The Black fan community noticed that many of these articles were written by White columnists and began to respond to the challenges, alleging a form of unconscious racism. One of the major *Scandal* Tumblr sites, SabiaCoruja, articulated the long-standing racial tensions that make the desire of many White columnists to replace Olivia with Mellie problematic:

> The last two posts [the recaps that favored Mellie at Olivia's expense] may seem somewhat disconnected, but I specifically posted them both to emphasize that, on a much smaller scale, what we're seeing happen regarding Olivia and Mellie on *Scandal* and the need by some in the media to downplay, if not

outright dismiss, Olivia is a very real and not uncommon phenomenon. For centuries, there have been those who have a need to downplay the accomplishments of people of color in The Americas, Europe and the world. I'm by no means trying to say that what we're seeing on *Scandal* is in any way on the same level of importance as the systematic and deliberate whitewashing of history that has been perpetuated in the world. What I am saying is that for those who read about the opinions and concerns that many of us have expressed towards segments of the media and society in general that seem all too eager to discount Olivia for Mellie at every opportunity, before you roll your eyes and dismiss it, take a step back and look at the broader picture.[32]

For fans like SabiaCoruja, being part of a community of subordinate, marginalized people is central to fandom, and to *Scandal* fandom in particular. This fandom is not only about the pleasures of filling in racially specific gaps or engaging in the fantasy of desirability. It is also about being able to call out en masse when their objects of love and identification are threatened in a way that symbolically challenges their own positionalities.

My last illustration of Black female *Scandal* fandom is, interestingly enough, a small sliver of the fandom-at-large: the *SS Terry* ship. A portmanteau of Kerry and Tony, this ship is based on the conspiracy theory that Washington and her costar Tony Goldwyn are in a secret relationship. Most of the fandom does not hold this belief but I wanted to bring "Terrys" out to demonstrate how this fandom runs parallel to mainstream fandoms that have their own "real people ships." The evidence that these shippers claim proves their ship is real varies from close analysis of stolen looks in photographs, body language in interviews, botched marriage certificates anonymously sent to TMZ, cryptic Twitter messages, the flirty banter between the two actors in publicity for the series, or at the time of this writing, the fact that no one has seen Washington's new baby Isabelle.[33] What also merits as evidence for the group is Washington's standard response when asked about her relationship status: "I don't talk about my personal life." She has said that so many times that it's become a hashtagged acronym within the fandom—#IDTAMPL. It does not matter that both Washington and Goldwyn repeatedly articulate that they are each married to other people. It does not matter that *Scandal* costar Josh Malina claims that Terrys are "dumb." How, then, to explain this belief? Is it purely stubborn insanity?

I argue that this example of shipping fandom actually functions much as other fan efforts to move peripheral characters of color to the mainstream to maintain visibility. It relies upon the inherent drama of a potential Terry ship to maintain Washington's visibility as a star, especially given the actress' trademark intelligence, beauty, and lack of Hollywood-style drama. In a media environment where there are precious few prominent Black actresses, Washington's ascendancy to fame without scandal has allowed her to easily maneuver through White mainstream spaces as well as Black urban ones. History has taught us that Black actors and actresses are not necessarily imbued with staying power—not for any fault of their own but as a consequence of the systemic discriminatory practices long held within the film and television industry. Thus, finding ways to keep Washington's fame central seems to be a strategy fans have taken on to extend her star cycle. As they figure, what better way to maintain legitimacy than through coupling? While not a logical solution, for fans who by and large have little influence in shaping celebrity futures, insisting that Washington has taken up with a man whose last name is central to Hollywood history is their best play to maintain her visibility. Moreover, since the two have such chemistry onscreen, for many of the Terrys, it just makes sense that they are together offscreen. The legitimacy of chemistry has thus become the marker of authenticity for Terry, a chemistry fans claim is so real that if they themselves could not resist it, how could the people involved remain immune?

In conclusion, more research on women of color in fandom needs to be conducted as online communities continue to thrive and allow a varied number of voices to be heard. *Scandal* is just one community to study but the fans that inhabit it go about fan labor in ways that speak to specific cultural experiences that traditional fan studies has yet to consider. The pleasures of Black women and, more broadly, women of color should not need to remain invisible. The internet and social media have allowed these bodies to find community. Taking those medium-specific platforms and not only feminizing them but racially feminizing them, provides us with a glimpse into how powerful these intersectional spaces can be for empowering these marginalized bodies. Until we revisit not just the gender uses of fandom but also the intersections of race and gender, it can never be, in the words of Olivia Pope, "handled."

Notes

1. Gifs are animated image files that loop a sequence of shots repeatedly.

2. Fans of Olivia and Fitz's relationship gave them the portmanteau "Olitz."

3. Awesomely Luvvie, "Vermont Is for Lovers, Too: Scandal Episode 308 Recap," AwesomelyLuvvie.com, November 22, 2013, http://www.awesomelyluvvie.com/2013/11/vermont-lovers-scandal-episode-308-recap.html (accessed January 3, 2015).

4. The penultimate scene in the episode is a tastefully filmed yet extremely sensual love scene between Olivia and Fitz.

5. A nickname created by fans for season two love interest Senator Edison Davis. Davis looks eerily like Bill Cosby, precipitating that nickname as well as "Edison Huxtable" after Cosby's character in *The Cosby Show*.

6. Awesomely Luvvie, "Vermont Is for Lovers."

7. John Fiske, "The Cultural Economy of Fandom," *The Adoring Audience: Fan Culture and Popular Media* (Routledge: New York, 1992), 32.

8. The notion of subordination and disempowerment is informed largely by Fiske's work on fandom.

9. Jonathan Gray, Cornel Sandvoss, and C. Lee Harrington, Introduction, *Fandom: Identities and Communities in a Mediated World* (New York: New York University Press, 2007), 2.

10. Mel Stanfill, "Doing Fandom, (Mis)doing Whiteness: Heteronormativity, Racialization, and the Discursive Construction of Fandom," in "Race and Ethnicity in Fandom," edited by Robin Anne Reid and Sarah Gatson, special issue, *Transformative Works and Cultures*, no. 8, 2011.

11. Fiske, 30.

12. Darlene Rose Hampton, *Beyond Resistance: Gender, Performance, and Fannish Practice in Digital Culture* (Dissertation, University of Oregon, 2010), 3.

13. Jacqueline Bobo, *Black Women as Cultural Readers* (New York: Columbia University Press, 1995), 27.

14. Ibid.

15. *Meta* is defined by Fanlore as "discussion of fanworks of all kinds, fan work in relation to the source text, fan fiction characters and their motivation and psychology, fan behavior, or fandom itself." "Meta," *Fanlore*, http://fanlore.org/wiki/Meta (accessed January 3, 2015).

16. For variations on *racebending*, see http://www.racebending.org (accessed January 3, 2015).

17. Diana Taylor, *The Archive and the Repertoire: Performing Cultural Memory in the Americas* (Durham, N.C.: Duke University Press, 2003), 2.

18. The Chamber, http://vchamber.livejournal.com (accessed January 3, 2015).

19. I am summarizing the plot points from TokenBlkgirl's *Pride and Prejudice* fan fiction. Since its original posting, it has been taken down but the synopsis can still be found at http://blue-skies-fic.livejournal.com/1347.html#cutid1 (accessed January 3, 2015).

20. Necole Bitchie, "TV Guide Responds to Taraji P. Henson's Claims that She Was 'Snubbed,'" Necole Bitchie (blog), http://necolebitchie.com/2011/09/22/tv-guide -responds-to-taraji-p-hensons-claims-that-she-was-snubbed (accessed January 3, 2015).

21. An Nicholson, "Taraji P. Henson and *Person of Interest* Cast Give Insight on season 3, *Starpulse*, http://www.starpulse.com/news/An_Nicholson/2013/11/20/interviewing_ taraji_p_henson_and_perso (accessed January 3, 2015).

22. Carlita Rizzo, "Shonda Rhimes Talks about Her New Show *Scandal*: 'The Cast Is a Dream'—Exclusive," *Wetpaint*, April 12, 2012, http://www.wetpaint.com/news/articles /shonda-rhimes-talks-about-her-new-show-scandal-the-cast-is-a-dream-exclusive (accessed January 3, 2015).

23. "White Hats Back On," May 16, 2013, *Scandal*, ABC, 2012–.

24. Willa Paskin, "Network TV Is Broken. So How Does Shonda Rhimes Keep Making Hits?" *New York Times Magazine*, May 9, 2013, http://www.nytimes.com/2013/05/12 /magazine/shonda-rhimes.html?pagewanted=all&_r=1& (accessed January 3, 2015).

25. Tanya Steele, "The Trouble with *Scandal*," *Shadow and Act*, May 22, 2012, http:// blogs.indiewire.com/shadowandact/0d245890-a445–11e1-bcc4–123138165f92 (accessed January 3, 2015).

26. Lesley Goldberg, "How ABC's *Scandal* Gets 2,200 Tweets per Minute," *Hollywood Reporter*, February 7, 2013, http://www.hollywoodreporter.com/news /kerry-washington-abcs-scandal-gets-418091 (accessed January 3, 2015). Jordan Chariton, "Scandal Jumps Five Spots on Twitter Nielsen Ratings," *Lost Remote*, November 18, 2013, http://lostremote.com/scandal-jumps-five-spots-on-twitter-nielsen-ratings_b39443 (accessed January 3, 2015).

27. "It's Handled," *Scandal*, October 3, 2013, ABC, 2012–.

28. "Feeling These Feelings," October 4, 2013, http://itshandled.tumblr.com /post/63088687769/baronessvondengler-sbrown82-kef12345 (accessed January 3, 2015).

29. Phoebe Robinson, "*Scandal*: Instead of Saving the Drama for My Momma, Shonda Rhimes Gave the Drama to Me, My Momma, and My Momma's Momma," *Glamour*, May 3, 2013, http://www.glamour.com/entertainment/blogs/obsessed/2013/05/scandal -recap-instead-of-savin.html (accessed January 3, 2015).

30. Ibid.

31. Billy Nilles, "*Scandal* Recap: 'Everything's Coming Up Mellie' Reveals the True Hero of This Series," *Zap2It*, November 15, 2013, http://blog.zap2it.com/frominsidethebox /2013/11/scandal-recap-everythings-coming-up-mellie-reveals-the-true-hero-of-this -series.html (accessed January 3, 2015).

32. SabiaCoruja, "Olivia Pope and the Whitewashing of History," *SabiaCoruja.com*, December 19, 2013, http://sabiacoruja.com/post/70476219953/olivia-pope-and-the -whitewashing-of-history (accessed January 3, 2015).

33. The Terrys contend that in addition to Washington actually being married to Goldwyn (she is in a sham relationship with retired NFL player Nnamdi Asamougha and he has been quietly divorced from his wife Jane Musky for years), he is also the father of her baby—a child who months after her birth has still not been allowed to be photographed or even discussed by the cast and crew at *Scandal*.

CHAPTER 3

Television for *All* Women?

Watching Lifetime's Devious Maids

JILLIAN BÁEZ

Even before the series premiered in summer 2013, Lifetime Television's *Devious Maids* garnered much attention for its ensemble Latina cast and the presupposition of stereotypical representations of Latinas. *Devious Maids* deploys familiar television Latina actresses like Judy Reyes from *Scrubs* (2001–2010), Ana Ortiz from *Ugly Betty* (2006–2010), Roselyn Sanchez from *Without a Trace* (2002–2009) and emerging stars Dania Ramirez and Edy Ganem along with the iconic soap star Susan Lucci. An adaptation of the Mexican telenovela, *Ellas son la alegría del hogar* (2009–2010),[1] this prime-time serial was created by *Desperate Housewives* (2004–2012) writer and producer Marc Cherry and executive-produced by Mexican American actress Eva Longoria (see Figure 3.1). The show immediately generated excitement among industry professionals, media advocacy organizations, and fans because the series showcased Latina talent. At the same time, the series received criticism from bloggers and journalists for drawing on long-standing stereotypes of Latinas as both maids and spitfires so prevalent in film and television.

The central controversy surrounding *Devious Maids* is that while it does offer a Latina ensemble cast of both fresh and familiar faces, it also depicts these characters as maids.[2] Latina/o film scholars have long noted the Latina maid as a ubiquitous archetype in U.S. film and television.[3] Indeed, long-standing Chicana actress Lupe Ontiveros noted that she was cast as a maid at least 150

FIGURE 3.1. Advertising for season 1 of *Devious Maids* emphasized the program's connection to *Desperate Housewives* as well as the "sexy Latina maid" stereotype. Used with permission of Lifetime Television/Photofest.

times in her career.[4] As such, the series producers' choice to cast their protagonists as maids is problematic given the history of Latina cinematic and televisual representation and further amplified by the way in which the fictional maids are sexualized. Similar to longtime representations of African American women as domestic workers, earlier depictions of Latina maids on television and film were more asexual or sexually undesirable.[5] However, as portrayed in the recent films *Maid in Manhattan* (2002) and *Spanglish* (2004), *Devious Maids* melds the maid with the spitfire archetype where Latina characters are sexualized and sassy servants.[6] This amalgam of the maid and spitfire archetypes is particularly evident in the promotional materials for the series.

This criticism has not gone unchallenged. While the creator Marc Cherry has rarely addressed the controversy surrounding *Devious Maids* in the press, executive producer Eva Longoria has responded in several outlets,[7] notably in the *Huffington Post*, where she states: "The stereotype we are grappling with here is that as Latinas, *all* we are is maids. And yet, this is a show that deconstructs the stereotype by showing us that maids are so much more."[8] Essentially, Longoria argues that the series seeks to develop dynamic stories about Latina domestic workers. Certainly, maids are deserving of having their stories told in nuanced ways, but in her response Longoria sidesteps the legacy of the archetype of the maid in Hollywood. Despite the early criticism of the show, *Devious Maids* did well in terms of ratings, especially after the first few episodes.[9] It was renewed for a second season in August 2013.

In this chapter, I analyze the content and reception of the first season of *Devious Maids* within an institutional context. In doing so, I view the series as a contested form of feminized popular culture that is emblematic of the cable television industry's incessant search for new audiences in the early twenty-first century. More specifically, I ask: What do the production, content, and reception of *Devious Maids* reveal about Lifetime's strategies as "television for women"? In order to answer this question I perform a textual analysis of the first season and briefly explore the show's public official Facebook fan page (moderated by Lifetime). The textual analysis pays close attention to the narrative and how the protagonists are portrayed in terms of race, class, and gender in order to under-stand Lifetime's shifting programming strategies to capture new audiences.

The reception analysis, while preliminary, offers some insight into viewers' varied investments in melodramatic media texts (i.e., as a form of fantasy and escapism and a focus on female characters and women's issues)[10] while also deconstructing how various segments of the series' audience approach the program in both transgressive and problematic ways. The Facebook fan page does not offer a comprehensive view of *Devious Maids*' reception, but with over 301,000 "Likes" and over 3,000 posts with anywhere between 30 to over 400 comments responding to each post (as of January 3, 2014)[11] it does offer a window into why audiences watch the series. The posts come from a great variety of viewers in conversation with one another, especially in comparison to fan-operated sites that involve only the participation of a handful of very committed fans. After reading each post and comment shared on the Facebook page (as of January 3, 2014), I determined that most of the users are fans and only a few are nonfans or anti-fans.

I study both the content and reception of the series within the broader institutional context of Lifetime as a cable network that creates media content specifically for women. In doing so, I argue that while *Devious Maids* is a complex text that portrays Latina womanhood in some nuanced ways, the postfeminist and postracial sensibilities of the show discourage most audience members from engaging with the potentially transgressive aspects of the series. Feminist media scholars, such as Susan Douglas[12] and Yvonne Tasker and Diane Negra,[13] have amply documented that, in the twenty-first century, postfeminist discourses are rampant in mainstream media. Postfeminist media discourses emphasize that women's equality has been achieved and therefore feminism is no longer needed. In rendering feminism unnecessary, postfeminist media encourage hypersexualized images of women (especially young women) and legitimize the mocking of women in general. Similarly, media scholarship on race indicates that postracial media discourses are commonplace. Postracial media discourses espouse that racism is over and as such there is no need to discuss race. Furthermore, as Catherine Squires argues, postracial media discourses not only locate racism in the past, but also relegate any references to race as personal, individual instances of how one chooses to identify.[14] Lifetime draws on these postfeminist and postracial media discourses in its newer programming, eager to expand its appeal to a wide range of audiences. Ultimately, in trying to simultaneously appeal to a broader female audience *and* a narrow Latina/o audience segment, *Devious Maids* illustrates the difficulties cable networks like Lifetime experience in trying to diversify programming that will attract highly segmented audiences, while also maintaining their larger audience base.

Lifetime's "Television for Women"

Lifetime Television was launched in 1984 as the first cable network to target women as a niche market. In the early twenty-first century, Lifetime operates two cable channels, Lifetime Television and Lifetime Movie Networks, and has been one of the most watched cable networks for both its original programming and syndicated fare. *Devious Maids* is certainly not the first original programming created by Lifetime that foregrounds women of color, and Latinas in particular. While Lifetime has historically favored representations of traditional white femininity and heteronormativity,[15] the network has more recently forayed into depictions of working-class women and/or women of color.[16] Beginning with the original series *Any Day Now* (1998–2002) that was centered around a friendship between a white woman and a black woman from the 1960s to 1990s in Birmingham, Alabama,[17] Lifetime produced a number of original series and films that include ethnically diverse casts.[18] Some of these representations have ensemble casts that feature one Latina protagonist among women of other ethnicities (e.g., *Strong Medicine* and *The Division*), while some programming exclusively has focused on Latina characters (e.g., the film *One Hot Summer*).

Devious Maids was originally produced for ABC, but the broadcast network passed after the pilot production stage. It is unclear from the trade press exactly why ABC dropped the series, but Lifetime made an offer to pick up *Devious Maids* immediately after ABC passed on the serial. ABC Studios agreed to continue producing the show, a logical strategy given that ABC's parent company, Disney, is also part owner of Lifetime. Compared to a broadcast network, Lifetime was better positioned to take this risk, given that cable networks can focus on more segmented markets than can broadcasters.[19] As a cable network that is part of larger media conglomerates like ABC-Disney and Hearst (as an affiliate of A&E Networks), Lifetime is in a powerful position to be able to produce narrowcast programming that specifically targets women, and sometimes women of color, and can take risks given its financial backing. Launched in 1984, Lifetime has remained steadfast in attracting audiences and, in early 2014, reported that they reach more than 98 million households.[20] Lifetime deliberately targets women (particularly middle-class to upper-class women ages 18–49) and, following the industry lore that melodramatic material captivates women, tends to produce female-centered dramas. Eileen Meehan and Jackie Byers have found that during its early years (1984–1997) Lifetime coopted liberal feminist discourses,[21] but I demonstrate that in the early twenty-first century the cable network is departing from this approach, reifying postfeminist and postracial discourses that are commonplace in the larger media landscape.

Lifetime executives expressed interest in *Devious Maids* for several reasons.[22] First, Lifetime perceived that *Devious Maids* would be a good fit with their most recent original programming that has focused on appealing to younger audiences with more sexualized content, such as *The Client List* (2012–2013), starring Jennifer Love Hewitt. Fueled by competition with other networks that cater to female audiences, such as WE, Oxygen, and OWN, Lifetime has tried to obtain edgier programming that foregrounds sex and scandal, in the spirit of programs such as Bravo's *Real Housewives*[23] franchise and the CW's *Gossip Girl* (2007–2012), in an attempt to capture lucrative younger audiences.[24]

Within this context, *Devious Maids* adheres to Lifetime's longtime generic convention of female-centered dramas, and more specifically taps into formulas used by popular prime-time soap operas and reality series to attract younger female audiences. Secondly, Lifetime was interested in *Devious Maids* in order to work with Marc Cherry, as part of the network's larger goals have been to work with A-list creative talent to create programming with high production values that are competitive with the broadcast networks. Lastly, Lifetime executives hoped that *Devious Maids* would draw more Latina/o viewers, an audience segment that has become highly attractive to mainstream media companies since the late 1990s when the trade press began to emphasize Latina/o's buying power and the popularity of Spanish-language media in the United States.[25]

In addition to *Devious Maids'* Latina cast and adaptation of a popular telenovela, Lifetime courted Latina/o audiences in the United States and abroad by offering the series in English and Spanish. As such, *Devious Maids* gave Lifetime the opportunity to continue to attract its established audience base by using a formulaic genre, while tailoring content to even more segmented portions of the potential audience (i.e., youth and Latina/o audiences). Overall, Lifetime's investment in *Devious Maids* is indicative of the network's early-twenty-first-century strategy of diversifying programming through postfeminist and postracial content that appeals to both mainstream and niche audiences. Such programming de-emphasizes gender and racial inequality within the narrative, but appears inclusive through a racially diverse cast.

Deconstructing *Devious Maids*

Set in Beverly Hills, *Devious Maids* narrates the story of five Latina domestic workers laboring for the rich and famous. Zoila Diaz (Judy Reyes), in her forties, has worked for her helpless and childlike employer Genevieve Delatour (Susan Lucci) for decades. The relationship between Zoila and Genevieve is playful, with Zoila often giving Genevieve snide, sarcastic remarks and telling her what is best for her. Zoila's teenage daughter, Valentina (Edy Ganem), also works for Genevieve under her mother's watchful eye. Early in the season it is revealed that Valentina is in love with Genevieve's son, Remi. Tension ensues between Zoila and Valentina as the mother warns her daughter that, "Rich boys, they never fall in love with the help." Carmen Luna (Roselyn Sanchez), an aspiring recording artist in her thirties from Puerto Rico, works for Alejandro, a Ricky Martin–esque Latin pop star in hopes to gain entry into the music business. Rosie Falta is a nanny to the infant of the Westmore couple, both B-list actors, after leaving her son behind in Mexico in search of work.[26] Lastly, but certainly not least as she is positioned as the central character, Marisol Suarez (Ana Ortiz) is a mysterious, new maid who begins to work for the Stappord couple.[27] From the beginning of the series it is obvious that Marisol is not like

56

the other maids, particularly in her accentless English, wide vocabulary, and curiosity about a recently murdered maid.

Like *Desperate Housewives*, the series opens with a murder mystery. Flora (Paula Garcés), a maid to the Powell couple, was brutally murdered in their home and the killer is unknown. As the series progresses it becomes obvious that Marisol is undercover in search of Flora's killer because her son is accused of the murder. Halfway into the season, audiences find out that Marisol is a prestigious English professor. The mystery surrounding Flora's murder drives the plot in the first season, and class struggle is central to this narrative. Essentially, the maids are positioned as foils to their employers. More specifically, the series depicts the rich as narcissistic, selfish, and helpless without their maids. In particular, Evelyn Powell (Rebecca Wisocky) executes witty lines that cement the campy tone of the series and reinforce stereotypes of the rich as irrational and out of touch. For example, immediately after Flora's death, Evelyn yells at the police: "I don't care about photos. I don't care about evidence. My maid was murdered! Who's going to clean it up?"

In order to establish the faults of the wealthy employers, the maids are depicted as the moral compass of the show. This is especially the case with Rosie, who is positioned as more selfless and nurturing than her boss Peri Westmore (Mariana Klaveno), who is so career-obsessed that she barely pays attention to her son and constantly complains about her good-natured husband. Rosie's moral superiority is solidified when Peri has an affair and refuses to take responsibility for a hit-and-run accident. In this way, audiences are invited to view the maids as endearing and unlikely heroes. The series' focus on working poor Latinas as morally superior to white women harkens back to dominant narratives in cinematic representations of the Latina señorita of the Good Neighbor period in the 1930s and 1940s and more recently the Latina maids in mainstream films like *Spanglish* and *Maid in Manhattan*, where domestic servants are placed in juxtaposition to their self-obsessed and clueless white and upper-class female employers.[28]

A perusal of two of the maid protagonists reveals that some of the characters are one-dimensional while others subvert and complicate the stereotype of the maid-spitfire. Compared to the other maids, Carmen is visually the most sexualized maid and embodies the spitfire with her sassy attitude. In particular, Carmen is always willing to use her sexuality to her advantage. She wears tight, revealing clothing and flirts with her African American coworker and later boyfriend, Sam, to manipulate him into covering for her at work. In the episode "Wiping Away the Past," it is also implied that Carmen considers not only dating a music industry executive in exchange for a recording contract but offering sexual favors. Carmen's embodying of the Latina spitfire is also intricately tied to her specific ethnicity.[29] At one point, Carmen tells her boss Alejandro, "Don't ever tell a Puerto Rican woman to calm down. It's a waste of time." Later, at a party Alejandro hosts for music industry professionals, Carmen exclaims to the guests: "Of course I can dance! I'm Puerto Rican!" In these ways, Carmen reifies the tropicalized Latina sexpot in her performance of excess in terms of her speech, dress, and dancing.[30]

Marisol is unlike Carmen and the other maids because she is highly educated and it is assumed that prior to going undercover she enjoyed a comfortable middle- to upper-class lifestyle. Marisol is a single mother and there is no mention of a husband or partner. Halfway through the season Marisol explains to her employer Taylor Stappford (Brianna Brown) that she adopted her son (who is coded as white) after experiencing infertility. It is notable that Marisol is depicted as infertile, breaking with dominant media myths of Latinas as hyperfertile.[31] Overall, in the first season Marisol is rendered as different than the other maids, made most notable in her interview with the Stappords when Mrs. Stappord tells Marisol, "You don't sound like a maid. You sound like someone that went to college." Throughout the season the audience is not privy to Marisol's background in terms of ethnicity, generation, or class background prior to becoming a professor, and so she occupies an ambivalent, in-between space where she neither completely fits in with her upper-class white employers nor with her working-poor maid counterparts. Indeed, she is the only maid that converses with her employer, Taylor, as an equal in terms of issues of marriage and motherhood.[32]

As evident in these brief sketches of two protagonists, the characters simultaneously embody stereotypes of the maid and spitfire and subvert and complicate those same stereotypes. The hybrid genre of soap/telenovela/dramedy tends to flatten characters that potentially could be more dynamic. As a dramedy that is an adaptation of a Mexican telenovela, *Devious Maids* is campy and melodramatic. It draws on conventions of soap operas and telenovelas in its focus on interpersonal conflicts. In keeping with telenovela narrative strategies, maids are central characters that embody a rags-to-riches fairy tale, especially in the case of Valentina and Carmen. Like *Desperate Housewives*, the series lightens more serious issues, like class struggles, with the element of humor. Within this hybrid generic structure, most of the characters embody archetypes (e.g., Carmen as the spitfire, Rosie as the docile nanny, and Evelyn and Genevieve as narcissistic rich women) because these roles allow for narratives around sex, family, and scandals to easily develop. At the same time, there are moments of subversion, as in the character of Marisol who is not quite who we think she is.

Devious Maids' use of a hybrid genre draws from earlier television series, namely *Desperate Housewives* and *Ugly Betty*. *Devious Maids* echoes *Desperate Housewives* through its use of a hybrid melodramatic genre that, like its predecessor, melds dramedy, murder mystery, and U.S. soap opera formulas while also infusing elements of the Latin American telenovela. Riding on the success of *Desperate Housewives*, and in particular the appeal of Eva Longoria's Latina spitfire character Gabrielle Solis,[33] *Devious Maids* also features female-centered narratives that can be funny, absurd, and tragic. However, while *Desperate Housewives* is thematically focused on domesticity in the form of marriage and motherhood, *Devious Maids* is decidedly more concerned with class struggles, employing a postracial and postfeminist lens to underscore class as the central tension in the larger narrative. As such, *Devious Maids* both reproduces and departs from the themes and generic conventions of *Desperate Housewives*, a strategy that has enabled the show to draw in already established *Desperate Housewives* fans and newer audiences, particularly working-class and middle-class women of color. At the same time that *Devious Maids* has drawn on generic conventions established by *Desperate Housewives*, *Devious Maids'* fusion of the dramedy and telenovela harks back to the generic conventions and aesthetics of *Ugly Betty*, such as the use of bright colors on Latina/o bodies and homes contrasted with the white, sterile colors on the bodies and space of the white, upper-class characters.

Despite the constraints of the series' hybrid genre on its narrative structure, as *Devious Maids* unfolded its character development became more rich and complex than critics and audiences anticipated. By the end of season one, the series addressed some salient class-based issues, such as immigration and labor (exemplified in Rosie's story), Valentina's struggle to gain access to higher education, and sexual exploitation (in Adrian Powell's chasing after Marisol to engage in his pornographic enterprise). Audiences also get to indulge in the fantasy of the maids talking back to their employers without much reprimand, something that only seems possible in fictional television and film.[34] Certainly, this talking back is limited to interpersonal relationships and does not question or challenge the dominant order. Nonetheless, these are some of the few moments when we see Latina maids as agents. Indeed, the depiction of gendered working-class struggles and the maids' talking back to and with their employers (in the case of Marisol and Taylor) are the most transgressive elements of the series and seem to be the comedic force of the show. As Susan Douglas describes in relation to watching "sassy" black women who verbally challenge racism and patriarchy in comedy, there is a subversive element to women of color who talk back to their superiors, even if this power is only symbolic.[35]

However, these ruptures are undermined by the promotional material supporting the show. First, the title of the series, "Devious Maids," suggests that the protagonists are not just mischievous, but malevolent. Flora and Carmen especially seem to embody this devious attribute because they are often scheming to get what they want. Second, the initial promotional materials, including print advertisements and commercials, depicted the characters as extremely sexual. For example, an outdoor ad for *Devious Maids* that was placed in East Harlem, a predominantly Latino neighborhood in New York City, displays the word "SEX" written on a misty glass door at the center of the ad. A faceless maid with a plunging neckline and short maid's uniform stands on the left of the frame, prepared to wipe the door with a sponge (see Figure 3.2). Ultimately, there seems to be a discrepancy between the show's representation of the protagonists

FIGURE 3.2. Bus shelter ad for *Devious Maids*, season 1. Photo by author.

as both sexual objects *and* agents and the promotion of the series as overtly sexualized with Latina maids as the main object to be consumed.[36]

In addition, *Devious Maids* operates as a postfeminist and postracial text. While the maids are somewhat less sexualized within the show than in the promotional materials, all of the maids adhere to hegemonic notions of femininity such as wearing dresses, high heels, and makeup, and are adorned with long hair. Notably, the maids' career aspirations are also feminized (e.g., Carmen's desire to become a pop star and Valentina's hopes to be a fashion designer). These types of representations replicate formulaic conventions of how younger women are portrayed in contemporary postfeminist television—as hyperfeminine, sexy, and ambitious.[37] In addition, *Devious Maids* follows the trend of using racially ambiguous casts, but at the same time carefully avoiding any references to racism. This strategy hinges on not offending mainstream audiences who may be uninterested in issues of race while also appeasing audiences of color who are desperate for more racially diverse programming. In particular, the series draws on familiar images of the "Latin look" of olive-skinned (not too dark or too light) complexion and dark hair that mark the Latina actresses as different, but as not too threatening. This postracial positioning also materializes in the narrative as the central tension in the plot concerns class struggles, not gender or racial inequality. Overall, the postfeminist and postracial sensibility of *Devious Maids* sharply limits the transgressive possibilities of the show, keeping it "safe" for both mainstream (white, middle- and upper-class) audiences and Latino/a audiences.

Devious Maids Fandom

Given *Devious Maids'* polysemic structure, in this section I consider what has drawn audiences to the series and how they have interpreted the series. As mentioned earlier, Lifetime attempts to target two niche audience segments: (white) female audiences (with hopes of also capturing these women's male partners) and Latina/o audiences. Analyzing reception of both of these audience segments (female fans overall and Latina fans in particular[38]) reveals the ways that Lifetime's "Television for Women" takes on multiple meanings within different fan contexts.

In analyzing the Facebook fan page, it is clear that *Devious Maids'* fan base is very international, with many fans mentioning that they are watching the series in the United Kingdom (where the show is syndicated on TLC), Canada, and Brazil. On the fan page the majority of the comments are in English, but there are also some posts in Spanish or Portuguese. The show's ratings reveal that although the series is on a network that specifically produces programming for and targets women, at least half of the audience is composed of men.[39] Although it is not clear how many of these men are heterosexual, female Facebook fans speculate that some men might tune in to watch the sexualized imagery. For example, while less than 5 percent of the comments on the fan page are from men, another 10 percent of the Facebook fans mentioned regularly viewing *Devious Maids* with their husbands. Some of these women speculated that their husbands are probably watching the show because of the sexual appeal of the Latina actresses. For example, one fan writes, "I think he watches it for all the hot latina's." (Monica Daniel, 8/5/13). A few men on the Facebook fan page also posted similar comments about watching the show in order to view the "sexy" actresses. These fans' posts suggest that *Devious Maids* invites a patriarchal and heterosexual male gaze while also appealing to women and gay men.

My analysis of the Facebook fan page reveals that the majority of fans watch *Devious Maids* because they are *Desperate Housewives* fans and are looking for a show with similar themes and aesthetic qualities. At least one-third of the comments posted on the Facebook fan page are references to how *Devious Maids* reminds audiences of *Desperate Housewives* and/or "fills the gap" left by the former show's end. In keeping with other derivative women's genres, namely soap opera, fans indicate that the "sex and drama" is one of the main sources of pleasure, albeit a guilty pleasure, of watching *Devious Maids*. In addition, about 10 percent of Facebook fans, particularly those with Spanish surnames, referred to *Devious Maids* as an "English novella," noting the melodramatic quality of the series and its occasional use of recognizable telenovela actors. As such, fans found pleasure in *Devious Maids'* blending of the two feminine genres of dramedy (as an extension of the soap opera) and the telenovela. One fan put the show's blended genre appeal this way: "I love this show! I was so sad when Desperate Housewives & Ugly Betty went off the air. This show is their love child and I am hoping it sticks around." (Arielle Michèle, 7/28/13). Overall, Lifetime's strategy of combining multiple forms of feminine genres to appeal to numerous segments of the female audience seems to appeal to both mainstream (men and women) and Latina/o viewers.

Latina/o audiences comprise 17 percent of *Devious Maids'* viewership, compared to only 12 percent in other Lifetime programming.[40] Very few Latino men comment on the fan page (and when they do they are largely sexualized comments about the Latina cast members), but nearly one-third of the posts on Facebook are from Latina-identified women. Latina fans tend to fall into three categories: 1) those who take pride in the series' ensemble Latina cast, 2) women who find pleasure in the maids' talking back, and 3) domestic workers who identify with or are sympathetic toward the characters. Latina fandom based on the Latina cast is informed by the historical underrepresentation of Latinas on television, particularly prime-time television. Excitement and pride in the show's Latina cast was voiced in at least twenty posts by Latina fans. Examples include the following on the Facebook fan page:

> "Love this show......Man [Cherry] putting Latinas on the map with bold letters" (Piel Morena, 8/13/13)

> "I am so glad this is a hit. Latinos deserve to be recognized. We can make good television" (Gladymar Rodriguez, 8/8/13)

Although non-Latina/o fans rarely indicated finding pleasure in watching the maids talk back to and undermine their employers, some Latina fans enjoyed this more transgressive element of the show. For example, in response to a scene where Carmen tells her employer, Alejandro, "Never tell a Puerto Rican woman to calm down," several fans cheered and wrote comments such as the following:

> "Let' em know Carmen!!!!" (Margie Muniz, 8/18/13)

> "I loved it when Carmen puts Alexandro in his place!" (Iris Magana, 8/19/13)

These types of comments indicate that while mainstream fans did not identify with the element of class struggle in *Devious Maids*, this was an important moment of rupture for some Latina audience members.[41] The maids' attempt to subvert their subordinate position through talking back is certainly the least realistic aspect of the series, as scholars have amply documented how domestic workers are often invisible at their places of employment,[42] but the fantasy of domestic workers challenging their employers is arguably the most transgressive element of the show.

A few Latina domestic workers also commented on the Facebook fan page that they liked the Latina protagonists because they are positioned as morally superior to their female employers. The following two posts are from fans that identified with the show's protagonists because they also work as domestic maids:[43]

> We're servants and mothers. In these women's houses they don't know anything—their children nor their house! They're only concerned with their friends and society." (translation from Spanish, Matyrosa Saldana, 6/23/13)

> "Luv this show!!!! there's nothing wrong with being a maid. maids don't just clean house. they also keep the family together, help raise the kids etc. i don't see this show as racist. besides the crazies r the people they work for." (Diana Prince, 7/21/13)

In these posts, fans acknowledge the physical and emotional labor that domestic workers perform while reifying the image of employers as superficial, clueless, and mentally unstable. These comments suggest that for this fan segment, *Devious Maids'* narrative strategy of positioning the maids as morally superior to their employers humanizes domestic workers and provides a key point of identification for some women who work in the service industry.

There were also ruptures present on the Facebook fan page by what Jonathan Gray calls "anti-fans," or audiences "who strongly dislike a given text" and who are "variously bothered, insulted or otherwise assaulted by its presence."[44] Gray notes that most anti-fans never view the text. Instead, anti-fans are usually exposed to the text via paratexts that include trailers and advertisements. As such, anti-fans respond not necessarily to the text itself but instead to "what might be 'in' the text."[45] This is certainly the case regarding some of the strongest reactions to *Devious Maids*. For example, several Latina Facebook users critiqued the show for its stereotypical portrayal of Latinas. In particular, it appears that these anti-fans often had not viewed the series and, instead, based their critiques on the promotional material provided by Lifetime which, as mentioned earlier, is highly sexualized and does not reveal the scope of the characters or narrative of the show. Here is a sampling of some of these posts:

> When I saw an ad for Devious Maids on television the other day I was so disappointed and frustrated. Not only is this show encouraging the stereotype of all Latinas as maids, but it is also depicting all Latinas as devious, sexualized playthings. I am a proud Latina for the reason that we are hardworking, good, and ethical people. None of these characteristics were being portrayed in the commercial for this show. I am currently pursuing a BS in Civil Engineering and for Latinas to be represented as Devious Maids is horrifying, backwards, and demeaning. I hope this show never airs and that this type of thinking about Latino women will come to an end. (Julita del Peruvian, 5/18/13)

> Wow, what a bunch of complete and utter nonsense by Ms. Longoria. . . . five maids? There ARE no maids in my family so I can't relate. A show based on popular stereotypes that Latin women fight against every day in this country and this show is for our benefit? As a Latina all I see is Eva Longoria's true goal. . . . which is money! (Diana Pilar, 5/18/13)

> There is way better things that a tv show can talk about Latinas. To me [this] is another show where Latinas are exposed looking hot with a bunch of

drama. And Latinas actresses should work harder to change that perspective, but this is easy to sell. ashamed for them. (Sandra de la Torre, 6/16/13)

The show looks good but I just don't appreciate the fact that its all Latinas. Why do we always have to be the hired help . . . Can't we rise above that??? (Elda Guadalupe Esquivel, 6/17/13)

These critiques of the show provide a counterpoint to the fans' uncritical celebration of the series, but these ruptures are limited because they view the show within a positive/negative binary that does not capture the nuances nor the complexities of this serial. While anti-fans' critique of *Devious Maids* is valuable in its questioning of the show's use of stereotypes (i.e., hypersexual Latina maids), the backlash is informed by middle-class respectability politics that seek to privilege the experiences of professional women, thereby erasing the visibility of poor and working-class women (i.e., domestic workers).

Overall, reception analysis reveals that while most female fans are watching *Devious Maids* as a source of feminine pleasure derived from its similarities to the generic qualities of *Desperate Housewives*, Latina fans view the series for its Latina cast and story lines that humanize female domestic workers. In particular, Latina fans revel in how the show positions the maids as morally superior to their employers and capable of subverting power relations through talking back and creating "devious" plots to outsmart their rich counterparts. Mainstream female fans rarely mention enjoying this more transgressive aspect of the show, perhaps because many posted that they view the serial as "not serious." Interestingly, Rosie and Carmen, who reify the most familiar immigrant and spitfire Latina archetypes, are the most popular with mainstream female fans. Arguably, Rosie and Carmen are the most likeable characters because they are the most recognizable characters to mainstream audiences. Characters such as Marisol are unintelligible as they run counter to dominant televisual representations of Latinas. Ultimately, analysis of the reception of the series suggests that *Devious Maids* takes on different meanings for varying segments of the female audience. Mainstream female fans rarely discuss the show in terms of feminism or antiracism, while Latina fans and anti-fans sometimes disrupt the series' postfeminist and postracial sensibility. At best the show only marginally ruptures dominant notions of Latina womanhood for mainstream audiences who watch it largely as a feminine genre that integrates melodrama. While Latina fans also enjoy the show for its feminized generic conventions, *Devious Maids* nonetheless provides an unprecedented moment of Latina visibility in mainstream television.

Conclusion

In this chapter, I have explored the production, content, and reception of *Devious Maids* in order to understand how Lifetime, "Television for Women," is vying for even more segmented portions of the female audience in the early twenty-first century. In a revision of their earlier strategy of targeting "women" as a homogenous category, Lifetime was interested in *Devious Maids* as a strategy to draw in both younger and Latina audiences, along with a mainstream, white audience. This strategy of attracting an established, broad female audience and more specific segments of the audience is reflected in the show itself. *Devious Maids* is a contested text that is simultaneously conservative (in its keeping with long-standing archetypes of Latinas as the "señorita"/maid and the spitfire) *and* progressive (in its inclusion of an ensemble Latina cast that to some extent challenges dominant notions of Latina womanhood). More specifically, the show manages this dual address by inviting audiences to read it through a postfeminist and postracial lens that underscores class struggles. In concert with the show's postfeminist and postracial sensibility, its fusion of women's genres (soap opera, dramedy, and telenovela) renders the series less serious to mainstream female viewers who overlook some of its more transgressive aspects. Eva Longoria reinforces this postracial and postfeminist sensibility when she tells Fox News Latino, "The show has really nothing to do with race. . . . It's a really great drama, it's a great mystery and it's a lot of fun."[46]

Lifetime is drawing both mainstream female audiences and Latina audiences with this strategy, but these audiences are reading the show in somewhat different ways. Mainstream female fans comment on enjoying the melodramatic aspects of the show and its similar tone to *Desperate Housewives*. In keeping with the show's postfeminist and postracial sensibility, mainstream female fans rarely mention the maids' race or ethnicity and instead focus on the interpersonal conflicts among the characters. Latina fans also take pleasure in the soapy qualities of the show, but tend to equally express enthusiasm in the Latina cast, telenovelaesque aesthetics of the show, and the maids' agency. In other words, while *Devious Maids* audiences are invited to consume Latina maids in familiar and sanitized forms through the nonthreatening, feminized genre of melodrama, Latina fans read the series through a more nuanced and transgressive lens than the broader female audience. At the same time, anti-fans develop strong responses to *Devious Maids* primarily based on paratextual materials such as the trailer and advertisements. These audience readings are emblematic of Lifetime's current attempts to draw in multiple segments of the female audience through postfeminist and postracial content that is intentionally polysemic.

These differences in audience responses also challenge the monolithic category of "women" in both feminist media scholarship and the media industries. In the late 1990s and early 2000s, feminist media scholars critiqued Lifetime for its minimal feminist content and its insistence on privileging white, middle-class, heterosexual female characters. Whereas Eileen Meehan and Jackie Byars found that Lifetime's earlier programming (1984–1997) coopted liberal feminism, in the early twenty-first century, Lifetime's original series reproduce postfeminism and postracism. *Devious Maids* suggests that Lifetime's "Television for Women" has become somewhat more inclusive, but that its success still relies on using formulaic women's genres that decenter gender and racial equality.

Notes

1. Translation: "They Are the Happiness of the Home."

2. Michelle Herrera Mulligan, "Devious Maids Misrepresents Latinas," *Huffington Post*, May 9, 2013, accessed December 1, 2013, http://www.huffingtonpost.com/michelle -herrera-mulligan/devious-maids-eva-longoria_b_3248787.html; Mary McNamara, "Review: 'Devious Maids Are Sexy, Scheming and Stereotypical,'" *Los Angeles Times*, June 22, 2013, accessed December 1, 2013, http://articles.latimes.com/2013/jun/22 /entertainment/la-et-st-devious-maids-review; Tanisha L. Ramirez, "Eva Longoria's *Devious Maids* Is a Wasted Opportunity," *Huffington Post*, May 3, 2013, accessed December 1, 2013, http://www.huffingtonpost.com/tanisha-l-ramirez/eva-longorias-devious -maids_b_3210204.html; Raul Reyes, "'Devious Maids' Does a Disservice to Latinos," *USA Today*, July 9, 2013, accessed December 1, 2013, http://www.usatoday.com/story /opinion/2013/07/09/devious-maids-latinos-tv-show-column/2461193/; Alisa Rodri-guez Valdes, "Opinion: The Problem with 'Devious Maids' Goes Far beyond Hollywood," *NBC Latino*, June 7, 2013, accessed December 1, 2013, http://nbclatino.com/2013/06/07 /opinion-the-problem-with-devious-maids-goes-far-beyond-hollywood/.

3. Mary Beltrán, *Latina/o Stars in U.S. Eyes: The Making and Meanings of Film and TV Stardom* (Urbana: University of Illinois Press, 2009); Isabel Molina-Guzmán, *Dangerous Curves: Latina Bodies in the Media* (New York: New York University Press, 2010); L. S. Kim, "Invisible and Undocumented: The Latina Maid on Network Television," *Atzlan* 24 (1999): 107–128; Steve Nava, *Working the Affect Shift: Latina Service Workers in U.S. Film* (Boca Raton, Fla.: Brown Walker Press, 2011); Charles Ramirez Berg, *Latino Images in Film: Stereotypes, Subversion, and Resistance* (Austin: University of Texas Press, 2002); Angharad N. Valdivia, *Latina/os and the Media* (Malden, Mass.: Polity, 2010).

4. Valdivia, 93.

5. Kim; Nava; Ramirez Berg.

6. Rosario from the television series *Will and Grace* (1998–2006) is an exception to this as she is depicted as sexually undesirable, yet sassy.

7. Jeanne Jakle, "Longoria Lauds 'Devious Maids' amid Heated Debate," MySanAntonio .com, http://www.mysanantonio.com/entertainment/entertainment_columnists

/jeanne_jakle/article/Longoria-lauds-Devious-Maids-amid-heated-debate-4613193.php;
Eva Longoria, "There's No Such Thing as a Wasted Opportunity," *Huffington Post*, May 7,
2013, accessed December 1, 2013, http://www.huffingtonpost.com/eva-longoria/theres
-no-such-thing_b_3233346.html; Tanzina Vega, "Eva Longoria Defends 'Devious Maids'
Against Critics," *Ledger*, June 29, 2013, accessed December 1, 2013, http://www.theledger
.com/article/20130629/news/130629425; "Eva Longoria's 'Devious Maids' to Release Preview in English and Spanish to Attract Latinos," *Fox News Latino*, June 5, 2013,
accessed December 1, 2013, http://latino.foxnews.com/latino/entertainment/2013/06/05
/eva-longorias-show-devious-maids-to-release-sneak-peak-in-english-and-spanish/.

8. Longoria.

9. Sheridan Watson, "'Devious Maids' Reaches Series-High Viewership," *Entertainment
Weekly*, July 29, 2013, accessed December 1, 2013, http://insidetv.ew.com/2013/07/29
/devious-maids-increases-viewership/.

10. Ien Ang, *Watching* Dallas: *Soap Opera and the Melodramatic Imagination* (New York:
Methuen, 1985); Charlotte Brunsdon, *The Feminist, the Housewife, and the Soap Opera*
(Oxford: Oxford University Press, 2000).

11. It is impossible to determine how many fans follow the page as Facebook no longer
reports this information to users. However, the "Likes" the fan page receives is an indicator of the series' popularity.

12. Susan J. Douglas, *The Rise of Enlightened Sexism: How Pop Culture Took Us from Girl
Power to Girls Gone Wild* (New York: Times Books, 2010), 126–153.

13. Yvonne Tasker and Diane Negra, eds., *Interrogating Postfeminism: Gender and the
Politics of Popular Culture* (Durham, N.C.: Duke University Press, 2007).

14. Catherine R. Squires, *The Post-Racial Mystique: Media and Race in the Twenty-First
Century* (New York: New York University Press, 2014).

15. Julie D'Acci, Introduction, Special Issue: "Lifetime: A Cable Network 'for
Women,'" *Camera Obscura* 33–34 (1994): 7–12; Heather Hundley, "The Evolution of
Gendercasting: The Lifetime Television Network—'Television for Women,'" *Journal of
Popular Film and Television* 29, no. 4 (Winter 2002): 174–181; Amanda D. Lotz, "Textual
(Im)Possibilities in the U.S. Post-Network Era: Negotiating Production and Promotion
Processes on Lifetime's *Any Day Now*," *Critical Studies in Media Communication* 21, no. 1
(2004): 22–43; Eileen R. Meehan and Jackie Byars, "Telefeminism: How Lifetime Got
Its Groove, 1984–1997," *Television and New Media* 1, no. 1 (2000): 33–51.

16. Lotz, 22–43.

17. Ibid.

18. Some of the original movies include *Little Girl Lost: The Delimar Vera Story* (2008),
which documents the true story kidnapping of the baby Delimar Vera; *One Hot Summer*
(2009) a romantic comedy about four middle-class Cuban American women in Miami;
the remade *Steel Magnolias* (2012), which features an all–black woman cast; and *Coretta
and Betty* (2013), a biopic on Coretta Scott King and Betty Shabazz. Examples of original
series with ethnically diverse casts include *Strong Medicine* (2000–2006) and *The Division*
(2001–2004).

19. Lotz, "Textual (Im)Possibilities," 22–43; Amanda D. Lotz, *Redesigning Women: Television after the Network Era* (Urbana: University of Illinois Press, 2006), 37–67.

20. Lifetime also reports on its website that there are even more audiences tuning in online, with 3.9 million unique visitors/93 million page views as of 2009, accessed December 1, 2013, http://www.mylifetime.com/about-us/about-lifetime.

21. Meehan and Byars, 34.

22. Cynthia Littleton, "Lifetime Orders Marc Cherry's 'Devious Maids,'" *Variety*, June 22, 2012, accessed December 1, 2013, http://variety.com/2012/tv/news/lifetime -orders-marc-cherry-s-devious-maids-1118055861/.

23. It should be noted that *Desperate Housewives* paved the road for the *Real Housewives* series in its focus on mothers and wives and an all-female cast. *Devious Maids* also tangentially draws from *Real Housewives* in its rendering of affluent women as emotionally and materially excessive. In addition, like *Devious Maids*, *Real Housewives of Miami* featured an all-Latina cast and simultaneously sought to target Latina viewers in particular while continuing to attract mainstream female audiences.

24. Lacey Rose, "Marc Cherry's ABC Pilot 'Devious Maids' Lands at Lifetime with Series Order," *Hollywood Reporter*, June 22, 2013, accessed December 1, 2013, http://www .hollywoodreporter.com/news/marc-cherrys-devious-maids-ana-ortiz-lifetime-341185.

25. Arlene Dávila, *Latinos, Inc.: The Marketing and Making of a People*, 2nd ed. (Berkeley: University of California Press, 2012); *Latino Spin: Public Image and the Whitewashing of Race* (New York: New York University Press, 2008).

26. Rosie's surname is significant as it translates into "missing" or "lost" and she is the one character who is widowed and her son is still in Mexico.

27. Marisol's surname is an intertextual reference harking back to Ana Ortiz's role as Hilda Suarez in *Ugly Betty*. However, Hilda is a foil to Marisol. Hilda was a working-class spitfire, while Marisol fits more within the Latina dark lady archetype as a mysterious middle- to upper-class character.

28. Molina-Guzmán, 159–161.

29. It is notable that Carmen is only one of two of the maids (Rosie is the other) whose ethnicity is made explicit. This ambivalent and homogenized representation of Latinidad is reinforced by the flamenco-pop theme music (instead of music that is more nationally specific such as salsa, merengue, banda, or cumbia). See Dávila, *Latinos, Inc.*, for a more thorough discussion of how mainstream media producers prefer to use panethnic representations of Latinos that erase differences within Latino communities.

30. Frances Aparicio and Susana Chávez-Silverman, eds., *Tropicalizations: Transcultural Representations of Latinidad* (Hanover: University Press of New England, 1997); Ana M. López, "Are All Latinos from Manhattan? Hollywood, Ethnography and Cultural Colonialism," in *Unspeakable Images*, Lester Friedman, ed. (Urbana: University of Illinois Press, 1993), 67–80; Priscilla P. Ovalle, *Dance and the Hollywood Latina: Race, Sex, and Stardom* (New Brunswick: Rutgers University Press, 2011); Valdivia, *Latina/os and the Media*; Angharad N. Valdivia, *A Latina in the Land of Hollywood: And Other Essays on Media Culture* (Tucson: University of Arizona Press, 2000).

31. Leo Chavez, *The Latino Threat: Constructing Immigrants, Citizens, and the Nation* (Stanford: Stanford University Press, 2008).

32. Zoila does discuss similar issues with Genevieve, but it is in a more condescending manner, as it is apparent that Zoila views Genevieve as incapable.

33. Debra Merskin, "Three Faces of Eva: Perpetuation of the Hot-Latina Stereotype in *Desperate Housewives*," *Howard Journal of Communications* 18, no. 2 (2007): 133–151.

34. Ibid., 91–109.

35. Douglas, 126–153.

36. Lotz describes similar discrepancies between the writers and promoters on Lifetime's *Any Day Now*, where the network's promotion depoliticized the content of the show. Lotz, "Textual (Im)Possibilities," 35–38.

37. Douglas.

38. It was difficult to identify Latina audiences because while many Latina/os have a Spanish surname, not all do due to non-Spanish European ancestors or through intermarriage. Also, use of Spanish or Spanglish is not always an indicator of a Latina/o background. As such, I identify Latina audiences only when the posters identify themselves as Hispanic, Latina, or from a specific Latin American country.

39. Watson.

40. Joanne Ostrow, "The Rise of the Upscale Hispanic TV Audience, the 'New Baby Boomers,'" *Denver Post*, July 28, 2013, accessed December 1, 2013, http://www.denverpost.com/ci_23746421/rise-upscale-hispanic-tv-audience-new-baby-boomers.

41. Susan Douglas argues that white women derive pleasure from watching black women challenge patriarchy in media, especially in comedic roles. Douglas asserts that because black women are generally not expected to conform to chaste and docile white femininity, black women are allowed more freedom to challenge gender norms within mainstream media. As such, white women may take pleasure in viewing these contestations to patriarchy precisely because they are not encouraged to voice these same concerns without being disciplined. While white viewers did not explicitly express pleasure in the maids' talking back to their employers on the Facebook fan page, this also might play a role in the popularity of the show among non-Latina viewers.

42. Nilda Flores-González, Anna Romina Guevarra, Maura Toro-Morn, and Grace Chang, eds., *Immigrant Women Workers in the Neoliberal Age* (Urbana: University of Illinois Press, 2013); Pierette Hondagneu-Sotelo, *Doméstica: Immigrant Workers Cleaning and Caring in the Shadows of Affluence* (Berkeley: University of California Press, 2001); Mary Romero, *Maid in the U.S.A.* (New York: Routledge, 2002).

43. In earlier posts on the Facebook page these users identified as Latinas and domestic workers.

44. Jonathan Gray, "New Audiences, New Textualities," *International Journal of Cultural Studies* 6, no. 1 (2003): 64–81, 70.

45. Ibid., 70.

46. "Eva Longoria's 'Devious Maids' to Release Preview."

CHAPTER 4

Women, Gossip, and Celebrity Online

Celebrity Gossip Blogs as Feminized Popular Culture

ERIN A. MEYERS

Gossip, as a form of communication, is socially frowned upon if not outright reviled. Though both men and women regularly engage in gossip talk, it is generally dismissed as the mindless pastime of bored and malicious housewives or a pernicious form of social control carried out by catty teenage mean girls. Yet gossip's bad reputation belies its importance as space to make and circulate meaning outside of the dominant culture. According to Jörg Bergmann, gossip is an informal mode of talk between two or more individuals about an absent third person known to all participants.[1] While such talk certainly has the potential to work as a means of social control, Bergmann suggests the primary function of gossip is to generate a sense of intimacy and connection between gossipers through the creation of shared meaning about their shared world. By negotiating and evaluating the social behaviors of others, gossipers form a social bond and, drawing on their own experiences and standpoints, forge an understanding of the way the world works. Patricia Meyer Spacks claims gossip talk "provides a resource for the subordinated [and] a crucial form of solidarity."[2] In this view, gossip is a form of talk that enables women "to reflect about themselves, to express wonder and uncertainty and to locate certainties, to enlarge their knowledge of one another."[3] Such private talk prioritizes women's voices and concerns and allows gossipers to negotiate dominant culture together.

Gossip's contradictory cultural standing is also at the forefront of its role within the media and entertainment industries. Gossip media, such as tabloids, are a central player in the production and circulation of celebrity precisely because they focus the revelation of the private and "real" individual behind the screen persona through gossip talk. Though audiences never actually know the celebrities they admire (or revile), celebrity culture is built upon an "insistent question of 'really'" in which the mediated image is searched for the "true" individual at its core.[4] Gossip about celebrities negotiates the boundaries between the public and private selves, allowing audiences to use these images as anchors for discussion of larger social issues that shape everyday life. This draws us into the star's image and, not coincidentally, works to sell a range of commodities— including the star's films or albums, consumer goods, and, of course, the tabloid magazines themselves. Yet, despite the important economic role gossip media and its primarily female audiences play in the media industry, celebrity gossip is routinely denounced as a meaningless and feminized distraction responsible for the "tabloidization" of contemporary media that privileges entertainment and sensation over information and reason.[5]

But to take celebrity gossip seriously as a form of feminized communication recognizes how gossip about celebrities is more than just distraction; rather it helps audiences make sense of the wider world and their place within it. Karen Sternheimer says, "[C]elebrity stories can help us make sense of our identities—not simply by telling us how we should look, feel, think, or act, but through a social process of negotiation."[6] For example, gossiping about whether or not Miley Cyrus's over-the-top displays of sexuality in her public and private life allows the gossipers to negotiate social expectations around sexuality and intimate relationships. In other words, gossip is not simply the pursuit of truth. It is a process of narrativizing and judging the contrast between the public and private celebrity image as markers of larger social ideologies, particularly around gender, race, sexuality, and class.[7] While such talk is not inherently resistant to dominant norms, the fact that it offers a space where women's concerns are negotiated and made meaningful makes it, and celebrity culture, important sites of cultural analysis.[8]

It is within this notion of gossip as "women's talk" and as a form of shared social meaning-making that I wish to explore the rise of the celebrity gossip blog as a unique form of feminized popular culture that speaks to the broader shifts in media cultures in the early twenty-first century. Drawing stylistically on the tabloid magazines and Hollywood gossip columns that have long offered a purportedly unauthorized and behind-the-scenes look at the lives of celebrities, particularly through a focus on stereotypically feminine concerns such as relationships, children, fashion, and beauty, celebrity gossip blogs foreground gossip talk as the primary way in which celebrities are made meaningful by and for audiences. But gossip blogs are distinct from print magazines because of the ways in which they engage the technological and social possibilities of the internet, and it is within these two lenses that I examine the rise and influence of the celebrity gossip blog. Though print gossip magazines, like *Us Weekly* and *People*, now also offer online content and other online outlets, such as Yahoo's OMG.yahoo.com and *HuffPost Celebrity*, certainly focus on celebrity content, the gossip blog is a specific and influential form of celebrity media precisely because of its focus on the social practice of gossip talk. That is, rather than simply reporting the latest dish, gossip blogs are platforms for commentary and meaning-making by the blogger and his or her audience. These digital spaces bring the private talk of gossip into the public sphere, highlighting the shared negotiation of celebrity images as both a place of audience pleasure and an intervention into the established industrial processes of celebrity culture.

A primary challenge of studying new media forms like gossip blogs is that they are marked by constant technological change, and certainly the various interactive features of the celebrity gossip blogs that emerged in the early twenty-first century have changed and will continue to change as new technological formats are developed. Yet such constant change should not preclude the close study of the underlying social and historical contexts that shape the social use of these technologies within popular culture. The technologies of the internet open new public spaces for the gossip talk, but these interactive spaces rely upon the existing social practices of gossip that have long shaped audience engagement with celebrity culture. What female audiences *do* in these spaces, namely negotiate broader social meanings through gossip about celebrity culture, is not new, even as the technological features of gossip blogs push this once private form of communication into the public sphere in new and more interactive ways. Drawing on the more in-depth analysis of gossip blogs in my book, *Dishing Dirt in the Digital Age*, I here offer a brief analysis of the initial ascendency of celebrity gossip blogs into popular culture during the early twenty-first century.[9] My goal is to explore the gossip blog as a particularly feminized form of new media through attention to the existing social practices of gossip that continue to shape the place of gossip blogs within the celebrity media industry and the everyday lives of their predominantly female readers.

Gossip Blogs and the Celebrity Media Industry

Extratextual forms of celebrity gossip have been a central force in celebrity culture since the early days of cinema. Early movie fan magazines like *Photoplay*, *Modern Screen*, and *Silver Screen* revealed the star's "'real' personality—his or her life, loves and most intimate of thoughts."[10] Sternheimer argues that bringing the private lives of stars into the public purview reinforced "that the American Dream of rising from the bottom of the economic ladder is real for those willing to work hard."[11] While these magazines humanized stars through these glimpses of their private lives, such "real" access served to idealize the glamorous and extraordinary lifestyles of the Hollywood elite as the norm to which all should aspire. However, beginning in 1950, celebrity gossip media took a dramatic turn away from studio control and toward unauthorized gossip with the emergence of *Confidential* magazine. Anthony Slide says *Confidential* rejected the fan magazine mode of fawning over celebrities and instead offered readers the purported "truth" about stars "in all their scandalous modes, without apology and without restraint."[12] No longer primarily a space of aspiration, celebrity media now also offered audiences a space to police and reject social norms embodied by celebrities through gossip talk. By positioning itself outside of the control of the studios and other official celebrity producers, relying on unauthorized visual images in the form of paparazzi-style photographs of stars and narratives that break down the façade of celebrity rather than reinforce it, *Confidential* changed the game of celebrity gossip and set the stage for contemporary tabloids.

Contemporary gossip tabloids, like *People*, *Us Weekly*, or *Star*, all focus on the private side of the celebrity, but each forwards a particular perspective on celebrity culture and has varying (and often hidden) levels of official access to the stars they cover. Most contemporary tabloids fall somewhere between the Hollywood studio lapdog position of early fan magazines and the scandalmongering of *Confidential*, but retain a clear focus on the private and "real" lives of the rich and famous. For example, Graeme Turner points out that while a title like *People* is less focused on titillation and scandal than other tabloids, its stories remain gossip-oriented, offering up narratives of celebrity lifestyles "with an occasional coating of skepticism and the photos can be used to set celebrities up as objects of ridicule as well as admiration."[13] These texts are based in gossip talk and are used by audiences as sources for their own meaning-making processes, offering sites of identification or dis-identification with the values embodied by celebrities.

Though both gossip talk and celebrity culture are generally denigrated as "guilty pleasures" that serve as little more than distractions, the media market for such distractions was booming at the beginning of the twenty-first century. According to the *New York Times*, the average total sales of popular celebrity tabloids *Star*, *People*, *Us Weekly*, and *In Touch* combined were up 11.6 percent at the end of 2004, with *Star* and *In Touch* sales each rising about 80 percent from the previous year.[14] Surging subscription and single-issue sales across the genre led to the introduction of new titles, including *Life and Style Weekly* in 2004 and an American version of British celeb-weekly *OK!* in 2005.[15] However, after this surge in sales in the early 2000s, the print tabloid genre has been in decline since 2005. In 2007, the magazine industry reported an 11 percent decline in sales of all titles on newsstands.[16] Once the core sales site of the celebrity media industry, single-issue sales of tabloids continued to drop as the decade progressed. *Us Weekly's* single-issue sales declined nearly 16 percent between 2007 and 2008 and *In Touch Weekly's* numbers fell a staggering 30 percent in the same period.[17]

The global economic downturn that began in the mid-2000s certainly played a role in declining ad sales and reduced circulation of these titles. But the print tabloids' descent has been hastened by the advent of online sources of celebrity gossip that allow audiences to turn to the internet instead of the newsstand for the latest dish. At a time when print magazines were downsizing staff and decreasing page numbers, online sources of gossip were flourishing, and a new form, the celebrity gossip blog, was at the forefront of this popularity. For example, Perez Hilton's eponymous blog, perhaps the best known celebrity gossip blog of the early twenty-first century, was among the top five most popular celebrity news sites in 2007, beating out online sites of established print tabloids like *Us Weekly* a mere two years after its launch.[18] Perez's audience increased an astonishing 215 percent between July 2006 and July 2007, positioning the site in the overall top ten most visited entertainment (not just celebrity) sites in August 2007.[19] Since this career high, the popularity of PerezHilton.com has been on the wane. The blog no longer places on Technorati's top 100 overall blogs and has fallen to number 8 on top 100 celebrity blogs and number 26 on the top 100 entertainment blogs.[20] Yet this is not an indication that blogs are disappearing, as other gossip blogs have simply usurped Perez's once dominant position and, of course, his site continues to draw audiences and generate revenue. Furthermore, since their initial ascendancy in the early twenty-first century, gossip blogs continue to influence celebrity media culture.

But what makes a gossip blog a unique celebrity media form and how has it drawn audiences from print tabloids? Like their tabloid predecessors, celebrity gossip blogs foreground "feminine" concerns through their alternating focus on the fashion, beauty, and glamour of stardom and the unauthorized glimpses of the private lives and relationships of the stars in their "real" lives. On a technological level, the speed at which gossip blogs deliver this gossip has impacted celebrity culture. Audiences no longer have to wait a week between issues of print tabloids, as gossip blogs offer frequently updated content throughout the day. But this content is not always "news" or even new information about a star, as gossip blogs rely heavily on paparazzi photos of banal and everyday moments in celebrities' lives to feed the need for content. Su Holmes and Sean Redmond suggest the age of new media has "increased the range and nature of surveillance" of celebrities, bringing every moment of their private lives, no matter how mundane, to audiences at the click of the mouse.[21] However, the speed of digital platforms also allows blogs to "break" stories well before a print magazine can publish. For example, when Britney Spears shaved her head on the night of February 16, 2008, JustJared.com (as with many other blogs) was able to post the story (notably sourced from a Los Angeles ABC affiliate) and paparazzi pictures of the newly bald Spears in the wee hours of February 17 with updates on her condition following throughout the day, whereas magazines had to wait for their next print issue to cover the story.[22]

These technological features are not the only unique aspect of celebrity gossip blogs. Instead, it is the ways in which these features promote the social aspects of gossip talk as part of the blog texts themselves. Blogs do not simply report the latest news about celebrities, as tabloids long have done. Instead, they explicitly open space for gossip-oriented interpretation of that news by both the blogger and the audience. The stories themselves are coated in a thick layer of gossip commentary from a blogger who, like his or her readers, is an onlooker to celebrity culture. Early bloggers had little, if any, tie to the established "professional" celebrity media industry that produces tabloids or other entertainment news media. Whereas the more hierarchical structures of commercial print media limit access to media production, essentially anyone with an internet connection and something to say about celebrity culture could start a blog. Certainly not all gossip blogs became popular or profitable, but the ways in which a few gossip bloggers were able to harness the technological and social potentials of new media to intervene into the established celebrity media industry points to broader shifts in media culture in the early twenty-first century.

Bloggers are not journalists breaking new stories, as most get their content by scouring the internet for existing celebrity news stories and then offering their own unique gossipy spin. For example, a site like PerezHilton (perezhilton.com) offers snarky and often mean-spirited takedowns of celebrities while PopSugar (popsugar.com) takes a more women's magazine style approach, highlighting celebrity style and fashion as well as fawning over celebrity couples and babies. In contrast, The Young Black and Fabulous (theybf.com) focuses exclusively on black celebrities (and audiences) who are often left out of mainstream celebrity media. Other popular blogs of the early twenty-first century include Pink is the New Blog (pitnb.com), Jossip (jossip.com), Jezebel

(jezebel.com), LaineyGossip (laineygossip.com) and DListed (dlisted.com).[23] By highlighting his or her individual perspective on celebrity culture, bloggers act as mouthpieces for particular segments of the audience, publicly speaking the meanings made through gossip talk. In other words, readers turn to Perez Hilton not simply for the latest dish on Britney Spears, but for what Perez has to say about it. Additionally, blogs explicitly enable audiences to engage in this public meaning-making around the celebrity image. Unlike the generally more private and individualized experience of reading a print tabloid, gossip blogs offer comment sections and other interactive spaces for audience members to participate in gossip talk (with the blogger and with each other) as part of their reading practices. Ultimately, gossip blogs are built around what audiences, including the blogger him/herself as well as the readers, do with celebrity content or how they engage gossip talk as a way to make meaning through celebrity culture.

Gossip Blogs as Women's Media

Since the days of the fan magazine, the focus of extratextual media has primarily been on women as both subjects of the magazines and their assumed audiences. Male celebrities, such as Tom Cruise or Mel Gibson, are not completely exempt from the scrutiny of the gossip media, but even a casual glance at a magazine rack or gossip blog page illustrates that stories about female celebrities drive the gossip genre. Sternheimer points out that, "[W]omen appeared on movie fan magazine covers far more often than men, and women were more likely to be the subject of magazine features."[24] Christine Geraghty argues that this focus on female stars is tied to gossip media's focus on the private lives of stars. She says, "[T]he common association in popular culture between women and the private sphere of personal relationships and domesticity fits with the emphasis, in the discourse of celebrity, on the private life and the leisure activity of the [female] star."[25] In particular, Geraghty sees stories of "love affairs, weddings and divorces" as well as an emphasis on children and child-raising as primary concerns of the tabloid media, tying female stars, much more than their male counterparts, to the domestic and private spheres.[26]

These same preoccupations dominate celebrity gossip blogs in ways that both elevate the importance of women's concerns into the public sphere and work to reify these gendered distinctions. Topics including fashion, beauty, family, and relationships are given central importance to understanding the "real" star on gossip blogs, thereby validating women's private sphere concerns as having value within the public sphere. At the same time, however, the quotidian and private side of the celebrity is held up for judgment and potential ridicule though gossip talk. Susan Douglas says this media attention gives female celebrities "a voice and a platform [audiences] don't have, [but] it also constantly polices them and their femininity" in exchange for this public visibility.[27] The contradictory discourses of celebrity gossip position celebrity gossip blogs, as well as their print tabloid contemporaries, as central media texts in which the similarly contradictory narratives of postfeminist culture are reinforced. On one hand, female celebrities are admired for their rich and successful lifestyles, evidenced by their consumption of the "right" sort of fashion and beauty products. This offers female audiences a seductive message that women really can "have it all," but in ways that tie success and empowerment to constant self-maintenance and conspicuous consumption. Here, female audiences are drawn to celebrities and gossip as a mode of fantasy and aspiration, of how to "do it right" in contemporary culture.

On the other hand, the intense scrutiny of these women's private lives also suggests that, despite their enviable lifestyles, these female celebrities actually cannot have it all. Within gossip media, female celebrities, "have what we wish we had, will never have, and yet even they—the most beautiful, admired, deferred-to women in the world—are also subject to the vicissitudes of living in a man's world."[28] Similarly, Kirsty Fairclough sees gossip blogs as reinforcing postfeminist discourses within celebrity culture. She says:

> Being correctly "feminine" is a concept that pervades both makeover and celebrity culture. One of the functions of the gossip blog within this landscape is to reinforce and police such conservative conceptions, while wrapping a deeply derogatory discourse in a cloak of reflexivity and irony which allows the blog to become an "acceptable" and normalized part of celebrity representation.[29]

The participatory nature of blogs invite female readers to take up the contradictory fantasies of postfeminist culture in which women have the freedom to make their own choices and achieve success in a range of venues, but only through the proper and constantly policed expression of femininity.

Hegemonic struggles around questions of femininity are apparent throughout celebrity media's coverage of the personal lives of female celebrities, but are particularly marked in the constant scrutiny of the female body as the site of the "real" celebrity and, more perniciously, as a marker of that celebrity's cultural value. Holmes and Redmond argue:

> The famous body is often the medium through which dominant ideological messages about gender, race, class, and sexuality are transmitted. The body

of the star or celebrity is often implicated in the construction of hegemonic notions of masculinity and femininity; in stereotypical ideas about racial difference and Otherness; and in normative assertions about sexual desire and class relations.[30]

The female celebrity body is positioned in gossip media as a site of visual spectacle that is policed for authenticity of both the individual star and the values she embodies. That audiences are explicitly given space to gossip as part of their engagement with gossip blogs implicates female audiences in the circulation of gendered norms within popular culture but may also offer a space for resistance.

"She's a Hot Mess": Policing Femininity through Fashion and Beauty

Most gossip blog posts begin with an image, typically a paparazzi photo, to anchor and catalyze gossip talk, often with very little additional information. The visual image is typically used to judge the beauty norms reflected by a celebrity, in particular to determine whether she successfully meets the "acceptable" standards of attractiveness through a judgment of her body. This reinforces the celebrity's role as a model of proper consumption for female audiences, providing a space to police the femininity of the star through her fashion and beauty choices. As with tabloid magazines, gossip blogs frequently use red carpet appearances, inviting audiences to scrutinize the celebrity image and judge her value in terms of successful display of feminine beauty as part of her public performance as a celebrity. In other words, that part of her job as both a celebrity and as a woman in the public sphere is simply to be appropriately beautiful.

For example, on February 8, 2008, Perez Hilton posted a picture of Beyoncé Knowles on the red carpet at the Grammys along with a reader poll explicitly inviting readers to judge her new look, which featured long blonde hair (for a similar image of Beyoncé at the Grammys, though not the exact one that appeared on PerezHilton.com, see Figure 4.1). In keeping with his snarky style that mocks celebrity rather than celebrates it, the title of the post is "Beyowulf Gets a Makeover."[31] The post reflects the general private-focused nature of blogs, as it offered no new information about Beyoncé's life or career; rather, it simply served as a space for readers to judge her "success" as a woman through the photo. The image is the central element of the post, as the text merely states, "Beyoncé debuted a new look at the Grammy's on Sunday night" and invites readers to participate in a poll to decide "Does Beyoncé look good as a blonde" by choosing either "Yes," "No," or "Who cares? She kept her armpits down!"[32]

Though the poll prompts reader engagement, the short nature of Perez's comments makes policing the image for evidence of Beyoncé's value in terms of beauty the real focus of the post.

Some readers are supportive and make positive comments, such as "joey" suggesting "it looks great" or "Alena" saying "very fresh"; many of the comments turn snarky or outright derogatory.[33] "Rumfallo" says, "No, don't go blond! You are black, black girls are NOT blond! Looks fake!"[34] This sentiment is intensified by OMGSHELOOKSAWFUL's comment:

> OMG she looks aweful!!!! i hate it when white blacks think they can pull blonde hair just because their less darker than others. I'm black and i think she's just wrong! she also bleaches her skin.[35]

FIGURE 4.1. Beyoncé Knowles at the 2008 Grammy Awards. Used with permission of Bauer-Griffin.

While it may be a reasonable expectation for a celebrity to look glamorous and beautiful at a red carpet event, a space where the public performing celebrity self is central, the commenters here go beyond critiquing a fashion choice and instead use Beyoncé's image to negotiate racialized and gendered norms about what constitutes acceptable standards of feminine appearance. Moreover, though Perez's initial post did not overtly address issues of race around Beyoncé's image, instead focusing the snark on the proper feminine behavior of "keeping her armpits down," many of the commenters' gossip talk used racialized norms to judge Beyoncé's image. This demonstrates both how gossip talk can still be used to police normative ideals about beauty and celebrity and how the meanings made on gossip blogs are shaped by the audience, not just the blogger. Put another way, though perhaps Perez did not intend to use gossip about Beyoncé's image to police acceptable forms of blackness or reinforce whiteness as the overwhelming standard for beauty and cultural value, the commenters' gossip kept such meanings circulating in both positive and negative ways.

Since female celebrities, as previously discussed, are more likely to be tied to their private lives instead of their public personas, it is no surprise that celebrity gossip blogs, like the tabloids, more generally focus on celebrities outside of the sphere of work or public appearances. In particular, they rely heavily on the unguarded moments in a celebrity's daily life as captured by paparazzi photos. While these seemingly unguarded and unstaged photos play an important role in accessing the "real" celebrity on multiple levels, one important function of the paparazzi photo is as a space to judge the celebrity's style, reinforcing the postfeminist discourse that women must look stylish and hot at every moment in order to be considered valuable.

In a PopSugar post from February 19, 2008, that features paparazzi photos of singer/actress Mandy Moore leaving a Los Angeles restaurant in her sweatpants, readers are given a glimpse of the quotidian and everyday life of the star (see Figures 4.2a and 4.2b). This post could be read as a humanizing moment where Moore is framed not as a glamorous and extraordinary individual, but as a "real" person who is just like the "normal" PopSugar readers in her preference for "comfy" sweats. PopSugar blogger Molly writes, "We're always bigger fans of Mandy's look when she's more put together, but the girl clearly loves her sweats. Can't say I blame her—some weekends are all about the comfy."[36] That a star is captured in what seems to be a truly unguarded and unglamorous moment and is read by the blogger and most of the PopSugar readers through a lens of identification points to the potential for resistance to some of the dominant norms of femininity typically forwarded on blogs. The claim that "some weekends are all about the comfy" opens up the gossip-oriented discussion of femininity on PopSugar beyond the typical trappings of Hollywood glamour as the only space of value for women. However, through links to earlier PopSugar posts of a glammed-up Moore at a red carpet event and, more tellingly, to other pictures of Moore wearing sweats, this post does invite a reading of the casual Moore as less than the glamorous Moore.

The commenters negotiate these distinctions through a policing of Moore's body, again reducing women's value to their physical appearance. It is notable that very few voice the overt opinion that Moore's casual look is unacceptable (evident, however, in the very first comment by creepupmytee that simply says, "ewwwwwwwwwwwwwwww").[37] Yet even the positive comments function as a mode of policing not just Moore's body, but those of other women as well. For example, JenniPoo says Moore has "not a speck of makeup and still looks awesome. I'm jealous of that skin," a positive comment that still serves to prioritize "natural" beauty as part of Moore's social value.[38] Others use Moore as an example of a female star who "gets it right" in contrast to those who fail at

FIGURES 4.2a and 4.2b. "Casual" Mandy Moore as appeared on *PopSugar*, February 19, 2008. Used with permission of Bauer-Griffin.

femininity, seeing physical appearance as a value in itself and as evidence of deeper values and behaviors:

> I love how casual she is . . . she doesn't need a cake of makeup on her face every day like Lindsay lohan . . . we should embrace how natural this girl is. :) when it's time to look good—she brings it! (so_dipped_in_love)
>
> at least she does work and not so care about her in-front-of-papa[razzi] looks not like some "my work is eating shopping hitting salon" papa addicts (XpsX)
>
> Better trackies than leggings as pants! (pink_magnetism)[39]

The "real"

As Richard Dyer suggests, celebrities, and gossip about them, are cultural markers for how to behave, think, and feel in contemporary culture—and how not to—with the celebrity body serving as the site for such negotiations of the self.[40] The notion that it is through the body of the celebrity that we can locate the "real" individual is also present in the PopSugar readings of Moore. In this instance, the gossip-based readings use the rejection of glamour as a space to reinforce other dominant norms of femininity. Many of the commenters see this dressed-down image of Moore as evidence of her "real" and "down to earth" self. BKNYGAL says, "I absolutely love Mandy Moore . . . she seems cool to hang around with. Not all stuck up and materialistic."[41] Here, as in the negative comparison comments above, standards of acceptable behavior are read through Moore's body. In this case, her more casual self is evidence that she possesses appropriate feminine values and behaviors at the inner core of her private self but nevertheless relies on her body as the site of such social value.

"Pregnant or Just Fat?"
The Baby Bump Watch and Body Snarking

P. David Marshall argues that the advent of new media technologies has disrupted "the symbiotic relationship between media and celebrity," allowing audiences to intervene in the production and circulation of celebrity in previously unprecedented ways.[42] Gossip blogs are marked by the constant flow of information, as bloggers post a steady stream of gossip tidbits and paparazzi photos of even the most quotidian and banal moments in the celebrity's life throughout the day. Readers are thus able to remain constantly abreast of new developments in a celebrity story or, as will be explored in more detail below, to create their own narratives through gossip talk based on the constant flow of images. Joshua Gamson suggests gossip "invites audiences to play games with meaning" and that such game playing is "a social activity in which relationships between players, more than relationships with celebrities are being established and reestablished."[43] But, while gossip media like tabloids have always been a space where audiences negotiate and make meanings from star images, the interactive and participatory spaces of gossip blogs have brought this once private and often individualized process of meaning-making into the public sphere through comments sections and other interactive features. The unique technological features of gossip blogs promote the same gossip "games" that have long defined audience engagement with celebrity culture, but within new and more publicly visible technological spaces.

An important gossip game that emerged within the interactive spaces of celebrity gossip blogs (and has since spread to gossip media more broadly) is the "baby bump watch." The "baby bump" refers to the small belly bulge associated with the early stages of pregnancy, and discovering the existence of the bump is the primary goal of this gossip game. As a physical manifestation of pregnancy uncovered through the scrutiny of the steady flow of images available on blogs, the bump is evidence of a truth about the celebrity's life and, importantly, one that is detected before she has publicly announced her pregnancy. Here, the audience intervenes into the typically controlled public presence of the celebrity by refusing to wait for the official announcement and, instead, circumvents the control of other celebrity workers in discovering an important aspect of the celebrity's "real" self. As a gossip game, the baby bump watch is premised on the contradictory discourses of postfeminism in its policing of the celebrity's proper expression of femininity through gossip about the bump.

The bump watch begins from an assumption that female celebrities necessarily possess idealized slender bodies, reinforcing celebrities as markers of "proper" femininity. To play the bump watch game, audiences scrutinize photos of the female celebrity for visual evidence that points to the existence of a bump. The presence of evidence, such as any additional curves on her body or even the decision to wear loose-fitting clothing, signals a potentially appropriate pregnancy, assuming the celebrity is properly contained with a heterosexual coupling, or, alternatively, signals a never-appropriate weight gain. During the bump watch, bloggers and readers publicly speculate if the female celebrity is "fat fat" or "preggers fat"[44] or if "chick just ate a cheeseburger,"[45] suggesting that female celebrities and indeed women in general must be constantly vigilant about the appearance of their bodies. Tellingly, feminist celebrity gossip blog, Jezebel, which explicitly bans "body snarking" and other forms of gossip talk that explicitly shame female celebrities, called up this body policing as a way to point out the problem of the bump watch.

During the baby bump watch surrounding Ashlee Simpson in April 2008, Jezebel blogger Tracie Egan writes:

> [Ashlee] tried to dress her belly down by wearing very loud pants, a slimming black top, and an opened blazer, but thanks to screen caps, we're able to get a look at her tummy, after the jump.... Lookit, I'm not one of those people that's like, "Is she pregnant or did she just eat a bagel?" I'm sensitive about body issues and if someone is a little bloated or something, it's pretty asshole-ish to assume they're pregnant. But these shots are sorta convincing.[46]

Despite the ban on body snarking, the inclusion of this post still invites readers, on some level, to scrutinize the female celebrity body as the site of social meaning. Yet this also illustrates the potential for gossip as a space of resistance, as Egan here points out the problem of judging women solely by their bodies and, along with the readers who are drawn to this particular blog, attempting to use gossip to challenge these oppressive norms.

The bump watch is not just, or even primarily, about motherhood, because many, if not most, of the female celebrities subjected to the bump watch are not pregnant, indicating the power of the bump watch as a mode of policing a range of gendered ideologies through the female celebrity body. The bump watch positions the female celebrity body as the embodiment of idealized slenderness and uses the potential of a bump as the means to police that body, recuperating wayward female subjects through ridicule and shame. Through a constant flow of paparazzi photos, blog readers use gossip about the female celebrity's body as a means to reinforce norms of feminine sexuality and physicality.[47] More specifically, readers report that only a pregnant woman could justifiably have a bump (otherwise she's "just fat") and only a woman in a heterosexual relationship (ideally marriage) could justifiably be pregnant (otherwise she's a slut). But it also foregrounds the female body (whether actually pregnant or not) as a site of spectacle that reveals the truth about the celebrity and a visual catalyst for the gossip game and its attendant social meaning-making. Thus, in order to refute the rumors of pregnancy, a female celebrity must put her body on proper display, again tying women's value back to their bodies within the narrow regime of postfeminist cultural discourses.

For example, in late February 2008, many gossip blogs began speculating that actress Kate Hudson was pregnant after multiple paparazzi photos surfaced showing the typically svelte actress appearing in public wearing baggy clothing. PopSugar mused that Hudson's "new baggy wardrobe" was "getting suspicious" even though she "hadn't had a serious boyfriend since her days with [actor/comedian] Dax [Shepard], but that doesn't rule out a surprise pregnancy."[48]

This sort of framing confirms that the bump watch is not simply about policing the appearance of the body, but also about policing the sexuality of the potentially pregnant celebrity, as Hudson's lack of a committed partner is a potential site of scandal should she be pregnant. Though an out-of-wedlock pregnancy would not have been inconsistent with Hudson's "free spirit" celebrity persona, it nevertheless enables gossipers to use her image as an anchor for gossip about whether or not such pregnancies are socially acceptable within the comments sections of various gossip blogs. It was only when several blogs, including PopSugar, published multiple paparazzi photos of a red bikini–clad Hudson poolside in Miami on March 3, 2008, that the game ended because her body looked like it "should" and, more importantly, that she put that body on display to prove it.[49] Her social value was thus reestablished by realigning her body with accepted standards of feminine behaviors and appearance. In both images, Hudson's body was the object of scrutiny and served as evidence to forward or stop the gossip game of the baby bump watch through which readers negotiate norms of femininity.

Print Gossip in the Digital Age

The rapid rise and continued presence of celebrity gossip blogs is indicative of broader changes within contemporary media culture in which traditional media forms, like newspapers and magazines, must adapt to the new demands for digital and interactive media content. The impact of gossip blogs on celebrity culture can be felt within the traditional gossip magazine industry, as magazine rack mainstays like *Us Weekly* and *People* have developed online portals that offer readers frequently updated and interactive content to satiate their desire for gossip between weekly issues. Instead of functioning as online versions of the print magazines, official tabloid sites like usmagazine.com and people.com act as supplements to their print counterparts, offering additional photos, gossip tidbits, and, most importantly, comments sections where audiences can get involved in the gossip talk about celebrities. That is, they act more like blogs in their snarky and participatory approach to celebrity culture, foregrounding shared gossip talk as a source of social meaning-making and the source of pleasure in celebrity culture. Yet unlike blogs that generally link to a range of outside sources, the additional content on official magazine sites is all located within its own site (or its subsidiaries), keeping readers within the economic and ideological worldview of the magazine. More tellingly, the additional online content frequently works to draw the online reader back to the print version of the magazine. Usmagazine.com, for example, prominently places teaser posts on the main home page to promote the next week's issue. These posts give sparse but juicy details of a current celebrity scandal and always end the post entreating the reader to "find out more" in the upcoming week's print edition rather than on the site. The reciprocal relationship between the print magazine and its online portal helps maintain the magazine's place of prominence within celebrity culture even as blogs continue to encroach on their readership.

Despite the rising popularity of all forms of digital media and the declining circulation of gossip magazines from their peak in the early twenty-first century, print magazines remain a central player within the celebrity media industry. This continued presence is, I suggest, tied to their continued "legitimacy" as purveyors of gossip compared to bloggers. Established celebrity gossip magazines still have the cultural and economic clout to access and circulate the latest gossip dish. Tabloids like *Us Weekly* have varying levels of insider access to celebrities and celebrity events as well as the greater economic resources to chase stories or pay paparazzi agencies. More tellingly, these magazines and their online counterparts originate the very stories bloggers then take up. PopSugar blogger Molly notes, "Bloggers are not really making the stories. But they're reporting *about* stories that are in [tabloids like the *New York Post's*] *Page Six*."[50] As outsiders to the celebrity industry, blogs rely on content from the official media industry, including tabloids and more legitimate entertainment media sources like *Vanity Fair*, to draw from in creating their own posts. Online portals of magazines may be changing in tone and interactive platforms to be more like blogs, but blogs simply could not continue should these legitimate print purveyors suddenly disappear.

Furthermore, though it is the case that overall circulation numbers are down for these magazines, celebrity gossip has weathered this downturn better than other print media. Even with their declining numbers, major titles like *People*, *In Touch Weekly*, and *Us Weekly* remain in the top 10 titles for single-copy sales, with *Star* and *Life and Style Weekly* also within the top 25 titles for single-copy sales from June 2012–June 2013, according to the Alliance for Audited Media.[51] Of course, these numbers do not represent the full number of readers, as the ubiquity of these magazines in everyday feminized spaces, such as the grocery store checkout lane, mean they are still often picked up and put down for a momentary pleasure. An ABC News poll suggests that 33 percent of women catch up on celebrity gossip in doctor's offices and 23 percent do so in hair salons, indicating these print magazines are still a pleasurable way to pass the time for many readers.[52] New media forms like blogs extend the options for getting the latest celebrity dish, but that same poll found that 34 percent of women named gossip magazines as their primary source for celebrity gossip, suggesting the enduring role these print media play in everyday engagements with celebrity culture.[53]

Conclusion

The early twenty-first century witnessed the rise of new interactive techno-logical spaces in which celebrity gossip takes place, offering female audiences a more publicly visible point of entry into celebrity culture. Celebrity gossip blogs enable audiences to quickly and easily engage with the latest celebrity gossip—and with each other—in ways not possible with print media. Thanks to digital technologies, gossip blogs offer a near constant stream of new infor-mation, from the mundane to the scandalous, that feeds the meaning-making processes of gossip. More crucially, celebrity gossip blogs offer comments sec-tions that, should the user choose to participate, bring the once private realm of gossip talk into the public space of the blog text. What was, for the print reader, a largely invisible and imagined community of like-minded readers now becomes a public virtual space of shared meaning-making between the blogger and readers and between readers.

Though these technological spaces that shape engagement on celebrity gos-sip blogs have already changed since they first emerged—and will continue to change as new technologies are developed—the underlying social practices of gossip remain central to understanding blogs as spaces of cultural production. The pleasures of gossip lie in the active judgment and evaluation of the celebrity image, as evidenced in both the scrutiny of a paparazzi photo for evidence, as in the baby bump watch, or the more general negotiation of information in a blog post and the comments sections. This remains a socially oriented form of communication, in which gossipers use their shared cultural production to connect to others and make the larger world more meaningful.

Despite the technological bells and whistles of celebrity gossip blogs as digital and interactive media forms, gossip about celebrities remains, as Turner argues, "an important social process through which relationships, identity, and social and cultural norms are debated, evaluated, modified and shared."[54] The pervasiveness of celebrity gossip is far from just a meaningless distraction; it provides important narratives about women's everyday lives in contemporary culture. Gossip offers both opportunities for resistance to postfeminist dis-courses and, more commonly, reinscription of the norms they forward. The shared practice of meaning-making and the communities forged around those meanings may offer female audiences a space to challenge dominant norms of femininity. But, as seen in the examples discussed here, gossip may also reinscribe those same norms under the guise of the pleasures and connections of gossip talk. Taking these blogs seriously as cultural forms recognizes the complex and often contradictory nature of feminized popular culture.

Notes

1. Jörg Bergmann, *Discreet Indiscretions: The Social Organization of Gossip* (New York: Aldine de Gruyter, 1993).

2. Patricia Meyer Spacks, *Gossip* (New York: Knopf, 1986), 4–5.

3. Ibid.

4. Richard Dyer, *Heavenly Bodies: Film Stars and Society* (London: Macmillan Press, 1986), 2.

5. Graeme Turner, *Understanding Celebrity* (London: Sage Publications, 2004), 76.

6. Karen Sternheimer, *Celebrity Culture and the American Dream: Stardom and Social Mobility* (New York: Routledge, 2011), 5.

7. Joshua Gamson, *Claims to Fame: Celebrity in Contemporary America* (Berkeley: University of California Press, 1994), 176.

8. Meyer Spacks, *Gossip*, 5.

9. Erin A. Meyers, *Dishing Dirt in the Digital Age: Celebrity Gossip Blogs and Participatory Media Culture* (New York: Peter Lang, 2013).

10. Anthony Slide, *Inside the Hollywood Fan Magazine: A History of Star Makers, Fabricators, and Gossip Mongers* (Jackson: University of Mississippi Press, 2010), 6.

11. Sternheimer, *Celebrity Culture and the American Dream*, 6.

12. Ibid., 179.

13. Turner, *Understanding Celebrity*, 73.

14. Louise Story, "Forget about Milk and Bread. Give Me Gossip!" *New York Times*, June 13, 2005.

15. Ibid.

16. Association of Magazine Media, "Average Single Copy Circulation for Top 100 ABC Magazines," *Association of Magazine Media*, accessed September 30, 2008, http://www.magazine.org/insights-resources/research-publications/trends-data/magazine-industry-facts-data/2006-average.

17. The Association of Magazine Media, "Average Single Copy Circulation for Top 100 ABC Magazines," accessed June 28, 2014, http://www.magazine.org/CONSUMER_MARKETING/CIRC_TRENDS/2008ABCsinglecopyrank.aspx.

18. Suzy Bausch, "Popular Celebrity News Sites Grow 40 Percent Year over Year, According to Nielsen//Netratings," Nielsen//NetRatings, Inc., last modified March 29, 2007, accessed December 19, 2014, http://www.nielsen-online.com/pr/pr_070329.pdf.

19. Laura Tiffany, "The Gossip Artist," *Entrepreneur*, last modified December 1, 2007, accessed December 19, 2014, http://www.entrepreneur.com/article/186508.

20. "Perez Hilton," Technorati.com, accessed November 15, 2009, http://technorati.com/blogs/perezhilton.

21. Su Holmes and Sean Redmond, "Introduction: Understanding Celebrity Culture," in *Framing Celebrity: New Directions in Celebrity Culture*, eds. Su Holmes and Sean Redmond (London: Routledge, 2006), 28.

22. JustJared, "Britney Spears Is Bald—Video," JustJared (blog), February 17, 2008 (2:30 A.M.), accessed July 14, 2014, http://www.justjared.com/2007/02/17/britney-spears -bald/.

23. Though TMZ (tmz.com) launched in 2005 and is a well-known celebrity gossip site that shares a lot of the characteristics of the blogs examined here, I do not include it as a gossip blog because it began as a joint venture between established media industry players America Online and Telepictures. However, its success in using the blog format speaks to the importance of this new form of celebrity media in the early twenty-first century.

24. Sternheimer, *Celebrity Culture and the American Dream*, 4.

25. Christine Geraghty, "Re-examining Stardom: Questions of Texts, Bodies and Performance," in *Reinventing Film Studies*, eds. Christine Gledhill and Linda Williams (London: Arnold, 1979), 196.

26. Ibid.

27. Susan Douglas, *Enlightened Sexism: The Seductive Message that Feminism's Work Is Done* (New York: Times Books, 2010), 243.

28. Ibid.

29. Kirsty Fairclough, "Fame Is a Losing Game: Celebrity Gossip Blogging, Bitch Culture and Postfeminism," *Genders* 48 (2008), accessed December 19, 2014, http://www .genders.org/g48/g48_fairclough.html, para. 9.

30. Su Holmes and Sean Redmond, "Introduction: Fame Body" in *Framing Celebrity: New Directions in Celebrity Culture*, eds. Su Holmes and Sean Redmond (London: Routledge, 2006), 124.

31. Perez Hilton, "Beyowulf Gets a Makeover," Perez Hilton (blog), February 11, 2008 (12:13 P.M.), accessed December 19, 2014, http://perezhilton.com/2008-02-11-beyowulf -gets-a-makeover.

32. Ibid.

33. Comment 6 and 14 on ibid. All comments are presented as they appeared on the blogs, including any spelling or grammar mistakes.

34. Comment 8 on ibid.

35. Comment 32 on ibid.

36. Molly, "Mandy Goes Ultimately Casual," Pop Sugar (blog), February 19, 2008, accessed December 19, 2014, http://www.popsugar.com/Mandy-Goes-Ultimately-Casual -1050456.

37. Comment on ibid.

38. Comment on ibid.

39. Comments on ibid.

40. Dyer, *Heavenly Bodies*, 17.

41. Comment on Molly, "Mandy Goes Ultimately Casual."

42. P. David Marshall, "New Media—New Self: The Changing Power of Celebrity" in *The Celebrity Culture Reader*, ed. P. David Marshall (New York: Routledge, 2006), 634.

43. Gamson, *Claims to Fame*, 183.

44. Perez Hilton, "Fergie Is Just 'Fat,'" Perez Hilton (blog), November 25, 2008, accessed December 19, 2014, http://perezhilton.com/2008–11–25-fergie-is-just-fat.

45. Natasha Eubanks, "Couples Fab: Djimon and Kimora Are Still on Preggers Watch," The Young, Black and Fabulous (blog), March 5, 2008, accessed May 19, 2008, http://theybf.com/index.php/2008/03/05/couples-fab-djimon-kimora-are-still-on -preggers-watchkim-k-reggie-bush-still/.

46. Tracie Egan, "Ashlee Simpson Tries to Hide Baby Bump on Today," Jezebel (blog), April 18, 2008, accessed July 18, 2008, http://jezebel.com/381431/ashlee-simpson-tries-to -hide-baby-bump-on-today.

47. Erin Meyers, "Gossip Blogs and 'Baby Bumps': The New Visual Spectacle of Female Celebrity in Gossip Media" in *The Handbook of Gender, Sex and Media*, ed. Karen Ross (London: John Wiley and Sons Ltd., 2013), 53–70.

48. PopSugar, "Is Kate Hudson Pregnant?" Pop Sugar (blog), February 21, 2008, accessed February 21, 2008, http://www.popsugar.com/Kate-Hudson-Pregnant-1061814.

49. PopSugar, "Kate Hudson Is So Not Pregnant," Pop Sugar (blog), March 3, 2008, accessed March 3, 2008, http://www.popsugar.com/Kate-Hudson-So-Pregnant-1091151.

50. Molly Goodson, interview by Erin Meyers, May 26, 2007.

51. Neal Lulofs, "The Top 25 U.S. Consumer Magazines for June 2013," Alliance for Audited Media (blog), August 6, 2013, accessed June 26, 2014, http://www.auditedmedia .com/news/blog/2013/august/the-top-25-us-consumer-magazines-for-june-2013.aspx.

52. Josh Cohan, "Women Enjoy Reading Celebrity Gossip," ABCnewsradioonline.com, January 25, 2011, accessed June 26, 2014, http://abcnewsradioonline.com/health-news /women-enjoy-reading-celebrity-gossip.html.

53. Ibid.

54. Turner, *Understanding Celebrity*, 24.

PART II

Bodies

CHAPTER 5

Mothers, Fathers, and the Pregnancy App Experience

Designing with Expectant Users in Mind

BARBARA L. LEY

In April 2011, I posted a question on my Facebook wall asking whether anybody had used a smartphone application (*app*) that provides support during pregnancy. At the time, I had been researching online pregnancy and mothering support culture for five years, and I became interested in how this culture was increasingly "mobile." Within the hour, I received several responses from female friends raving about their apps. Kate, whom I hadn't seen in person since we graduated high school, was so eager to tell me about her app that she disclosed her seven-week pregnancy—even though she was still, in her own words, "on the down low" about it with her family and close friends.

Similar to the online experiences of other women that I have studied, Kate's pregnancy was "transmediated" from the start.[1] Soon after receiving her positive pregnancy test, she went to the website BabyCenter.com for information about managing her pregnancy. She signed up for the site's weekly emails that discussed her growing baby's development and joined its support group for women with December 2012 due dates. Yet her favorite BabyCenter.com tool was its free smartphone app, My Pregnancy Today: "The app on my phone is what I really LOVE," she explained. "I have synced my email messages to it. I use it all the time and it shows pics of where the development of the baby is . . . what to expect. And it will let me know how many days left until the big day! It also has a check list of things to remember . . . drink plenty of water, walk, make your prenatal appt. . . . I am excited about all of it so feel free to ask me questions about anything!!!"

In this essay, I examine the "usability" of pregnancy apps, particularly in terms of their usefulness and user satisfaction, to understand their appeal to Kate and a growing number of other expectant parents, most—but not all—of whom are women. To this end, I analyzed the aesthetic, therapeutic, and technical design of nine pregnancy apps available in the iTunes store. I also analyzed the user reviews that accompanied the apps.[2] On the one hand, I found that the architecture and design of pregnancy apps enhance satisfaction among many expectant parents, especially women, by providing them a range of support tools, options for personalization, and the ability to access support whenever and wherever they need it. On the other hand, the gendered and heteronormative assumptions built into the apps' designs perpetuate hegemonic discourses regarding pregnancy and parenting that can leave some expectant parents, especially fathers, frustrated with their app experience.

The Mobile Turn in Online Pregnancy Culture

Over the past two decades, an array of companies, health organizations, medical professionals, and everyday internet users have developed a range of online sites and tools to support expectant parents—particularly expectant mothers—during pregnancy, birth, and early infancy. The emergence and growth of this pregnancy support culture, which represents one facet of what Julie Wilson and Emily Chivers Yochim call the online "mamasphere,"[3] has gone hand in hand with technical developments. Some of the earliest (but still popular) online support resources were informational websites and web-based discussion forums. The "Web 2.0" platforms that emerged in the early twenty-first century led to new forms of online support, including blogs, YouTube videos, Facebook pages and groups, and Pinterest pins and boards.[4] Online virtual worlds also became home to pregnancy support sites. In Second Life, for instance, women with miscarriage histories can visit a pregnancy loss memory garden, and couples seeking affordable fertility treatments can consult with staff from a clinic in India that offers low-cost in vitro fertilization (IVF) to patients globally.

Mobile phones play a growing role in online support culture. This trend reflects increasing ownership rates over the first decade or so of the twenty-first century, with 90 percent of U.S. residents owning cell phones (88 percent of women and 93 percent of men) and 58 percent of them owning smartphones in particular (57 percent of women and 61 percent of men).[5] Just as importantly, it reflects our culture's increasing intimacy with—if not dependence on—cell phones, especially smartphones. Scholars and media critics have noted how women and men across racial, age, and socioeconomic lines have become, for better or for worse, "tethered" to their mobile devices, and that in many ways, such devices have become extensions of their everyday selves and lives.[6] In the realm of pregnancy support, for example, public health agencies have developed Text4Baby campaigns that use free texting services in conjunction with other online resources to provide prenatal and postnatal support to low-income women and at-risk teens.[7] Women use the talk and texting features of mobile phones to connect "offline" with individual members of their online support groups.[8] Moreover, mobile phones that provide internet access enable expectant mothers to visit their online support sites, tools, and communities. Indeed, accessing support resources via such phones has become so commonplace that many pregnancy sites have created mobile-friendly versions to make navigation easier.[9]

Smartphone apps constitute one of the most significant developments in mobile pregnancy support during the early twenty-first century. Apps are software programs for smartphones that provide users with various online and/or offline tools and services. All smartphone owners use apps "native" to their phone, and 84 percent of owners have downloaded at least one app, usually related to everyday activities such as news-seeking, social media use, banking, shopping, reading, and gaming.[10] Health-related apps constitute a growing segment of the overall app market,[11] with the iTunes store carrying more than 400 pregnancy-related apps alone. Whereas most health apps provide users with features that allow them to manage their physical, emotional, and mental well being, some of them offer medical professionals tools for managing the health of their patients. Yet health apps have commercial purposes, too. The companies that develop pregnancy apps, for example, use them to market their other parenting products such as child-rearing magazines, baby photo albums, and postpregnancy apps for infant care. Free health apps, including those for pregnancy, tend to generate revenue by running in-app ads from third-party marketers. Many companies also use their health apps to collect consumer data, which are sent to third-party analytics services for the purpose of improving the app user experience and to the aforementioned marketers to help them better target their in-app ads to particular users.[12]

Despite consumer groups' concerns about the commercial purposes of health apps,[13] their popularity is increasing, with almost one third of smartphone owners using them.[14] More specifically, a 2012 study found that 3 percent of all U.S. smartphone owners who have downloaded at least one health app have downloaded a pregnancy app,[15] and a 2013 mobile analytics report found that 47 percent of worldwide smartphone users who have downloaded at least one health app have downloaded a pregnancy or menstrual-tracking app.[16] Other studies have found that a substantial number of their pregnant female participants use or would like to use smartphone apps as part of their perinatal care,[17] and pregnancy apps have been touted by medical professionals as beneficial patient tools.[18] Furthermore, only a few users critiqued their app's commercial purposes in the reviews that I examined. The majority of them, like Kate, focused their comments—both positive and negative—on their app's support features.[19]

Usability and the Pleasures of Pregnancy Apps

The "love" that Kate felt for her pregnancy app was reflected in the user reviews that I examined. More than half of the apps had thousands—and in some cases, tens of thousands—of accompanying user reviews, with most of them written by women. The positive reviews far outweighed the negative ones, especially for the more popular apps. The average review score for most of the apps ranged from four to five (out of five) stars. Although some reviews were short (e.g., "I love this app!"), many reviewers provided detailed analyses of their app's features. Women frequently discussed what they liked and disliked between former and upgraded versions of the same app. Some reviews discussed the relative advantages and disadvantages of different apps, and of the paid and "lite" versions of the same app. Numerous reviewers also explained why they preferred using their smartphone's pregnancy app to seeking online support via their computer.

In certain respects, the enthusiasm expressed by expectant mothers for their pregnancy apps is not unique to apps per se but reflects a broader set of pleasures that they experience from their engagements with online pregnancy support more generally. Such pleasures relate to learning strategies for promoting a healthy pregnancy and baby; connecting with other pregnant women for emotional and social support; bonding with their growing baby; and preparing for their baby's birth, homecoming, and postnatal care. At the same time, the design of pregnancy apps and the smartphones for which they are developed provide users with particular modes of technological, therapeutic, and social engagement that shape their support experience in particular ways. Approaching the study of pregnancy apps in terms of their "usability," especially the specific notion of usefulness, helps to explain not only the interplay between app design and the user experience but also the enthusiasm that users have expressed about these apps. According to Jeffrey Rubin and Dana Chisnell, usability means developing and designing products with "users in mind" so that "the user can do what he/she wants to do in the way he/she expects to be able to do it, without hindrance, hesitation, or questions."[20] Although the software industry tends to view a product's usability in terms of its functionality (e.g., ease of use, learnability, and efficiency), Rubin and Chisnell argue that it also refers to a product's usefulness. A product can run smoothly and have an intuitive design, but it is not usable if it does not meet the consumer's needs.[21] Indeed, one study found that a product's usefulness is 1.5 times more important than its ease of use when it comes to a user's acceptance of and satisfaction with it. In other words, users will tolerate some functional difficulties if the product helps them achieve their goals.[22]

Fabien Miard highlights three design features—multimodality, personalization, and mobility—of cell phones and smartphones that make them useful for citizen political movements.[23] Interestingly, these same design features, especially in combination with one another, are central to the design and usefulness of pregnancy apps. First, pregnancy apps are multimodal, meaning that they—in conjunction with smartphone tools such as the inbuilt camera, internet connection, and keyboard—consist of a diverse set of support tools that women can access quickly and easily by pressing the app's icon on their phone. Second, pregnancy apps personalize the user experience by facilitating not only the person-to-person contact highlighted by Miard but also interactions between the app and user. Such interactions relate to interfaces that "speak" to users and inbuilt settings that require users to customize app features to reflect their specific needs. When it comes to mobility, users can access their app's online pregnancy support tools anywhere and anytime, as long as they have a charged smartphone with them. The support contexts that I discuss below highlight how these three design features can make the pregnancy app experience satisfying to expectant mothers.

TAKING CHARGE OF PREGNANCY AND BIRTH

Although feminist scholars have described how the early internet was a predominantly masculine space developed for and by men, the emergence of online pregnancy support culture demonstrates how the internet, including its so-called "information superhighway," has become a feminized space, too.[24] A wealth of women's health and pregnancy-related information and resources is available online, and women turn to the internet for health information purposes, including pregnancy-related information purposes, more than men do.[25] Two factors contribute to these interrelated trends. First, the changing dynamic of doctor-patient relationships over the past fifty years as result of the feminist and consumer health movements has encouraged patients, especially women, to play an active role in their health-care decision making.[26] Second, women have historically taken greater responsibility than men for their personal health and the health of their families due to cultural expectations surrounding gender and motherhood.[27] Thus, going online for pregnancy-information purposes can increase women's sense of self-efficacy and empowerment, in addition to validating their identity and worth as "good" mothers.

Pregnancy apps provide expectant mothers with another set of informational tools to help them take control of their health and the health of their baby. Expectant mothers, especially first-time ones, have many questions about topics such as the changes happening to their body, the stages of their baby's in utero development, and strategies for having a healthy pregnancy and birth. Through articles, photographs, video, charts, and/or interactive reference guides, pregnancy apps provide a broad range of pregnancy-related information in one central place. Moreover, apps require users to personalize their settings based on the baby's due date and (if known) gender, which then customizes much of the information to the user's own pregnancy timeline. Just as importantly, women can access this information wherever and whenever they need it, so long as they have their smartphone with them. "I absolutely love this app," a Sprout user stated. "It makes me feel like I've got a constant informational guide during my pregnancy." Another Sprout user explained, "This is such a wonderful app to keep all the info handy and ready to view whenever I feel like."

The informational support that pregnancy apps provide to expectant mothers can also enhance their sense of confidence and authority when it comes to their interactions with medical providers. Many apps include features such as appointment calendars, checklists, and birthing-plan templates designed to help women take charge of their medical appointments, feel on more equal footing with their medical providers, and advocate for their medical needs. One Sprout user recommended its medical appointment checklist "so that you don't forget to ask important questions." At the same time, pregnancy apps provide so much pregnancy-related information that some women become less dependent on medical providers for help and guidance in the first place. A Baby Bump Pro user noted, "It's so nice to see progress without always having to go to the doctor."

"Health-tracking" programs, including fetal kick counters, contraction timers, and weight trackers, are another set of pregnancy app tools that allow women to play an active role in managing the physical experience of pregnancy and birth. Rather than *providing* users with information, such tracking programs offer tools for *collecting* pregnancy-related information. Pregnancy app tracking tools are part of a broader movement toward the "quantified self" that promotes the use of digital devices to monitor and manage various aspects of one's physical health, emotional well being, and everyday behaviors and habits.[28] Such tracking tools can motivate users to engage in healthy behaviors and sustain them over time, but they also have the potential not only to reduce one's sense of self and well being to quantifiable data patterns but also to cause anxiety in users from the perpetual monitoring.[29] Such concerns may be especially pertinent to pregnancy apps that encourage expectant mothers to track their symptoms and bodily changes within a broader media and biomedical culture that fuels women's anxiety by marketing images, products, and services that pressure them to seek normative body and behavioral ideals.[30]

Although a few user reviews criticized their apps' weight trackers for these reasons, the vast majority of reviewers praised their app's tracking tools, and many even downloaded apps designed solely to track a particular facet of their pregnant body. Consider contraction timers. Many health professionals encourage expectant mothers to record the frequency and duration of their contractions in order to glean information about how far along they are in labor.[31] Tracking contractions may also appeal to women who seek control of their labor process by helping them birth at home or avoid going to the hospital until necessary. The painful nature, long duration, and ever-changing frequency of contractions, however, can make traditional tracking methods such as pen and paper, stopwatches, and computer-based programs difficult to use. In contrast, app timers make it convenient and easy to record contractions, wherever and whenever they occur, simply by pressing a button when each one starts and stops. "This worked great for me," a Labor and Contraction Timer user stated, "So much easier than trying to track with a clock or stop watch. Just what you need so you can concentrate on you and your baby's needs."

BONDING WITH THEIR BABY

Advances in biomedical ultrasound and fiber-optic photography during the second half of the twentieth century have not only deepened our general understanding of fetal development but also contributed to our culture's increasing visual, textual, and audio narratives of fetal personhood—that is, the socially constructed notion that the fetus is its own living being connected to, but ultimately separate from, the expectant mother. These "fetal imaginaries," as Rayna Rapp calls them, have complex implications for abortion politics, fetal rights debates, and other reproductive arenas of contestation that tend to pit the rights of women against the supposed rights of human embryos and fetuses. Such fetal imaginaries are also embedded within the experiences of women who may view their growing embryo as a "baby" from the start of their pregnancy and may feel that ultrasound enhances their ability to bond prenatally with their child.[32]

Not surprisingly, many online sites for pregnant women construct information about fetal development through the lens of fetal personhood. Similarly, pregnancy apps build on their online counterparts by constructing fetal imaginaries in ways that take advantage of design features unique to smartphone technology. Many apps, for example, include weekly descriptions of fetal development, with each entry often accompanied by an image of the appropriately aged fetus. Sprout's weekly 3D fetal images are particularly compelling due to their photographic quality, interactive features, and audio clip of a fetal heartbeat. In addition to personalizing this information by aligning its weekly updates to the user's pregnancy timeline, apps often refer to "your baby" in their textual descriptions of fetal development. Many apps also place the baby's name (if the user provided one) at the top of both the written updates and fetal images. Some even send weekly push notifications to the users' smartphones that remind them of their fetus' age and the number of weeks left until the due date.

Although the collective set of textual, visual, and audio representations that constitute the apps' fetal imaginaries are not the users' actual babies, users can experience them as windows into their own baby's development. "I absolutely love this app!" one woman stated. "This is my 1st pregnancy, and it's so incredible to watch the baby grow via Sprout!" Such fetal imaginaries also blur the spatial boundaries between the virtual fetus that expectant mothers carry around with them via their smartphone and the physical fetus that they carry in their uteruses. The experience of what Jason Farman might call one's "sensory-inscribed" fetus being located in two places simultaneously is especially evident among users who described their app's virtual fetus as "my" baby: "Love it!" another Sprout user wrote. "So helpful throughout the whole process! It's fun to say, 'you want to see a picture of my baby?'"[33]

CONNECTING WITH OTHERS

Hundreds of support groups for pregnant women and new mothers have formed online during the past twenty years. Many women turn to such online groups because their familial and friendship networks have become geographically dispersed, they increasingly work outside of the home and spend less time interacting with other women in their local communities, and they often view their mothers' advice about pregnancy and parenting as "out of date."[34] Women who participate in such online groups often experience comfort, validation, and empowerment from the emotional and instrumental support that they receive from other members.[35] Moreover, the collective identity and sense of "we-ness" that support groups develop over time can provide members with community, connection, and belonging that can extend beyond members' specific pregnancy-related needs.[36]

Due to the popularity of internet support groups, many pregnancy apps include an online forum. These forums are often structured around smaller subgroups devoted to specific topics, and users can join the subgroups that relate to their particular interests and needs. What to Expect's online community, for example, includes more than one thousand subgroups focused on topics such as due dates (e.g., April 2007 babies), birthing approaches (e.g., Bradley Method moms), and infant feeding (e.g., Breastfeeding). Certainly, many of the questions and concerns that women bring to their support group—such as what baby name to choose and what items to buy for their newborn—are ones that their apps' information guides and checklists address. However, many users also crave personalized responses and personal stories from other women experiencing similar issues. "Love both the posted information on each counted day of my pregnancy, and also the chat threads which allow moms-to-be to be grouped by baby's upcoming birth month and have conversations with other moms who are going through the same things as you are," a My Pregnancy Today user discussed.

Having mobile access to one's online support group can be especially helpful when faced with unexpected stresses such as spotting after a gym workout or sudden fears about becoming a mother while shopping for a crib. In such situations, women can, simply by touching their app's icon, turn to their group for reassurance and comfort. A Baby Bump Pro user explained, "The ladies are all very supportive of each other and it's nice to be able to talk to other women especially if you are waiting for a doctor's appointment and have quick questions before hand." Furthermore, such mobile access locates users' own "sensory-inscribed" bodies in two locations—the physical and virtual—at once.[37] Thus, users' ability to reach their support group regardless of their physical location can give them a sense of perpetual companionship and togetherness. "You can take your sisterhood wherever you go!" another Baby Bump Pro user noted. "I love it!"

Yet the support benefits of pregnancy apps go beyond these mobile "sisterhoods." They can also facilitate emotional support from an expectant mother's partner and other family members. Women can easily share information from their app by passing their smartphone to their loved one or by using their app's "share" function to send information to them electronically. A Sprout user stated, "This will be my husband's first [baby]. So to help him understand what I am going through, I email him the Dr. info." Moreover, spouses, grandparents, and other family members can download the apps onto their smartphones, keep track of what their expectant loved ones might be experiencing, and offer them support as needed. Some—though not all—pregnancy apps also offer support tips for expectant dads who use them. A My Pregnancy Today user explained, "I had my husband download the app as well and it helps him understand how women feel and the proper way to be a supportive partner."

To Whom Do Pregnancy Apps Speak?

Although usability can be defined in terms of what users can do and how well they can do it, another way to conceptualize it is "the absence of frustration."[38] User frustration, which can lead to dissatisfaction and displeasure with the product at hand, can result from numerous factors. On a technical level, bugs and other design flaws that make products faulty or glitchy can be one source of frustration. In the case of pregnancy apps, many negative user reviews, especially those written immediately after a new version of an app was released, focused on such bugs and flaws. A deeper source of frustration, however, can relate to a product's usefulness, particularly in terms of how it "speaks to" their users. Products are not simply designed with *general* users in mind but with *particular* users in mind. Characteristics about their target users, including their race, gender, age, sexual orientation, and cultural background, can be inscribed into their design. Thus, users whose values, needs, and experiences are not reflected back to them can experience frustration and dissatisfaction.[39]

When it comes to pregnancy apps, one set of user inscriptions revolves around what Michael Warner calls "default heteronormativity."[40] This default heteronormativity, which structures the apps' technical, aesthetic, and therapeutic design, assumes that users conform to heterosexual and gendered norms. Specifically, most apps construct their users as heterosexual females in married or partnered relationships with the baby's biological father. They also tend to embody traditional gender roles by constructing pregnancy, birth, and newborn care as feminized arenas in which fathers play a limited role. In many ways, this default heteronormativity extends to the user reviews. No self-identified lesbian or gay man wrote any of the reviews that I examined, and aside from one review written by a single (and self-identified heterosexual) woman, the vast majority of them appeared to be written by women and men in heterosexual relationships with the baby's biological parent. Furthermore, the user reviews written by women occasionally noted their app's limited attention to single mothers, gay couples, and fathers, but the vast majority of them took for granted their app's gendered construction. The reviews written by men yielded a different response pattern, however. Although many men seemed satisfied with their pregnancy app and did not question its gendered and heteronormative assumptions, a significant number of them felt frustrated and dissatisfied with the paucity of high-quality apps and specific app features geared toward expectant fathers.

HANGING OUT IN THE MOBILE MAMASPHERE

The gender dynamics in U.S. heterosexual households, especially middle- and upper-middle-class ones, have changed since the mid-twentieth century. To be sure, our culture still tends to construct pregnancy and childcare as feminized arenas, and mothers still take on the bulk of pregnancy and parenting-related responsibilities. That said, fathers have increasingly taken on a greater share of these responsibilities, and a small but growing number of them "stay at home" with their children while their wife or partner works.[41] These gender shifts have gone hand in hand with broader societal changes, including an increase in two-parent households with working mothers, a greater acceptance and implementation of paternal work leave policies, and the emergence of social support networks, both online and offline, for fathers.[42] Growing paternal involvement is also apparent in pregnancy app user reviews. Many reviews written by expectant mothers discuss how their husbands and boyfriends use their apps or have downloaded apps onto their own phones, and a substantial number of expectant fathers wrote their own reviews.

Despite the changing role of fathers and the fact that some of them use pregnancy apps, the vast majority of such apps target expectant mothers. Most apps embody a hegemonic feminine aesthetic, with both their thumbnails and content pages dominated by shades of pink or other pastels. The apps also speak primarily to pregnant women by directing most, if not all, of their information, checklists, and other features toward them. Consider Pregnancy ++, which was one of the only apps that I examined asking users to identify their parental status when configuring its settings instead of just assuming the users were expectant mothers. Even though this information allows the app to personalize the daily home page messages (see Figure 5.1), the icons that are listed at the bottom of the screen still speak to women. The "Me" icon, for example, directs users to support tools such as "My Belly" and "My Weight."

To varying degrees, however, most apps include a few support features devoted to expectant fathers, particularly in the form of occasional pregnancy

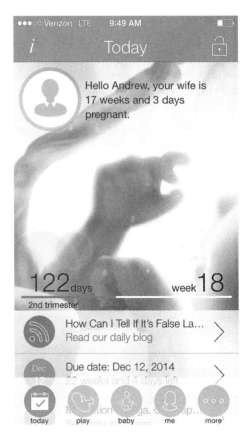

FIGURE 5.1. The homepage of Pregnancy++ personalized for the husband of an expectant mother. Used with permission of *Health and Parenting.*

and parenting tips interspersed throughout the daily or weekly information guides. Some of these tips discuss ways in which men can play an active role in their child's life before and after birth. Pregnancy ++, for example, suggests various strategies for bonding with their in utero baby, coping with pre-baby worries, and dividing infant care responsibilities with their pregnant partner. Yet most tips for dads approach paternal involvement as supporting their pregnant wives or girlfriends. Baby Bump Pro's "Just for Dad" tip on Day 62, for example, suggests that men should offer their partner a back rub to help ease the physical load of their growing baby, and What to Expect's Day 56 tip encourages fathers to be sensitive to their partner's pregnancy-related mood swings. Moreover, such tips sometimes reinforce traditional gender roles in parenting. For instance, Baby Bump Pro's "Just for Dad" tip on Day 202 encourages expectant fathers to "hammer out your post-baby budget. . . . Financial concerns are one of the biggest sources of anxiety for dads-to-be. . . . It's best to involve the mom-to-be, but only if it doesn't place added stress on her. Once you've crunched all the numbers and you know where you stand, you'll be able to welcome baby with open arms and not empty pockets."

Similarly, most app-based online support communities offer one or two subgroups for fathers (e.g., Baby Bump's "Just for Dads") or for mothers and fathers (e.g., My Pregnancy Today's "Mom and Dads at Home"). Such subgroups provide spaces for dads to socialize with one another, but their relegation to small sections of a multifeature app (or "corners," as What to Expect calls its two dads' groups) marginalizes fathers and their needs. Moreover, the user-driven content of these subgroups means that it is the users, rather than the app developers, who provide information and support to other members. Finally, some apps (e.g., Sprout and Pregnancy ++) have no online forum for men to connect with other dads.

Feminist scholars of gender and the internet have described how female users who participate in male-oriented spaces online—some of which Lori Kendall calls "virtual locker rooms"—can find ways to enjoy the experience despite feeling marginalized by their masculine, if not sexist, culture.[43] The use of pregnancy apps by expectant fathers reverses this gender dynamic in that men must navigate the mobile mamasphere and find pleasure in app features, content, and design elements that, for the most part, speak to and about women. Some men appreciate learning about the pregnancy process, even if most of the information is not geared toward them. A Pregnancy ++ user wrote, "What an awesome app to have during pregnancy, especially if it's your first. I'm the father, and it's been awesome and exciting to follow along and read about the things to expect." Other men embrace their app's maternal focus because they want to support their pregnant partner. "Me and my wife love using this app," a My Pregnancy Today user explained. "I downloaded it so I can understand what she's doing along the way and get an idea of what I need to be doing to help." Another set of male users appreciated the ability to learn about and bond with their baby. As one Sprout user stated, "This app makes me feel so happy and complete. Being able to . . . see what my baby looks like where ever I am is very rewarding." Yet the apps' overall focus on expectant mothers can leave some male users feeling left out of the pregnancy process and their newborn's care. Another Sprout user noted, "As a male, I have to admit it's pretty cool. Only problem for me is basically all the notes are for women." Perhaps not surprisingly, numerous male and female reviewers suggested that their mother-centered pregnancy apps should provide more features for heterosexual fathers and couples.

APPS FOR DADS

Although mothers are the target users for the vast majority of pregnancy apps, a few apps geared toward expectant fathers exist. In some regards, these latter apps speak to heterosexual fathers in ways that the mother-to-be apps do not. They embody traditional masculine colors such as dark blue, orange, and black, and a few include pictures of men holding their babies. They allow users to personalize the settings, and to varying degrees, provide men with tools and information that help them play an active role in their baby's life before and after birth. Duty Calls, for example, provides an interactive checklist of baby items to buy, and mPregnancy encourages men to attend ultrasound appointments in order to enhance prenatal bonding. Across the board, however, the dad-to-be apps primarily construct paternal involvement as supporting one's pregnant partner. Pregnant Dad's information guide for Day 13—right around the time that conception occurs—sets the stage for the expectant father's role: "Your job is done! Not really:). . . . You are entering a period of 280 days, where you can support your partner. Pay attention and show interest!" Duty Calls includes two partner support guides, including a list of "Do's and Don'ts" with tips such as "Rub her feet" and "[Don't] wake her up. She needs the sleep." Although all the dad-to-be apps mention the important role that fathers play in their newborn's life, none of them discusses what this role entails. In fact, Pregnant Dad assumes that paternity leave will consist of missing a few days of work for the baby's arrival: "Hopefully your employer is flexible to give you days off for the days of birth and after."

To be sure, some men experience great satisfaction from their father-to-be apps. The fact that such apps exist makes them feel as if they matter. "Just found out I'm going to be dad and this was exactly what I was looking for since it seems that guys get left out of this whole pregnancy thing," a Duty Calls user explains. Other dads feel satisfied with their app's approach to paternal involvement. Another Duty Calls user wrote, "Wow !!! That was my impression when I looked at the app. Awesome designs. I love the countdown. Knowledge section really is very helpful. Checklist really makes things easy, I can now remember and keep track of everything. Good job !!!!" Many others appreciate their app's emphases on supporting their pregnant partner and information about fetal development. "Great app for dads to be!!!," a Pregnant Dad user stated, "Lets you know what to expect from your mom to be, how she'll act, how she going to feel, where she is in progress!! Lets you track the babies progress from how big it is to what you expect when going to the doctor!!!"

Still, the potential of father-to-be apps to involve men in the pregnancy process only goes so far. By focusing the bulk of their content on how men can support their pregnant wives or girlfriends, the apps for dads—even more so than their mother-to-be counterparts—perpetuate the notion that their primary role is to be a "good" husband or boyfriend rather than an involved father. The apps' titles (e.g., "Duty Calls" and "Pregnant Dad: Surviving Pregnancy as a Father-to-be") reinforce this emphasis by constructing a father's role in pregnancy as an obligation to get through instead of a process worth experiencing for its own sake. Moreover, the apps' weekly updates focus more on technical facts regarding general fetal development and less on the fetal imaginaries that may help some expectant dads foster an emotional connection with their baby. Pregnant Dad's Week 14 updates, for example, explain the chances of having twins and spend several pages discussing famous twins. Instead of relying on images of human fetuses to illustrate their growth, Duty Calls uses fruit (e.g., strawberries for Week 3 and a cantaloupe for week 29). Yes, mPregnancy includes human images to highlight fetal development. However, its images dehumanize the growing fetus because they are jokingly positioned next to stereotypical masculine objects such as beer caps, cigarettes, and footballs to illustrate their growth (see Figure 5.2). Although the father-to-be apps occasionally address worries that men may have about pregnancy and about

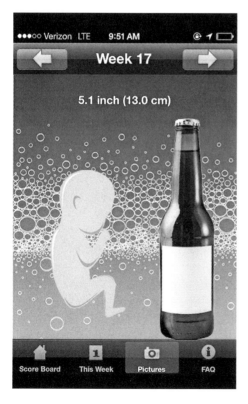

FIGURE 5.2. mPregnancy's image comparing the size of a 17-week-old fetus to the size of a beer bottle.

becoming dads, they spend more time discussing stereotypical concerns such as the impact of pregnancy on their sex lives.

Not surprisingly, men who download dad-to-be apps to become more involved in pregnancy and newborn care can feel condescended to or demeaned. As one Pregnant Dad user explained, "I was expecting so much more out of this app. I was disappointed with the lack of really relevant information given to a dad to be about topics that would help him feel involved in the pregnancy." An mPregnancy user stated, "It is shockingly bad. Almost offensive. I hate that men are portrayed as buffoons with interests only in beer, cigarettes, football and pizza." The devaluing of fathers is further evident by the spelling and grammar mistakes, design flaws, and limited features that tend to occur more frequently in the apps for fathers compared to the apps geared toward mothers.

The dearth of dad-to-be apps—let alone good ones—can leave some expectant fathers in a state of conflict: To where do they turn when the best designed and most informative apps are geared toward mothers yet the apps for dads meet their needs even less? Based on my user review analysis, most men are making do, for better or worse, with the mother-to-be apps. A Pregnant Dad user highlights this tension: "An app for the father-to-be who wants to be only slightly more informed than one who knows nothing . . . [My Pregnancy Today] is much better and provides more insight even though it's geared towards the mother." Although both types of apps have their own particular benefits and drawbacks when it comes to the needs of expectant dads, each one ultimately constructs pregnancy and infant care as feminized spaces in which fathers play a secondary role.

Transforming Pregnancy and Parenting Culture

The gendered and heteronormative contexts in which pregnancy apps are produced and used highlight the ways in which their usability, particularly in terms of their usefulness, is socially constructed. Given that some reviewers expressed frustration that their apps did not speak to single women and same-sex couples, perhaps it is not surprising that I found only one review written by a self-identified single woman and no reviews written by self-identified lesbians and gay men. I do not know whether these individuals wrote reviews without identifying their single status or sexual orientation, whether they decided not to write reviews about the apps that they used, or whether they tend not to use pregnancy apps in the first place. Although answering these questions would require a different type of user study, it is likely that the default heteronormativity of the apps and their reviews co-construct one another in some way.

The vast majority of user reviews, which were written by men and women in heterosexual relationships, highlight the ways in which the usability and usefulness of pregnancy apps is socially constructed in a different way. On the one hand, design features such as multimodality, personalization, and mobility can enhance satisfaction among many users, especially heterosexual (and partnered) women, by allowing them to take charge of their pregnancy and birthing experience, by fostering immediate online and offline emotional support from others, and by promoting an ongoing bond with their growing baby. On the other, the hegemonic assumptions built into the apps' aesthetic, technical, and therapeutic design can conflict with the needs and experiences of other users, particularly expectant fathers who feel marginalized by their app's focus on women and traditional gender norms. Furthermore, the design features that enhance satisfaction among users who see themselves in their apps' content can exacerbate the frustrations of such expectant fathers. Yes, men can bring their apps wherever they go, but how useful is their portability when their features do not speak to them as fathers, overlook their pregnancy and parenting support needs, and provide few support tools in the first place?

Despite the frustrations expressed by users about their app's treatment of fathers, their reviews tended to highlight other ways in which their app brought them satisfaction and joy. Thus, pregnancy apps seem to fulfill—at least to some degree—the needs of many expectant mothers and fathers, even with their design limitations. To ease these frustrations and increase user satisfaction, developers could design quality apps (aimed at women, men, or both) that construct heterosexual couples as "co-parents" who want to play active and equitable roles in preparing for their new child's arrival and in caring for their newborn infant. For example, apps could provide expectant fathers with strategies for negotiating extended paternal leave in workplaces that look down on men for taking such leave. They could provide strategies for how mothers and fathers can share parenting responsibilities so that they both can take time for self-care, work, or other personal activities. Such apps could also offer tips for expectant women on how to embrace their partner's prenatal and postnatal parenting efforts given that many women feel guilty about sharing these responsibilities with them due to long-standing cultural messages constructing good mothers as selfless.

Just as importantly, the benefits of designing pregnancy apps that challenge traditional gender roles may go beyond increased user satisfaction. The user inscriptions built into the apps are both descriptive and prescriptive; that is, they not only reflect who developers think their target users are but also tell users what types of mothers and fathers they are supposed to be.[44] Thus, constructing their apps' multiple features and personalization options through a co-parenting framework transforms hegemonic narratives regarding pregnancy and parenting into more equitable ones that expectant mothers and fathers can access wherever they go. At minimum, users who feel frustrated with their apps' traditional gender assumptions may feel validated by apps that approach them and their partners as co-parents. More optimistically, such apps may encourage users who lean toward hegemonic gender roles to interact with models of motherhood and fatherhood that they may not have previously considered for themselves or their partners.

The online and offline social networks in which pregnancy apps are embedded may help to facilitate broader societal change, too. The portability and information-sharing options of pregnancy apps allow users to disseminate their support features and content to others in person, by email, and on social media sites. Given that some users already share their app's content with others in these ways, it is likely that some would continue to do so with apps that promote more gender equitable approaches to parenting. Moreover, pregnancy apps are often developed by companies offering an array of online and offline support resources. Revamping their app's gendered parenting narratives may lead them to do the same across their range of support offerings—many of which draw audiences that go beyond their app's users. The biggest impact of revamping the gendered assumptions built into pregnancy apps, however, may consist of empowering users to live out more equitable models of motherhood and fatherhood at prenatal doctor appointments, at home, at so-called "mommy and me" classes, at work, and in the world more generally, regardless of whether they have their smartphone with them.

Notes

1. Barbara L. Ley, "Beyond Discussion Forums: The Transmediated Support Culture of an Online Pregnancy and Mothering Group," in *Motherhood Online*, ed. Michelle Moravec (Newcastle upon Tyne: Cambridge Scholars Press, 2011), 23–44.

2. The apps that I chose are among the most downloaded, although I also chose a few less popular ones that had specialized features. For apps that come in both paid and free versions, I chose the former, as those usually have more tools than the latter. For the user reviews, I focused on ones written between January and September 2013, but for some apps I went as far back as 2010.

3. Julie Wilson and Emily Chivers Yochim, "Pinning Happiness: Affect, Social Media, and the Work of Mothers," in this volume.

4. May Friedman and Shana L. Calixte, eds. *Mothering and Blogging: The Radical Art of the MommyBlog* (Bradford, Ontario: Demeter Press, 2009); Lori K. Lopez, "The Radical

Act of 'Mommy Blogging': Redefining Motherhood through the Blogosphere," *New Media and Society* 11 (2009): 729–747; Robyn Longhurst, "YouTube: A New Space for Birth?" *Feminist Review* 93 (2009): 46–63; Ley, "Beyond Discussion Forums," 30–34; Jessica Reed and Becky Gardiner, "The Beautiful Breastfeeding Images Facebook Is Missing Out On," *The Guardian*, February, 23, 2012, accessed January 6, 2015, http://www.theguardian.com/commentisfree/2012/feb/23/breastfeeding-images-facebook-missing.

5. "Mobile Technology Fact Sheet," Pew Internet, accessed January 6, 2015, http://www.pewinternet.org/fact-sheets/mobile-technology-fact-sheet/.

6. Sherry Turkle, *Alone Together: Why We Expect More from Technology and Less from Each Other* (Boston: Basic Books, 2011), 171–186.

7. W. Douglas Evans, Lorien C. Abroms, Ronald Poropatich, Peter E. Nielsen, and Jasmine L. Wallace, "Mobile Health Evaluation Methods: The Text4baby Case Study," *Journal of Health Communication: International Perspectives* 17 (2012): 22–29; Robyn Whittaker, Sabrina Matoff-Stepp, Judy Meehan, Juliette Kendrick, Elizabeth Jordan, Paul Stange, Amanda Cash, Paul Meyer, Julie Baitty, Pamela Johnson, Scott Ratzan, and Kyu Rhee, "Text4baby: Development and Implementation of a National Text Messaging Health Information Service," *American Journal of Public Health* 102 (2012): 2207–2213.

8. Ley, "Beyond Discussion Forums," 27–30.

9. Ibid., 30–34. Also, 33 percent of female cell phone owners, and 52 percent of smartphone owners, have used their device to access online health information. See Suzannah Fox and Maeve Duggan, *Mobile Health 2012* (Washington, D.C.: Pew Internet, 2012), 5–9, accessed January 6, 2015, http://www.pewinternet.org/files/old-media//Files/Reports/2012/PIP_MobileHealth2012_FINAL.pdf.

10. Fox and Duggan, *Mobile Health 2012*, 11.

11. Chantal Tode, "Mobile Health App Marketplace to Take Off, Expected to Reach $26B by 2017," *Mobile Marketer*, March 25, 2013, accessed January 6, 2015, http://www.mobilemarketer.com/cms/news/research/15023.html.

12. "Fact Sheet 39: Mobile Health and Fitness Apps: What Are the Privacy Risks?" Privacy Rights Clearinghouse, accessed January 6, 2015, https://www.privacyrights.org/mobile-health-and-fitness-apps-what-are-privacy-risks#section%204.

13. Ibid.

14. Nielsen, "Hacking Health: How Consumers Use Smartphones and Wearable Tech to Track Their Health," April 16, 2014, accessed January 6, 2015, http://www.nielsen.com/us/en/newswire/2014/hacking-health-how-consumers-use-smartphones-and-wearable-tech-to-track-their-health.html.

15. Fox and Duggan, *Mobile Health 2012*, 12–14.

16. Citrix, *Mobile Analytics Report*, February 2013, 8, accessed January 6, 2015, http://www.citrix.com/content/dam/citrix/en_us/documents/products-solutions/bytemobile-mobile-analytics-report-february-2013.pdf?accessmode=direct.

17. Hearn et al. found that 10.5 percent of pregnant women signed up for a government-sponsored app to help manage weight gain during pregnancy, and O'Higgin et al. found that 44 percent of pregnant women wanted to use a smartphone app. See Lydia Hearn,

Margaret Miller, and Anna Fletcher, "Online Healthy Lifestyle Support in the Perinatal Period: What Do Women Want and Do They Use It?" *Australian Journal of Primary Health*, accessed October 4, 2013, http://dx.doi.org/10.1071/PY13039; A. C. O'Higgins, C. O'Connor, N. Daly, E. Kent, M. Kennelly, and M. Turner, "PP. 40: The Potential of Digital Media to Improve Fetal and Maternal Outcomes," *Archives of Disease in Childhood: Fetal and Neonatal Edition* 98 (2013): A93.

18. Jennifer Gunter, "An App to Help Your Patient Track Her Pregnancy," *OBG Management* 24 (2012): 63–66, accessed January 6, 2015, http://www.obgmanagement.com/uploads/media/2409OBG_Gunter.pdf.

19. The few users that mentioned their app's industry purposes tended to critique the in-app advertisements for infant formula, as they believed that their apps did not adequately promote breastfeeding.

20. Jeffrey Rubin and Dana Chisnell, *Handbook of Usability Testing: How to Plan, Design, and Conduct Effective Tests* (Hoboken, N.J.: Wiley, 2008), 4–6.

21. Ibid., 4–6.

22. Fred D. Davis, "User Acceptance of Information Technology: System Characteristics, User Perceptions, and Behavioral Impacts," *International Journal of Man-Machine Studies* 38 (1993): 475–487; Jeff Sauro, "Measuring Usefulness: The Technology Acceptance Model (TAM)," November 1, 2011, accessed January 6, 2015, http://www.measuringu.com/blog/usefulness.php.

23. Fabien Miard, "Call for Power? Mobile Phones as Facilitators of Political Activism," in *Cyberspaces and Global Affairs*, eds. Sean S. Costigan and Jake Perry (London: Ashgate Press, 2012), 119–144.

24. Mia Consalvo, "Selling the Internet to Women: The Early Years," in *Women and Everyday Uses of the Internet: Agency and Identity*, eds. Mia Consalvo and Susanna Paasonen (New York: Peter Lang, 2002), 111–138.

25. Susannah Fox and Maeve Duggan, *Health Online 2013* (Washington, D.C.: Pew Internet, 2013), 6–14, accessed January 6, 2015, http://www.pewinternet.org/files/old-media/Files/Reports/PIP_HealthOnline.pdf.

26. Carol S. Weisman, *Women's Health Care: Activist Traditions and Institutional Change* (Baltimore: Johns Hopkins University Press, 1998).

27. Fox and Duggan, *Health Online 2013*, 6–14.

28. Quantified Self: Self Knowledge through Numbers, accessed January 6, 2015, http://quantifiedself.com/about/.

29. Mark Joseph Stern, "Weight, Watched," *Slate*, November 11, 2013, accessed January 6, 2015, http://www.slate.com/articles/technology/future_tense/2013/11/smartphone_diet_apps_are_they_helping_us_lose_weight.html.

30. Gail Dines, "Growing Up Female in a Celebrity-Based Pop Culture," in *Gender, Race, and Class in Media: A Critical Reader*, eds. Gail Dines and Jean M. Humez (Los Angeles: Sage, 2015), 433–440.

31. "Stages of Labor: Stage 1," American Pregnancy Association, accessed January 6, 2015, http://americanpregnancy.org/labor-and-birth/first-stage-of-labor/.

32. Rayna Rapp, *Testing Women, Testing the Fetus: The Social Impact of Amniocentesis in America* (New York: Routledge, 2000), 124–164.

33. Jason Farman, *Mobile Interface Theory: Embodied Space and Locative Media* (New York: Routledge, 2012), 16–34.

34. Barbara L. Ley, "'Vive les Roses!': The Architecture of Commitment in an Online Pregnancy and Mothering Group," *Journal of Computer-Mediated Communication* 12 (2007): 1395; Patricia Drentea and Jennifer L. Moren-Cross, "Social Capital and Social Support on the Web: The Case of an Internet Mother Site," *Sociology of Health and Illness* 27 (2005): 920–943; Henrietta O'Connor and Clare Madge, "'My Mum's Thirty Years out of Date': The Role of the Internet in the Transition to Motherhood," *Community, Work, and Family* 7 (2004): 351–369.

35. Ley, "'Vive les Roses!'"; Drentea and Moren-Cross, "Social Capital."

36. Ley, "'Vive les Roses!'" 1388–1393.

37. Farman, *Mobile Interface*, 16–34.

38. Rubin and Chisnell, *Handbook*, 4–6.

39. Ibid. Also, there are different opinions about the relationship between user satisfaction, usefulness, and usability. Whereas some definitions of usability view these as separate issues, Rubin and Chisnell bridge them. I am taking this latter approach.

40. Michael Warner, "Introduction: Fear of a Queer Planet," *Social Text* 29 (1991): 3–17.

41. Kim Parker and Wendy Wang, *Modern Parenthood: Roles of Moms and Dads Converge as They Balance Work and Family* (Washington, D.C.: Pew Social Trends, 2013), accessed January 6, 2015, http://www.pewsocialtrends.org/files/2013/03/FINAL_modern_parenthood_03-2013.pdf.

42. Curtis B. Livesay, "The Other Side of the (Gender Coin): Stay-at-Home Fathers' Use of Online Discussion Groups," in *Motherhood Online*, ed. Michelle Moravec (Newcastle upon Tyne: Cambridge Scholars Press, 2011), 168–179; "The Changing Role of the Modern Day Father," American Psychological Association, accessed January 6, 2015, https://www.apa.org/pi/families/resources/changing-father.aspx.

43. Lori Kendall, *Hanging Out in the Virtual Pub: Masculinities and Relationships Online* (Berkeley: University of California Press, 2002), 71–108; T. L. Taylor, *Play between Worlds: Exploring Online Game Culture* (Cambridge: MIT Press, 2006), 93–124.

44. Nelly Oudshoorn and Trevor Pinch, "How Users and Non-Users Matter," in *How Users Matter: The Co-Construction of Users and Technologies*, eds. Nelly Oudshoorn and Trevor Pinch (Cambridge: MIT Press, 2003), 7–11.

CHAPTER 6

Fashioning Feminine Fandom

Fashion Blogging
and the Expression of Mediated Identity

KYRA HUNTING

It's *just* "dress-up for gamer gurlz" is one of many critiques the blogger behind *Console to Closet* reports being levied at her whenever her blog is featured on a video game's social media.[1] That "dress-up" would be used dismissively points to one of the problems in approaching fashion blogging seriously. Although dress-up is a fundamental form of play and identity formation that most children engage in, it is rarely treated seriously. Its grown-up equivalent—fashion—is similarly devalued. At best fashion is seen as "frivolous," at worst actively sexist or regressive. Fashion and fashion media are too rarely afforded serious consideration as important spaces for creativity, social engagement, and self-expression—all functions made more visible by fashion blogging.

The love of fashion has inspired some to express their media fandom through blogs that examine the intersection between fashion and media. Despite a tendency among some commentators to flatten fashion blogging into a single phenomenon, there is tremendous diversity within fashion blogging. While fandom-centered fashion blogging represents only a small sliver of fashion blogs and fan blogs, its unique focus points to the importance of this diversity when evaluating the function of fashion blogging. My study looks at fifteen fashion blogs whose themes focus on media and fictional texts in order to focus on the gender politics of the relationship between fashion and media fandom. While fashion blogging has been critiqued as problematic in relationship to gender and class, I argue that fashion blogging not only creates opportunities for women's

self expression through technology but can in fact destabilize normative relationships to gender, beauty norms, and consumption that are often assumed
to be part of an interest in fashion culture. As an important subset of fashion
blogging, fan-fashion blogs place fandom and media texts at the center of their
focus, often deemphasizing images of the blogger, presenting opportunities for
a more playful and complex relationship to the ideological issues that accom-
pany fashion. Focusing on the specifics of *form* and *focus* that are shared by a
particular subset of fashion blogging reveals the complexity present in these
websites and the potential for feminist and feminine expression and creativity
that such blogs represent. By combining fandom with fashion blogging, female
fans are able to create a space where they can express their taste and where they
can refashion their relationship to fashion and embodiment as one in which
their media passions and identifications can be expressed through the body.
These spaces allow for fans to engage with their favorite media texts, the material world of fashion, and concepts of the body in creative, diverse, and even
political ways that would not have been as viable in contexts other than the
platform that fashion blogging provides. Indeed, the way in which the interface
used by many fashion bloggers provides fan-fashion bloggers with a wealth of
raw materials to construct fan-based outfits allows for possibilities that pre-
internet or text-based expression of fan culture would not have allowed for.

In this chapter, I consider how the platform provided by fan-fashion blogs
and the affordances of the technology allow fan-fashion bloggers to play with
media and fashion in a way that is less constrained by a blogger's financial or
physical limitations than previous engagements with fandom and fashion—
like cosplay or collecting. Fan-fashion blogs can also destabilize some of the
assumptions about scarcity, competition, and authenticity that accompanied
these preceding fan practices. Further, I argue that the focus on *fandom* and
its distinct set of values and priorities in these blogs shifts their orientation in
relationship to several issues associated with fashion and fashion blogging more
broadly, including displacing traditional approaches to issues like consumption,
body policing, and "normative femininity."

Although journalists recognized the phenomenon of fashion blogging as
early as 2002, and fashion bloggers were invited to Fashion Week in 2003, the
academic consideration of fashion blogging has been sparse. Within the academic scholarship on the subject there is considerable disagreement about
whether or not fashion blogging has the potential to be a disruptive influence.[2]
Some scholars suggest that fashion bloggers are often a part of the industry
and prioritize normative images of attractiveness and "style"[3] or rely heavily on
values of "consumption and . . . normative femininity"[4] that are already central

to critiques of the fashion industry. These discrepancies reflect the difficulty in making definitive claims about the potential and politics of fashion blogging. These difficulties emerge from the tremendous diversity of fashion blogs on the web. While there has not been a systematic cataloguing of fashion blogs, it is clear that there are thousands of fashion blogs in the early twenty-first century. Fashion blogs have become prevalent enough to splinter into specialty subcategories; there are mommy fashion blogs, eco fashion blogs, academic fashion blogs, Mormon fashion blogs, and, the focus of this study, fan-fashion blogs. Fashion blogging represents a *media form*, one with shared attributes and investments that provide certain affordances impacting content—content that may vary wildly from case to case and subcategory to subcategory. As a result, the particular *form* and thematic *focus* of fashion blogging are pivotal in terms of the ways in which fashion blogging interacts with crucial ideologies of gender and identity. Fashion blogging can function as a site of tension and negotiation over ideologies of gender and embodiment, where women bloggers can engage creatively with fashion in order to explore questions of taste, fandom, and identity as part of a community of fans and bloggers. The goal of this chapter is to demonstrate the potential and pleasures provided by fan-fashion blogging and to explore the impact of these blogs' specific themes and formal elements on their ideological relationship to the problems and possibilities presented by fashion culture.

A Taxonomy of Fashion Blogs

A key challenge for those who study fashion blogging is its tremendous diversity. Categorizing the types of fashion blogs can be a complex task because there are a number of different ways in which they can be classified. Frequently, fashion blogs are classified by their dominant themes—high fashion, alternative, modest, eco-themed, vintage, and so forth. In Table 6.1, I provide a taxonomy that is based on the format of a blog and the types of content that the blog features. Within a category there are a number of shared elements in relationship to form and content, but there may also be a significant amount of thematic variety. A single type of fashion blog, such as the personal style blog, may have examples focusing on every theme listed earlier. This taxonomy was developed based on the analysis of 166 fashion blogs;[5] Table 6.1 focuses on the nine most common types of blogs in my sample, a description of their main focus, and examples; however there are many more specialized categories of blogs. Although distinct categories are listed in the table, many blogs may fit into more than one of these categories or include elements of multiple categories. The taxonomy not only serves to illustrate the diversity of a phenomenon that

TABLE 6.1. Fashion Blog Taxonomy

Category	Descriptions	Examples
Personal Style	Blogs that focus on photographs of the blogger in outfits, usually in diverse/attractive settings.	*Fashion Toast, Man Repeller, Atlantic Pacific, Avant Blargh*
Street Style	Blogs that focus on photographs of subjects captured "on the street." These focus on interesting outfits in global cities and may have favorite subjects.	*The Sartorialist, Advanced Style, Street Peeper, Tommy Ton*
Photologues	These blogs use photographs to capture the blogger's life. Fashion images are mixed with travel, setting, and food images. While blogs devoted to this are relatively rare, many blogs in other categories feature this as part of their blog.	*Ann Street Studio, The Daily Prep*
Online Fashion Magazines	Online fashion magazines contain articles, images, and slide shows on a variety of topics. These feature a number of contributors. Some commentators may not consider these blogs, because many are linked to publishing companies.	*Refinery 29, Racked, Fashion Indie, The Coveteur*
Potpourri Blogs	Like online fashion magazines, potpourri blogs include content on diverse topics including fashion, beauty, recipes, interior design, art, and lifestyle. Unlike online fashion magazines, these blogs are the work of a single or small number of bloggers.	*Cupcakes and Cashmere, College Fashion, The Glamourai, Park and Cube*
DIY/Tutorial	These blogs provide instruction for their readers. DIY blogs focus on apparel, clothing, and decor craft projects that their readers can complete. Many other blogs focus on tutorials for hair and makeup looks and for making beauty products.	*P.S. I Made This...., A Beautiful Mess, Love Maegen, Makeup Geek*
Shopper/ Review	These blogs provide shopping guidance for readers. They include profiles of products, reviews, lookbooks, and information about sales or store openings.	*In the Gloss, Racked, She Finds, Bag Snob*
Style-Spotting/ Celebrity Fashion	These blogs focus on celebrity style and style on film and television. These "spot" and locate items seen on celebrities or media texts, comment on the outfits worn at events or in photo shoots, and provide recaps of media texts.	*Tom & Lorenzo, Who What Wear, You Know You Love Fashion, Clothes on Fashion*
Collage-Style Fashion Blogs	These blogs primarily feature collections of items compiled into a collage, generally to represent outfits. While blogs that focus on this form are relatively rare, many blogs include this within their larger purpose.	*Nerd Boyfriend, DisneyBound, Console to Closet, Fiction to Fashion*

is often discussed only in relationship to its most prominent representatives but also seeks to demonstrate the differing "scripts" or approaches to fashion blogging from which fan-fashion blogs are able to draw.

While the table features many of the most common types of fashion blogs, there are a number of categories that are less common but point to the incredible variety within the term. There are blogs that function as a trade press focusing on the industry, like *The Business of Fashion*; blogs that focus on fashion as a space for art, film, and illustration, like *A Shaded View of Fashion* and *Fifi Lapin*; and even fashion blogs with activist or social issue foci, like *The Curvy Fashionista*, *Threadbared*, and *DapperQ*.

The focus and structure of these blogs often indicate a predisposition to approach these issues in particular ways. Shopping and Review blogs have a tendency to place an emphasis on consumption, while DIY and Tutorial blogs push back against a consumerist norm by encouraging readers to make their own versions of expensive designer or beauty goods. Blogs that focus on the industry may critique aspects of fashion culture, but by and large buy into the business' goals and values, while Activist blogs may question norms of physical attractiveness in fashion or question the racial or gender politics of the industry. Most clear in my sample, however, was the tremendous diversity that occurred within categories that allowed for vastly varying approaches to ideological and gender issues. Personal Style Blogs, because they focus on photographs of the blogger, had a strong tendency to privilege norms of physical attractiveness and the presentation of one's body for appreciation. However, certain blogs, like *Gabi Fresh*, subverted this norm by focusing on plus size bloggers. Similarly, while many beauty blogs provide information on how to meet a western beauty ideal, the successful blog *Curly Nikki* focuses on how to grow, nurture, and cultivate natural hair for women of color as both an ideological and beauty norm. Examining categories of fashion blogs can help us identify norms within fashion blogging and ideological tendencies within a category. However, it also is important to be aware that within any of these categories there are blogs that push against norms of beauty and consumption that are associated with the fashion industry.

This kind of resistance is particularly frequent in collage-style fashion blogs, which often remove the embodied element of fashion and instead focus on sets of items that are "collaged" together, usually to make a specific outfit. Fan-fashion blogs, which form the majority of this category, center on media and fan culture's intersection with fashion as their primary theme (see Figure 6.1). Since this category is thematic it can overlap with many of the format categories listed. There are fan-fashion personal-style blogs, like *The Stylish Geek*, featuring

FIGURE 6.1. A typical fan-fashion collage-style blog, taking inspiration from the video game, *Gears of War*. Used with permission of *Console to Closet*.

the blogger in media-themed clothing, and a large number of "style-spotting" fan-fashion blogs dedicated to locating the items of clothing worn on film or television. However, interestingly, in my analysis of the 166 fashion blogs that formed the basis of this taxonomy, while a large number of the blog types intersected with media or fandoms in some way,[6] even if it was simply pulling in the image of a celebrity's style, fan-fashion blogs overwhelmingly favored one category of fashion blogs: the collage-style fashion blogs. The preponderance of fan-fashion blogs choosing the collage style, otherwise a not particularly popular format, is particularly telling insofar as it dovetails with other aspects of fan-fashion blogging. These include the use of clothing to express something about a character or to play with a character's traditional form, a general de-emphasis on the blogger's body—a key feature of many other fashion blogs, and an interest in fan expression as self expression over traditional notions of trends and "attractiveness." Here, we can see that while there is a broad diversity of fashion blogs and that fashion blogs can serve diverse functions and provide diverse messages, not all formats of fashion blogs are equally well suited to all functions and messages. This points to the significance of both thematic and format type to the kinds of creative expression and ideological messages expressed in a given fashion blog.

Most of the blogs that I will consider here are collage-style fashion blogs that belong to a subcategory of fan-fashion blogs that I call "interpretive" blogs. Interpretive fan-fashion blogs use a media text, character, or setting as their inspiration and then create an original outfit based on this inspiration. The collage-style blog that is used in my primary case study, "interpretive fashion blogs," disembodies fashion and allows it to be considered outside of the context of physical norms. Although collage-style blogs are relatively limited, collage elements are common to a wide variety of blogs and many of the possibilities of the collage-style "interpretive" blogs can be seen within blogs whose format may tend to privilege "idealized" beauty and body images.

Fashion Blogging's Ideological Flexibility

Given the potential that some observers of fashion and fashion blogging have noted for fashion blogging to reinforce norms of physical attractiveness and consumerism,[7] it may seem problematic to consider fashion blogging as an important site of feminized popular culture, and even feminist engagement. However, the complexity and diversity of fashion blogs, and fashion bloggers and their goals, reveal the extensive potential fashion blogging has for fashion bloggers and its many fans. These mostly female bloggers exist at an important nexus of individual expression and creativity, technological mastery, and community, all of which impact feminist questions of access and voice.

The potential benefits for the individual bloggers in this respect are clear. The mostly young women who run many of the fashion blogs build spaces where they can articulate their tastes and their fashion fantasies and share important parts of their lives. While some fashion bloggers only post images of themselves in clothing, others talk about their families, their jobs, or even their beliefs. Even when blogs focus solely on fashion, they may serve as an important platform for women's voices. While fashion is "seen as frivolous and anti-intellectual" by many scholars, it can in fact be an important space for self-expression.[8] Mormon fashion blogs, in their focus on fashionable dressing that is also modest, express religious beliefs and conviction through fashion choices. Eco-fashion blogs express political values through the fashion on display. Indeed, given the complexity of embodiment and gender performance for women where, according to Jo Reger, "the female body is a site of both oppression and resistance," one could argue that any fashion choice, any presentation of the gendered body, speaks to more than the items being worn but to a complex relationship to gender, identity, and the self.[9]

While only an extremely small number of fashion bloggers in my sample specifically identified themselves as wanting a career in fashion, fashion blogging presents an opportunity for professionalization and technical skill building. Some famous fashion blogs, like *The Man Repeller*, have led to book deals and capsule collections, and some of the bloggers in my sample sell T-shirts and merchandise related to their blog. Many fan-fashion sites are developed using Polyvore, a social media site that allows for the creation of collages of fashion items, whose interface encourages a particular kind of collage style that mimics the layouts used in magazines like *Real Simple* or *InStyle*, gathering the elements of a themed outfit together onto a blank background. Here, the technology lends itself to a visual vocabulary already associated with the professional world of fashion. Further, these bloggers exhibit technological proficiency in the service of fashion. Most use at least three or four social media platforms and engines employing blog websites, Polyvore and Tumblr and often maintaining social media presence on Instagram, Facebook, and Twitter, as well. Many fashion bloggers also include web video on their sites, further extending the technological competency they exhibit. The leveraging of technology, an often discursively masculinized realm, to create communities and self-expression around fashion, a discursively feminized realm, is emblematic of the contradictions that are constitutive of fashion blogging. While fashion blogs may, to some, simply calcify the limited spaces of female voices and self-expression in the areas of consumption and fashion/beauty, they require not only competency in the area of fashion but also in the use of a variety of media technologies, including the use of social media to increase the visibility of their blogs and their own brands or digital identities and to increase their interaction with a larger community of bloggers and followers.

The importance of community has a long history in feminism, and it is telling that many critiques of fashion, and fashion blogging, define it as part of postfeminist or neoliberal ideologies focused on the self.[10] Laurie Ouellette critiques this focus on "self-fashioning" in makeover TV and Sarah Banet-Weiser and Inna Arzumanova see this problematic "entrepreneurship of the self" at play in fashion blogging.[11] However, despite the extent to which creative self-expression and entrepreneurship appear in some of the benefits of fashion blogging discussed earlier, in many fan-fashion blogs, community instead comes to the fore.

Most fan-fashion bloggers produce many of their posts in response to specific reader requests, often crediting reader suggestions. Many fashion bloggers actively include the reader communities throughout their site. For example, *DisneyBound* and *Companion Clothing* have featured photos of readers wearing their own interpretive outfits.[12] Fan-fashion blogs that focus on matching outfits seen in media often ask readers to help them locate hard-to-find items and credit them when they do.[13] The blogger behind *Console to Closet* created a Polyvore account that readers have used to contribute their own outfits, and she prominently has given credit to community submissions. Some fashion blogs even extend their interest in community to providing opportunities for offline interaction. *DisneyBound* organized a meet-up of readers in conjunction with the Disney Parks' Dapper Days event, where hundreds of fans met one another (many for the first time) and were photographed for the blog.[14] Less formally, *DisneyBound* has featured numerous photos from followers who met someone who was also DisneyBounding (dressing inspired by a Disney character). While some forms of fashion blogging may seem to privilege a me-centric, neoliberal, and postfeminist ideology by offering the individual blogger's taste, body, and personal experiences as a commodity, fan-fashion bloggers trouble this assumption by placing their engagement with their readers and fan communities at the center of their projects. While most of the blogs in this sample, with the exception of *You Know You Love Fashion*, are primarily visual, many devote the little writing that does appear to responding to members of their community of readers.

Occasionally these responses take on explicitly political dimensions. The blogger who runs *Companion Clothing* unexpectedly hosted a conversation about the use of sexist language, in this case the term "slutty," and the problem of choosing outfits because of their sex appeal, after one reader asked for more "slutty" *Dr. Who* interpretive outfits.[15] Ultimately the blogger both changed the term to sexy, in response to her readers, and indicated that she would make very few "sexy outfits" because it was clearly a sensitive issue for many of her followers. Here, the issue of the possible interpretation of *Dr. Who* characters' fashion grew into questions about the gender politics of both language and clothing. While explicit instances like these make the political dimension of fashion more visible, the choices made in terms of fashion are substantive even when subtle, expressing a complex relationship to texts, gender, and embodiment.

Critics of fashion blogging rightfully point out that it is not enough to simply laud the opportunity for a voice for women, that the nature of this voice is also important.[16] However, having a voice in and of itself can still be a political act. Suzanne Scott's work on the marginalization of female comic-book fans notes how women and girls are subject to misogyny and harassment in geek, comic-book, and gamer culture and may feel silenced.[17] Many fan-fashion blogs focus on or feature media that are associated with male fandoms. Here, visibility itself is potentially political by allowing a space for female fans to speak. For many, the value placed on visibility, community, creativity, and technological literacy

as expressed through fashion is a problem in itself, because of fashion's association with normative femininity.[18] But this assumes an agreement with those that
"have argued that fashion is a means of controlling women," a phenomenon that
is oppressive both economically and in terms of women's identities.[19] Other
feminist scholars have argued that fashion is an important source of pleasure,
a space where women can "convey politics, personalities and preference" and
an important part of oppositional subcultures.[20] Fashion can be thought of as
conflicted: a problematic part of commodity culture and a venue for personal
creativity; a place where women are sexualized and where women play with
gender and identity; a place where women engage in an entrepreneurship of
the self and where they create communities over shared interests. The value
in fashion blogs is not that they somehow smooth over these conflicts; rather
it is that they provide opportunities for these tensions to be played with and
negotiated. Reger says of fashion that the issue is not to somehow avoid contradiction, but, instead, the "issue is wasting contradiction's *utility*."[21]

The connection between feminism and fashion can often be found in these
contradictions. In his study of fans, Matthew Hills argues for a "suspensionist
approach" that allows for contradictions and avoids the trap of moral dualism.[22]
At the nexus of fandom and fashion, the important issue is how individual
blogs' chosen goals impact the way they interact with these tensions and what
ideologies the blogs communicate. By articulating the culture of fandom onto
fashion, many fan-fashion blogs subvert the stereotypical relationship to consumption, embodiment, and sexualized femininity associated with fashion
by refocusing the goals of fashion away from creating an "attractive" personal
image and toward an interaction with media.

Interpretive Fashion Blogging

"Interpretive" fashion blogs take on a theme related to media—Disney, video
games, and so forth—and then develop outfits "inspired by" these media. The
nature of this inspiration and the abstractness of the interpretation can vary
widely. Some blogs, like *Dress Like Celebs*, take their inspiration literally; they
take a character from a television program, isolate key "signature" style elements, like baby doll dresses and cardigans on Quinn in *Glee*, then create an
outfit with these precise elements.[23] However, many of the blogs in this category are much more abstract in their translation of their inspiration into an
outfit, turning characters who are animals, aliens, anthropomorphized objects
or machines, and even settings or theme park rides into wearable outfits. I
describe these types of blogs as "interpretive" because the bloggers do not

Interpretive

start from a specific article of clothing but instead start from a character, idea, or world that they deconstruct into its core aesthetic, narrative, and symbolic parts and then reconstruct using clothing. Interpretive fashion blogs represent something of a semiotic exercise; they establish the core signifiers of a media text, character, or world and then refashion these elements into a sign that can be worn on the body. The fact that any given media icon can be interpreted in numerous ways on these blogs serves to highlight their semiotic flexibility while simultaneously reinforcing their core constituent elements. The character of Dumbo is interpreted into eighteen widely diverse outfits, for everything from prom to beach days, on *DisneyBound* (see Figure 6.2). Yet across this variety a clear vocabulary for what "Dumbo" is gets established: These outfits were all rendered in a palette of gray, yellow, and red or pink and generally included a feather necklace or bracelet, elephant jewelry, a yellow bow, and occasionally heart accessories.

FIGURE 6.2. *DisneyBound* presents an outfit collage interpreting the animated film, *Dumbo*. Used with permission of *DisneyBound*.

play

These outfits break down the important signifiers of Dumbo-ness; the color palette of the character and elephant items signify the character itself, while other items (Dumbo's magic feather, the heart jewelry) gesture to items or ideas that have important purchase in the text. In this way, an article of clothing is presented not as an end in itself but as a building block that allows for play with media texts. The ludic element of clothing is particularly evident in interpretive blog posts. These posts frequently respond to requests and combine disparate elements to figure out different answers to the puzzle of how to interpret a given text sartorially. Some of these blogs' followers explicitly define success as people recognizing the theme of their outfit despite its subtlety, placing value on this ludic possibility.

Interpretive fashion blogging provides a particularly rich site of inquiry for considering how some branches of fashion blogging might overturn some of the frequently critiqued aspects of fashion and blogging, like consumerism or body policing. In particular, the shift of focus to the fan text can allow for a greater variety of body types, physical appearance, and class positions than may commonly be associated with fashion blogging. The impact of the shift in focus is bolstered by the technology used by these fan-fashion blogs and their visual format, which shifts the focus of these blogs away from the body to a more purely digital realm where the idea of fashion as fan expression takes precedence over the fashion object itself.

Interpretive fashion blogging also distinguishes itself from other fan-centered engagements with fashion by displacing the core value of authenticity with creative interpretation. Authenticity is a core value in a number of areas in which fandom and fashion intersect. In cosplay, a practice where fans dress up as media characters to attend events and conventions, participants are judged, often literally, on how accurate the details of the costume and the physical appearance of the cosplayer are in relation to the character they are cosplaying. Because media texts popular in cosplay culture, particularly anime and video games, often depict women as scantily clad, slender, and extremely buxom, this emphasis on authenticity makes it uncomfortable or impossible for many women to "authentically" emulate this appearance.[24] This emphasis on authenticity can have a policing quality to it where individuals whose weight, race, or physical features prevent them from appearing "authentic" or whose financial resources don't allow for specialty wigs or leather armor are marginalized. Indeed, cosplay is often at its most visible through professional or competitive cosplayers, chronicled on the Syfy series *Heroes of Cosplay*, a dimension of cosplay practice that is *by definition* based on the judgment and ranking of participants. This dimension of competition is also present in some collecting practices that focus on collecting clothing used on a television show or film through auctions and specialty stores. Josh Stenger has documented the ways in which an auction of *Buffy the Vampire Slayer* costume items and the discourses it produced served to illustrate the financial and physical privilege implicit in the process and the way in which both the materiality of the clothing and the dramatic expense excluded most fans from participating.[25] Even when seeking out clothing that is not a collectible but rather a replica—the common fan practice of cataloging and hunting down fashion items—the barriers placed on fans with limited economic resources or whose body type or age might not match the cultural "ideal" may be significant.[26] In all of these cases the focus on the "authentic," replicating as closely as possible the appearance of media characters or possessing "authentic" articles of clothing, can require significant financial resources and exclude fans whose age, body type, or appearance may not be commensurate with media norms. This can be particularly significant in fan-fashion practices like cosplay that frequently figures characters that were originally animated and that are not only extremely slender but often also extremely buxom, representing an extreme of attractiveness very difficult to emulate for most women.

Because the goal of interpretive fashion blogs is imaginative engagement with the *idea* of a character, setting, and so forth, and not exact replication, the barriers for participation are much lower. The "About" section of *DisneyBound* describes the site as "inspiration for you to pull together your own outfits which work for *your body* and wallet *whether from your own closet* or local mall."[27] While not all interpretive sites are as explicit, the variety with which a single character might inspire multiple outfits generally sends the signal that the goal is not to copy the outfits on the site exactly but to use them as inspiration. As a result, women with a variety of body types, ages, modesty norms, or appearances can easily participate in their own "inspired" outfits. For example, the impossibly proportioned Jessica Rabbit is interpreted in such a way on *DisneyBound* that with a few adjustments (a plus-sized dress, longer hemline, or flatter shoe) a wide variety of different women could wear some variation of the outfit (see Figure 6.3). The variety of interpretations available on these sites is elastic enough that a woman with a less femme style might "do Jessica" in purple skinny jeans, a red sweater, and silver combat boots. Unlike cosplay, where the focus on authenticity would make a character like Rayne from *BloodRayne* difficult for those without an "ideal" body, an interpretive version of Rayne, such as that on *Console to Closet* allows for a variety of women to express their fandom through their body (see Figure 6.4).

This flexibility also allows for participation for those from diverse class positions. Across the numerous interpretive fan-fashion blogs, shared techniques

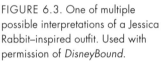

FIGURE 6.3. One of multiple possible interpretations of a Jessica Rabbit–inspired outfit. Used with permission of *DisneyBound*.

FIGURE 6.4. *Console to Closet*'s imagining of a Rayne outfit, inspired by the *BloodRayne* video game. Used with permission of *Console to Closet*.

can be observed. Characters are evoked through color, shapes, or symbolic elements; it is this combination of elements, rather than any particular clothing item, that is important in these blogs. The outfits presented on these blogs are presented as tools, rather than road maps, and the Rayne outfit could be used as a tool for inspiration just as easily at thrift stores as at Bloomingdale's or even as a way to reconceive one's own closet. Many fan sites are quite tuned into class; some present "budget" versions of outfits while those sites that recap or locate the actual fashions on the show often highlight programs like *Baby Daddy* or *The Vampire Diaries* because the costume designers try to choose pieces that their characters might actually be able to afford. However, the more subversive potential of interpretive fashion blogs is that they don't necessarily require consumption at all. As a result, their discursive register does not prioritize what is new or encourage shopping directly. The average follower's closet would likely already contain a number of items that could be combined into interpretive outfits or that could be made into one with a very inexpensive or homemade accessory. Consumption is not even required of the fashion bloggers themselves. Because Polyvore, the website used by most of the blogs in my sample to create collages, makes it easier to "clip" images found on the web than to add images of your own items, the collages are made up of items that are, or were once, on sale across the web. Whether or not the blogger owns any of these items is irrelevant and unknown. Unlike those fashion bloggers who depend on images of themselves in ensembles, there is no requirement for an interpretive fan-fashion blogger to buy anything at all to participate.

This is not to imply that these sites are anticonsumerist but that the focus of the sites does not encourage consumption to the same extent as many other fashion blogs. Indeed the technology that drives these sites creates a complex relationship to consumerism. The nature of Polyvore removes the need for a blogger to have access to the garments that they feature, but it also is set up to privilege items that are for sale as the "material" a Polyvore user can use. As a result, most of the collections trace back to Polyvore, where the items are linked to prices and the stores that sell them. In this way the consumerist element of fashion is certainly not erased, and is even encouraged, by the technological (and sometimes textual) aspects of media-inspired fan-fashion blogs. However, this apparent contradiction is a useful one and far more complex than it might appear. Because items are selected from Polyvore's immense library and items and posts are recirculated over time and across blogs, quite frequently when you click through, the item is no longer for sale. This phenomenon circumvents the flow of consumption that one might imagine the format could encourage. This does not, however, circumvent the blog's goals. *College Fashion*'s "Geek

Chic" back to school column illustrates how to create a first day of school outfit reminiscent of *Star Trek* or *Harry Potter*, and meeting this goal can be followed without the specific items in the post and even without any new purchases.[28]

The centrality of "interpretation" and responsiveness to media also allows these blogs to take on a complex and creative approach to gender performance. As Jo Reger has argued, "the body can . . . become a site of resisting cultural norms by reclaiming femininity through fashion,"[29] a practice that fan-fashion blogs engage in by playing with gender and placing a value on femininity as a choice and performance, one that is conscious and neither permanent nor essential, different from an unthinking obedience to gender norms. Many of the outfits created and circulated on these blogs could be considered "feminine," but they are not simply reflecting a sense of "normative" femininity. Rather, femininity is often a factor that is *introduced*, made space for, in a relatively masculine textual world. *Companion Clothing*, for example, took the aggressive, masculine figure of the cyberman—a character that erases femininity as it turns humans into a homogenized masculine/robotic form—and reimagined it as a light, feminine outfit interpreting its metal armor into a floaty silver dress, sequin silver oxfords, and feminine jewelry. Across these blogs "feminine" clothing is used to interpret even the most macho of male characters; the hypermasculine Gaston from *Beauty and the Beast* is interpreted through a red lace dress on *DisneyBound*, Sherlock is embodied in a pencil skirt and black pumps, along with his signature scarf, on *NERDYFASHIONBLOG*, and the gun-toting *Bioshock Infinite*'s protagonist Booker Dewitt's layers and dark red details are expressed in a lace corset top and red floral earrings on *Console to Closet*. In these instances, femininity is presented as a valuable option and one that is articulated with values of power and competency that many texts yoke to masculinity.

Moreover, these instances point to the ability to destabilize gender as an essential part of embodying a character. While the prevalence of female bloggers and readers results in a preponderance of outfits designed for women, these sites also include instances of female characters that are translated into men's outfits or into more masculine outfits for women. *DisneyBound* features a wide range of approaches to the extremely feminine character of Cinderella, particularly her poofy blue ball gown, including a set for men that includes blue slacks, a blue polo shirt, and sparkly silver high-top sneakers; a more androgynous version of a woman's outfit with a pair of jeans, a blue button-up shirt, and sparkly flats; and athletic gear featuring blue shorts, a blue top, and silver and blue sneakers—alongside the more obvious outfits of floaty blue dresses and high heels. Here, what makes Cinderella, *Cinderella*—a color palette, a special shoe, a slightly sweet or demure feeling—transcends a specific gender or model of gender performance. Loving *Cinderella* and wanting to express that through one's appearance does not, as one might expect, require the normative femininity expressed in the film. A fan could "be" Cinderella whether they were male or female, while playing basketball or while dressed in a pair of jeans. Subtly, then, these blogs present feminine gender performance through dress as play.

These blogs open up two important spaces to reconsider the relationship between gender and fandom. On the one hand, fandom is often discursively associated, with men (as with the term *fanboy*) or with genres (like sci-fi/fantasy) and media (like video games) that are associated with male audiences. On the other hand, when women participate in traditionally "masculine" fandoms, they are often either met with hostility or simply ignored. The prevalence of media fan-centered fashion blogs allows us to address both of these issues. On the one hand, they make visible the vibrant fandoms behind traditionally "feminine" texts. While some male-associated texts like *Star Wars* may make an occasional appearance on *DisneyBound*, most posts draw from Disney's animated films and musicals, which are often feminized or infantilized. The blog *Dress Like Celebs* and many of the media-inspired entries on *College Fashion* focus on comedy and drama series targeted largely at teen girls and young adult women. These sites make the creative, active fandom around feminized media not only visible but visible in a way that emphasizes its ability to support creative engagement with a text's distinct world.

On the other hand, these blogs also carve out space in stereotypically masculine fandoms not only for women to participate but to participate through traditionally feminized interests. Blogs like *Console to Closet*, *Companion Clothing*, and *NERDYFASHIONBLOG* focus on video games, *Dr. Who*, and traditional "geek culture" texts associated with highly visible male fandoms where female fans are often invisible, if not actively unwelcome.[30] These fan-fashion blogs demonstrate that pairing masculinized "geek culture" and feminized "fashion culture" is not only possible, but productive. Here, female video game, sci-fi, and fantasy fans carve out a space within these fandoms that insists on, rather than erases, their femininity. By focusing on fashion, a feminized interest, these female-run blogs invite the gathering of other women with a love of these media to create communities of female fans. These sites allow for the possibility of engaging with masculinized media without having to subjugate or deny femininity; instead femininity becomes a constituent part of one's video game, sci-fi, or superhero fandom. Given the harassment of women in some areas of geek and gamer culture and the policing of women's presentation through the narrative of "fake" geek or gamer girls, the creation of a space in which fashion and feminine style can be used as a tool to express geek or gamer fandom represents an important counterpoint. These sites not only allow for the compatibility of these two subcultures but illustrate how masculine iconography can be reimagined and articulated through the feminine.

A particularly strong example of this can be seen in *NERDYFASHION-BLOG's The Avengers* ball gown series, where superheroes are interpreted through women's formal wear (perhaps the most feminine-coded of all clothing). Here, the hypermasculine figures of comic-book culture, like the Hulk, are articulated through the hyperfeminine iconography of the ball gown and high heels. Rather than just creating a simple juxtaposition, the inclusion of chunky plastic jewelry blends references to the masculine with the femininity of the ball gown. These blogs do more than simply play with gender, they play with the gender norms of video-game, comic-book, and sci-fi/fantasy fandom, creating a playground where women are not only allowed but where femininity, feminized skills, and interests are valued.

These blogs create spaces where women, and "women's interests," can be valued as part of fan culture but without having to follow familiar scripts of self erasure or self objectification.[31] These blogs decenter familiar goals of fashion—to be "pretty," or "sexy," or "in style"—and replace them with their own goal: to creatively engage with a favorite media text. *Console to Closet* declares its goals as creating outfits that "are foremost, fashionable so that anyone could wear them and still feel 'geeky.'"[32] Unlike cosplay, which would be incompatible with everyday lives, the goal of interpretive fashion blogs is to create outfits that would allow people to integrate their love of these media into their life and fashion. While some sites note the possibility of the pleasure of recognition, the core goal is for the individuals themselves (and maybe some members of the community online) to know that they are embodying a given character or text. Being able to "pass" is implied here as individuals display the outfits that they plan to wear to work, weddings, and first days of school that subtly evoke a favorite video game, Hogwarts house, or Disney princess. The goal of the outfits created on *DisneyBound* or *Console to Closet* are not to appear sexy or attractive to others, or even to be immediately recognizable as Minnie Mouse or Lara Croft, but instead to embody one's fandom for oneself, to integrate fandom into everyday life. In interpretive fashion blogs, bodies are not policed for their adherence to cultural norms; rather, bodies can be taken ownership of as a space within which one's passions and fandom can be made visible, unobtrusively, for oneself and one's fan community.

Conclusion

I have looked at the potential of interpretive fashion blogs not to argue that fashion blogs are necessarily feminist or subversive; nor would I argue that fashion blogs are *never* consumerist or never reinforce gender and appearance norms. Instead, I argue here that fashion blogs can have a diverse relationship to feminist issues and that they have the potential to provide opportunities for self expression, creativity, and community building through technology that contains complex and even subversive relationships to issues like consumption and gender norms. What becomes crucial here is that it is not an interest in fashion that inherently drives the relationship of these blogs to issues of gender but the *focus* and *goals* of these blogs. Interpretive fashion blogs focus on the media texts that inspire the outfits created on the blogs, and as a result body norms and consumption are de-emphasized.

Marjorie Jolles and Shira Tarrant argue that, "Fashion contains the potential for pleasure and subjugation, expression and convention" and much the same can be said for fashion blogging.[33] The interest in fashion in and of itself should not be treated as predictive of these websites' gender politics. Rather, it is essential to consider the diversity within fashion blogs and how factors like a blog's form, element, or primary focus impacts the ideologies blogs convey. Grappling with the diversity of fashion blogging and the variation within the form may be a daunting task, but it is important to understand the tension and contradictions that emerge within this form of expression. As a result, fashion blogging should not be examined as a single phenomenon but as a form of expression with specific iterations, whose meanings and ideologies differ; fashion blogs can be disciplining or liberatory, conservative or subversive. Fashion provides a platform that women bloggers use to speak; we should be wary of dismissing this platform as frivolous or regressive before listening to what it is being used to *say*.

Notes

1. Amanda McGinnis, *Console to Closet*, last modified September 18, 2013, accessed September 25, 2013, http://consoletocloset.com/.

2. Susie Khamis and Alex Munt, "The Three Cs of Fashion Media Today: Convergence, Creativity and Control," *Scan Journal of Media Arts Culture* 7, 2 (2010): 3.

3. Esther Rosser, "Photographing Fashion: A Critical Look at the Sartorialist," *Image and Narrative* 11, 4 (2010): 167.

4. Sarah Banet-Weiser and Inna Arzumanova, "Creative Authorship: Self Actualizing Individuals and the Self Brand," in *Media Authorship*, ed. Cynthia Chris and David A. Gerstner (New York: Routledge, 2013).

5. This sample was developed based on the best and most influential blog lists, drawn from *Lucky Magazine, Signature 9, Look Magazine*, and *Fashionista*; the blogs in my case study sample; and a variety of blogs drawn from recommendations from colleagues and associates, in order to add variety to the sample beyond those blogs most recognized by the industry.

6. Fan/media content appeared particularly frequently in "Potpourri Blogs" and "Online Fashion Magazines."

7. Banet-Waiser and Arzumanova, 164.

8. Jo Reger, "DIY Fashion and Going Bust: Wearing Feminist Politics in the Twenty-First Century," in *Fashion Talks: Undressing the Power of Style*, ed. Marjorie Jolles and Shira Tarrant (Albany: State University of New York Press, 2012), 211.

9. Ibid., 212.

10. Banet-Weiser and Arzumanova; Laurie Ouellette and James Hay, *Better Living Through Reality TV* (Malden, Mass.: Blackwell, 2008).

11. Ouellette and Hay, 101; Banet-Weiser and Arzumanova, 169.

12. Leslie Kay, *DisneyBound: Where Fashion Geeks and Disney Nerds Collide*, last modified, September 19, 2013, accessed September 25, 2013, http://disneybound.tumblr.com/; McGinnis, *Console to Closet*.

13. This community activity can be traced back to Fan Forum practices as noted by Jennifer Gillian in "Fashion Sleuths and Aerie Girls: *Veronica Mars*' Fan Forums and Network Strategies of Fan Address," in *Teen Television: Essays on Programming and Fandom*, ed. Sharon Marie Ross and Louisa Stein (Jefferson, N.C.: Mcfarland, 2008), 191.

14. Kay, *DisneyBound*. The Facebook page for the event had over 500 individuals who claimed to be going, and well over 200 people are visible in the meet-up photo.

15. Katie, *Companion Clothing*, last modified September 16, 2013, accessed September 25, 2013, http://companionclothes.tumblr.com/.

16. Banet-Weiser and Arzumanova, 167.

17. Suzanne Scott, "Fangirls in Refrigerators: The Politics of (In)visibility in Comic Book Culture," *Transformative Works and Culture* 13 (2013): 1.

18. Banet-Weiser and Arzumanova, 164.

19. Astrid Henry, "Fashioning a Feminist Style, or, How I Learned to Dress from Reading Feminist Theory," in *Fashion Talks*, 17; Reger, 217.

20. Jolles and Tarrant, "Feminism Confronts Fashion," in *Fashion Talks*, 1; Reger, 209.

21. Reger, 238.

22. Matthew Hills, *Fan Cultures* (London: Routledge, 2002), 183.

23. *Dress Like Celebs*, last modified September 19, 2013, accessed September 25, 2013, http://dresslikecelebs.tumblr.com/.

24. Osmund Rahman, Liu Wing-sun, and Brittany Hei-man Cheung, "'Cosplay': Imaginative Self and Performing Identity," *Fashion Theory* 16, 3 (2012): 326–328.

25. Josh Stenger, "The Clothes Make the Fan: Fashion and Online Fandom When *Buffy the Vampire Slayer* Goes to eBay," *Cinema Journal* 45, 4 (2006): 26–44.

26. This phenomenon has been tracked by Jennifer Gillian in her study of *Veronica Mars* fans.

27. Kay, "About," *DisneyBound*, last modified September 19, 2013, accessed September 25, 2013, http://disneybound.tumblr.com/.

28. Shannon, "Geek Chic: Back-to-School Edition," *College Fashion*, last modified August 31, 2013, accessed September 25, 2013, http://www.collegefashion.net/inspiration/geek-chic-back-to-school-edition/.

29. Reger, 212.

30. Scott, 1.

31. Salter and Blodgett, "Hypermasculinity," *Journal of Broadcasting and Electronic Media* 56, 3 (2012): 410.

32. McGinnis, *Console to Closet*.

33. Jolles and Tarrant, "Feminism Confronts Fashion," in *Fashion Talks*, 1.

CHAPTER 7

Women's Nail Polish Blogging and Femininity

"The girliest you will ever see me"

MICHELE WHITE

The participants in the Polish or Perish blog have playfully redeployed the academic mandate to publish or perish as a means of emphasizing the importance of nail polish in their lives.[1] They have also featured a photographic banner with lined-up nail polish bottles on their website. Each bottle has been labeled with an academic degree (see Figure 7.1). The participants subtitled this group nail blog "WOMEN WHO HAVE ALMOST AS MUCH NAIL POLISH AS THEY HAVE EDUCATION" as a way of linking gender, nail polish, and intellectual pursuits. According to daydream222, one of the posters from Polish or Perish, some "fellow feminists look at" her as a "hypocrite" because investments in nail polish can "reinforce feminine stereotypes (such as that all women do and should wear makeup)."[2] Despite the "negativity surrounding nail polish," she has been "an active feminist." daydream222 has personally chosen to wear nail polish rather than for "any other reason." She has also resisted the "traditional 'rules' of nail polish such as wearing only French manicures, sheers, pinks, or reds." daydream222 thus provides a critical reflection on feminism and femininity, which repeats postfeminist claims that women have been able to freely choose their own interests in late-twentieth- and early-twenty-first-century society, without fully defining the feminine aspects of nail polish.

Megan from Blondes Love Cupcakes has deployed some of the features of femininity referenced by daydream222, including the association of pink with women, but she has not interrogated or defined the term. Instead, Megan started

FIGURE 7.1. Masthead image from the Polish or Perish blog, by Heidi Thomas. Used with permission of Polish or Perish.

the blog to "showcase" her "love of nail art."[3] She uses the title, the banner photograph of pink-frosted cupcakes, and a decorative pattern of pink polka dots to code the blog as feminine and woman-produced. In doing this, she repeats the cultural identification of cosmetic practices, pale colors, decorative patterns, and small and sweet foodstuffs as gendered feminine. Nail polish bloggers, informed by such cultural perceptions, understand polish as feminine. In a related manner, as daydream222 has suggested, society identifies nail polish as a low form. Yet nail bloggers also trouble cultural conceptions of normative femininity through their inability and resistance to wholly describing and identifying the feminine. These bloggers critique some aspects of feminine culture *and* identify the expectations that prevent them from moving beyond certain applications and norms. They emphasize the produced aspects of their nails and bodies and thereby undermine the idea that women and femininity are natural states. By demonstrating in this chapter the ways nail polish bloggers have conceptualized the limits and the limitations of femininity without narrowly defining femininity, I contribute to academic and popular debates about gender, beauty culture, and the internet.

Nail bloggers' images and posts indicate that a large number of them are white heterosexual women. However, bloggers' self-representations and comments have also shown that nail blogging draws participants from a wider range of social identity categories. There are GLBTQ participants with varied gender identifications. Pam Pastor, who is from the Philippines, argues that there are "nail polish bloggers from all corners of the world" and "polish addicts of all races, shapes and ages from teenage girls to cool grandmas."[4] Polish blogs like Polish or Perish include individuals who chronicle their experiences in Australia, the United Kingdom, and the United States and their cultural positions as

Asian, black, and Caucasian women. In a post about the "academic analysis of color," daydream222 has asserted, "Nail polish is very connected to ideas of race, socioeconomic class, and gender."[5] She underscores the relationship between cosmetics and identity and the reasons for writing about these practices.

My focus is on the relationship between nail polish and conceptions of femininity, but race and class intertwine with gender. As daydream222 describes, "Salons that cater to specific classes of women may have different products" and women of color are "stereotyped as wearing huge, chunky acrylics." In a comment on this post, B.Stone adds that the "louder" her "nails are, the more people might attribute it" to her "being black."[6] Perfect manicures have been associated with people who have the leisure and skill to paint their nails, the money to go to salons, and careers that will not damage the finish. However, people with a variety of jobs and lifestyles have blogged about nail polish. For instance, Cindi has worked in a "chemical factory with an all man crew" and used nail polish to "stand out as a girl in a men's world."[7] Nail bloggers raise questions about femininity and class when associating some applications and forms of nail maintenance with being classy and others as trashy, as in posts inquiring about the status of red polish.[8] These bloggers also articulate their raced, classed, and gendered identities through blog names and design choices, making a range of identities part of the nail blogging culture.

This community has certain regular features. Nail polish blogs often have witty titles, such as All Lacquered Up; Lacquer Buzz; Hey, Nice Nails!; and Kiss My Acetone.[9] These bloggers skillfully design their sites with lively colored borders and decorate them with scrollwork and other patterns. Some have included cartoon self-portraits, but stars, hearts, and images of nail polish bottles are more common. Most of them feature sequentially dated posts, with the recent posts at the top of the blog, and detailed titles for each post. They also write about, take photographs of, and upload close-up images of nail polish color swatches, nail art applications, and nail polish bottles. While there are diverse ways of representing nails, including swatch sticks and wheels with plastic nails, polish bloggers tend to feature cropped images of their own hands. Because bloggers have identified some hand poses as overused and unflattering many in the nail blogging community value coded poses as ways of imagining women's bodies.[10]

Researching Beauty Culture and Femininity

Feminists have often understood normative Western femininity as a cultural category that forms and controls women. For feminist activist and journalist

Susan Brownmiller, femininity is a "tradition of imposed limitations."[11] Feminist scholars have associated cosmetic practices with the body-centric forms of femininity that women have been encouraged to produce, including bodily comportment, grooming and beautification rituals, and maintaining a slender and toned physique. According to Kathy Davis's research on beauty practices, women's engagement with their appearance has been "one of the central ways that femininity is constructed."[12] Yet culture has not always coded these cosmetic procedures in the same way. Kathy Peiss has identified a shift in the twentieth century when makeup went from "signaling women's freedom" to "binding feminine identity to manufactured beauty."[13] Feminist philosopher Sandra L. Bartky has further critiqued cultural conceptions of cosmetics and argued that these procedures and conceptions have delimited women's identities and opportunities for self-expression. According to her, applying cosmetics should be understood as "a highly stylized activity that gives little rein to self-expression."[14] For instance, painting the face can "be described as painting the same picture over and over again with minor variations." The "woman who uses cosmetics in a genuinely novel and imaginative way is liable to be seen not as an artist but as an eccentric."[15] Such women are identified as aberrant and even mentally ill because they refuse cultural mandates about taste and class. While nail polish bloggers have been encouraged by other bloggers and their own interests and painted very different nail art applications on the same nails, they are still warned against wearing less conventional facial cosmetics. For instance, some bloggers caution against "too much" glitter makeup, especially eye shadow and dusting powder. These applications are culturally associated with girls, sex workers, and drag queens and can thus problematize women's claims to normative adult femininity.[16] Innovative nail polish applications may be more culturally acceptable because they are not applied to women's faces and do not intervene as directly in people's ability to assess women's physiognomy.

There has also been research on the ways women find enjoyment and agency in beauty culture. Beauty practices, according to Davis, cannot be separated from the "oppressive cultural constraints on women to be beautiful."[17] However, she also demonstrates how women find beauty practices to be pleasurable and use these tactics as methods of working within cultural limitations. Bartky refutes the cultural association of makeup applications with creativity and expressive processes, but many popular writers identify nail art as empowering and artistic. In an article on nail art, writer Tracie Egan Morrissey portrays it as "art for art's sake." Nail art, according to Morrissey, provides women with creative outlets that have not been delimited by cultural norms.[18] In a related manner, reporter Sarah Hampson describes nails as a "small, painted canvas of the mind and a silent, powerful voice of unapologetic femininity."[19] For Morrissey and Hampson, nail art outwardly reflects women's ideas and is a feminine form of creativity. They refute the sole articulation of nails as a bodily property and instead associate women and their nails with the mind and thinking. This is a reconceptualization of the usual binary that correlates women with the body and emotions and men with the mind and rationality.

This acceptance and even celebration of normative femininity has often been described as "postfeminist" and contrasted with feminist critiques of traditional women's roles.[20] Postfeminism has also been linked to sexual subjectification, reassertions about natural sexual differences, self-disciplining through such practices as makeovers, assertions about agency and choice, and consumerism.[21] As communication scholar D. Travers Scott has argued, postfeminism and interactive technologies provide similar narratives about equality and choice. Individuals have been assured that they are "'liberated' through interactive technologies, free to choose, surf, produce, remix," and find their place—"but to minimal results at best."[22] Virginia Braun has interrogated these promises and rightly points to the ways narratives about choice elide the normative pressures that women experience to make certain decisions.[23] Yet women should not be understood as passive dupes who have never been able to resist cultural directives or strive for their own forms of agency.

Female nail bloggers identify the personal options and cultural mandates that are part of polish and beauty culture. They suggest that nails express women's ideas and agency without quite being animate flesh. For Sophia Papadopoulos, bare nails offer a "canvas that can be used to create some intricate and amazing works of personal portable art." There "are endless possibilities" because of the many kinds of nail art.[24] Papadopoulos has portrayed nail art as a form of postfeminist empowerment and choice. In this formulation, nails are an open and incomplete surface that facilitates creative potentialities. Alaina conveyed these creative possibilities and called her blog "The Little Canvas."[25] Mr. Kate has advised her readers to "Treat your nails like tiny canvases!"[26] For these women, nails and nail polish applications are somewhat distinct from the body. Nails are surfaces that are waiting to be produced—canvases, effects, and nearly dead material that is attached to the body. Society has used nail polish and other beauty applications to further link femininity, naturalness, and beauty. However, the inanimate features of nails and bloggers' indications that nails are produced effects trouble these connections.

Nail polish bloggers often distinguish between nail polish applications and the rest of beauty culture. Lady Fancy Nails has specified, "Nails are a canvas that convey style and personality far differently than traditional elements of beauty, such as facial cosmetics, which has historically been defined by male notions."[27] Morrissey has also differentiated between nail polish applications, which satisfy women's interests and pleasures, and other beauty applications. She writes, "Men don't want to fuck you because of the design painted on your nails or the 3D acrylic flowers and bows attached to them." This has made nail art the "only form of primping and grooming that isn't rooted in making oneself more appealing to men or exploiting women's insecurities."[28] Olivia S. supports these ideas. She has not painted "big pink hexagons and hearts" to make herself "more attractive to men" and sexually subjectify herself.[29] These comments link women's tastes to the ways class is expressed through sexual identifications. Morrissey and Olivia S. code nail art practices as hyperfeminine and as exchanges between women. Morrissey has also too quickly presumed that the women involved in other forms of beauty culture are heterosexual and focused on men. Nevertheless, considerations of the women-centered and feminized aspects of nail polish culture are vital and point to the array of ways women engage with conceptions of the female, femininity, beauty, and artistry.

While Morrissey has situated female-focused polish culture in relationship to the work of nail artists and salons, she has not addressed the notable influence of bloggers. My study considers the ways nail polish bloggers have conceptualized femininity and can contribute to debates about the functions of nail artists and applications. The perceptions of these bloggers are distinct from individuals who have understood nail polish practices as resistant to conventional roles. Hampson has argued that nail art defiantly confronts "dated standards of demure femininity." When considering these issues, bloggers have indicated the ways that they do not personally embody femininity. Nail bloggers' refusal of aspects of the feminine/masculine binary could support a wider array of lived practices. However, bloggers' resistance to such categories as "girly" or "hyperfeminine," which challenge women's tastes and thereby some features of their class positions, poses further problems for people who have been culturally labeled as female and feminine. These categories are made into less viable identifiers. They provide conflicts for people who are told simultaneously that they should be feminine and that the related category of the girly is diminishing.

Nail Polish and Bodily Management

Nail art, according to Hampson and other popular proponents, has functioned as a kind of resistance to conceptions of women and how femininity should be performed. Yet most people find it difficult to ignore norms and standards, including cultural expectations about women's self-representations. As sociologist Diane Naugler has argued, "It is hard not to measure one's appearance in terms of its approximation to an ideal feminine or masculine body, even if one does not consciously accept such standards."[30] Individuals who conceptualize applications as resistant to conventions still recognize and to some extent address norms. Blog readers also measure their nail art applications and hand care in relationship to nail bloggers' images and narratives. They remark upon bloggers' skillful applications and compare these practices to their own abilities. For instance, Sharon Murrell has expressed her admiration for a blogger's nail art, which is "very feminine and classy" and "precise and neat."[31] She thereby points to the ways women's nail polish applications have been gendered, classed, and focused on painting within the lines of the nail and cuticle. Murrell hopes that one day she will achieve similarly mannered results and judges herself according to the represented norms and standards.[32] Painting has often been coded as an impassioned and expressive process, but Murrell associates nail painting with women's control over the body and its features. Her comments resonate with Bartky's description of the repetitive and normalizing aspects of applying cosmetics.

Most early-twenty-first-century nail polish bloggers privilege cleanliness and neatness. They have hopes of maintaining and fashioning themselves by neatly applying polish and taking care of their hands and nails. By having and expressing these desires, they follow cultural proscriptions about women sustaining bodily control. They try to avoid the negative associations of women with fluidity and filth. This has not always been successful. Mommy Loves Nail Polish has chronicled her attempts to remove nail stains.[33] She had "forgotten to use a proper base coat" and it appeared as if she had not "bathed in months." She indicates that her body only *seems* to deviate from social norms and distances herself from filth, which has been associated with laziness, slovenliness, lower-class behaviors, sex workers, and disease. She further insists that her hands and nails "really are not dirty!" In combination with these narratives about bodily control, Mommy Loves Nail Polish and other bloggers have offered tutorials and frequently asked questions sections (FAQs). Through these features, they articulate the expected condition of women's bodies and nails, provide pointers on how to achieve these states, and chronicle problems with polishes and nail maintenance. For instance, Nail Art 101 has chastised readers that, "It doesn't matter how cool your mani is if everyone is looking at your gross cuticles. This is especially true if you have a nail blog and are photographing your manicures."[34] In writing this, Nail Art 101 has asserted the importance of bodily maintenance over creativity. She also perpetuates the cultural emphasis on women's appearance.

Women use beauty practices to maintain the respect of their community and their claims to being culturally acceptable, according to Bernadette Wegenstein's research on late-twentieth- and early-twenty-first-century makeover culture.[35] Women's attempts to keep their hands soft and nails clean and manicured can be understood as part of their acknowledgment of societal rules, including nail blog engagements and conventions. Not performing such operations, as Wegenstein's research has shown, is imagined to indicate a lack of self-respect and makes women less properly visible. In a related manner, women, especially as they mature, have been expected to keep themselves up and to labor on their self-presentations. Feminist philosopher Susan Bordo has shown some of the ways that women are directed to shape their bodies.[36] Wegenstein and Bordo have argued that makeover culture articulates the self as a "project" that women are expected to positively change.

Readers respond to nail tutorials, express their appreciation of the information, and indicate that they have been following the instructions and trying to change for the "better." In doing this, they create a female culture of shared knowledge *and* extend bodily norms and expectations. McDiaz714 happily found a blog where she "can learn about taking care" of her nails.[37] She has been able to paint her nails, "but taking care of them is a whole different story." Through this account, McDiaz714 establishes her skills and limitations. Of course, Nail Art 101 indicates that such artistic skills are negligible unless women are managing the ways they look. Joy acknowledged this visual emphasis when complimenting a blogger on her "gorgeous nails!"[38] She wanted her nails to "grow like that" and planned to use the associated method. Women like McDiaz714 and Joy assess bloggers' hands, which are consistently featured in digital photographs. They compare bloggers' self-presentations to their own appearance and commit to working on their bodies, imagining a time when they can achieve similar results. For instance, In-The-Red-Nails admired a blogger's "perfect" nails, asked for advice, and stated that hers "would never grow" that "nicely."[39] Through these behaviors, she and other readers have articulated a contradictory culture of feminine skills and inabilities. In some cases, tutorial writers have encouragingly responded to posters' images and denied their own expertise. Posters counter this combination of compliment and negation by insisting that the blogger's nails are painted beautifully. This suggests that nail polish blogs, and potentially other female cultures that focus on creative production, have been rendered by the ways women praise others, note their own limitations, and receive validation in return.

Nail Polish and Femininity

A number of popular authors and bloggers have associated nail polish applications with normative femininity. According to Stylish Eve, "every woman loves to care about her nails as they express her femininity and elegance."[40] She articulates women's interest in their nails as "care" and also evokes maternal caregiving and feminine bodily maintenance. In a related manner, admin has advised that fingernails "clad in girlish nail polish" provide a "feminine touch."[41] This relates physically touching to women's aesthetics and ways of being. Nails continue to be part of women's tactile engagements and creative practices. This includes nail polish bloggers' production of bodies and media content and comparison of their applications to other bloggers' texts. However, nail bloggers have not ordinarily been able to specify what constitutes feminine nails and gendered ideals. Female nail polish bloggers mention femininity but have trouble articulating its features and their relationship to it.

Such confusion over defining femininity is evident in participants' struggle to create a manicure based on the theme of "Feminine Nails" in a 2012 nail bloggers' polish challenge.[42] In this kind of participatory challenge, bloggers respond to a series of topics and post about applications over a period of time. Nail challenges also provide opportunities for individuals to collaboratively communicate about and develop nail polish culture. In the case of the feminine nails challenge, this resulted in participants suggesting that cultural understandings of nail polish make it difficult to conceive of and produce something feminine. vicerimus had a "hard time" with the feminine nails theme because painting nails has usually been "considered feminine, so, basically, it was an open theme."[43] Cuti-CLUE-les found it difficult to differentiate among all the possible applications. She does not have her "own definition" of feminine and has "never seen a manicure and thought 'jaysus that looks awful masculine.'"[44] Fabby also had a hard time and asked, "[What the] heck are feminine nails?! Does that mean there are manicures that are not feminine" and "Where is the line?"[45] She inquired, "So, what's your verdict?" and sought validation for her manicure and her visual and physical instantiations of the feminine. The lack of replies to Fabby's query suggested other bloggers' confusion over the concept of the feminine and feminine nails.

Manicures have been linked to diverse femininities, including the association of glitter polishes with girlishness.[46] Black nail polish has been deemed more acceptable for men. However, nail polish bloggers have not articulated the qualities of unfeminine manicures in any detail. The women in the feminine nails challenge even suggested that they were prevented from rendering femininity because of nail polish's feminine position. This suggests that insistently feminine objects and roles can make it difficult to further self-present as and conceptualize the feminine. The challenge did not produce definitions of the feminine but it did provide varied means of interrogating gender conceptions and norms. Fitzy, who has identified as a "queer kid," declared that gender "deserves to be completely shaken up." He "had a hard time coming up with ANYTHING" for the challenge because "the word 'feminine' had" him "grumbling angrily" about "gender roles and expectations."[47] According to Sharra Farivar, "Gender rigidity needs to be LOOSENED!" She has identified the gendering of colors and other things as "almost ALL social construct."[48] Through such resistant comments and women's difficulties producing feminine designs, the challenge pointed to the social rather than natural features of identity construction and the ways binary categories make some people uncomfortable.

Many participants contested the instruction to create feminine nails. They could not associate this construct with their personal identities. Fashion Footing related feminine nails to "really delicate colors and patterns," which is not her style, so she "went in a different direction."[49] She claimed to have an understanding of feminine nails that could not be applied to her own identity and body. In a similar manner, Kate "decided against soft, fluffy pink nails which would probably be your archetypal feminine mani right?"[50] While Kate proposed what she believed to be an exemplary feminine nail art application, she still sought affirmation from her readers. Fashion Footing and Kate engaged with femininity by articulating their identity as something other than what they understand as classically feminine.

Other nail polish bloggers found it necessary to distinguish themselves from femininity and the "girly girl." Although most nail polish bloggers have used the term without defining it, Real_Girl_Fashion describes the "girly girl as someone who's very feminine and has feminine interests" and ways of "dressing/carrying herself."[51] Elana Levine relates third-wave feminist interest in the "girlie" to women's engagement with aspects of girl culture that are dismissed by late-twentieth- and early-twenty-first-century society, including investments in cosmetics, clothing, and the color pink.[52] Female bloggers have also contested cultural conceptualizations of femininity and how femininity is evaluated. For instance, LemonyEmily titled a nail blog post the "girliest you will ever see me."[53] In doing this, she distinguished herself from girly forms of femininity and placed limits on her normative gender self-presentation. LemonyEmily "would never call" herself a "girly-girl" even though she has a "blog centred entirely around nail polish art and makeup." She proposes understandings of nail polish culture that are not hinged to girlyness and hyperfemininity. Holly's "bottle blonde hair, love of make-up," and "handbag addiction" have linked her to the "real girly-girl" but she seldom wears dresses, has a "phobia of anything floral," and "all things glittery are usually a definite 'no no.'"[54] These bloggers use these distinctions to argue for a broader recognition of the differences between what culture understands as particular feminine positions and individual women's self-identifications. They point to the diverse gender positions constructed and experienced by women. Yet some of these women have also produced these positions as a way of preventing their tastes and the cultural associations of nail polish from negatively pigeonholing them.

Challenging Femininity

The 2012 and 2013 "Girly-Girl Nail Art Challenges" and associated posts offer one of the most elaborate nail blog narratives about femininity.[55] The participating bloggers proposed that the feminine aspects of nail polish challenge women's gendered experiences. The 2012 challenge was announced with a pink flower–decorated text and colored script. The involved women created applications that were motivated by "Think Pink," "Gimme That Bling," "Delicate and Elegant," "Inspired by the Runway," "Gotta Love Chick Flicks!" "Who Inspires You!" "Sugar, Spice, and Everything Nice," and "Girls Just Wanna Have Fun!"[56] The challenges referenced a range of femininities rather than producing a consolidated conception of gender or using the term "feminine." The challenges included aesthetic elements that are thought of as feminine, such as the color pink and sparkling things. They articulated women's cultures and connections through encouragements to honor the women who inspired female bloggers. More active and resistant gender self-presentations were proposed, such as the reference to singer Cyndi Lauper's feminist anthem that "girls just wanna have fun."

The women involved in the challenges' "Gimme That Bling" prompt were further informed, "Diamonds are a girls best friend, so put some sparkle on those nails." This statement associates women with diamonds and sparkles and codes these aesthetics as feminine. It references the song sung by Carol Channing in the Broadway production of *Gentlemen Prefer Blondes* and performed by Marilyn Monroe and Jane Russell in the film of the same name. The film portrays misunderstood and emotionally unaware women who appear to be seeking diamonds as a form of monetary support from men. However, the female characters end up in heterosexual marriages that are posed as the better and healthier outcome, at least in the case of Russell's character. The challenges have furthered and changed this media reference by suggesting that diamonds are a girl's best friends and that women's nails should sparkle. This mention of sparkling nails (and hands) evokes engagement rings and cultural assertions that marriage is the appropriate life course and position for women.

Many participants responded to the "Gimme That Bling" prompt and applied an image of a diamond to one of their fingers.[57] In doing this, they further associated women and femininity with diamond engagement rings, engagements, and marriages. This application of a diamond image is a form of accent nail. These accents have been painted in different ways or have more elaborate designs than the other nails. They have been used to emphasize the ring finger and underscore the prevalence and importance of heterosexual unions. According to Lauren M., the accent "nail of choice" has been "the ring finger" and has provided a "great way to show off your sparkler!"[58] Sarah Brown queered the accent nail with her account of femme lesbians who paint "their ring fingernails" or "fucking fingers" in a "different color" so that they are recognizable to other lesbians.[59] Sarah Kane has also complicated the issue by indicating that ring finger accents let "potential suitors know that you're single" by indicating that there is no engagement ring.[60] While Brown and Kane have offered different scenarios, most definitions of accent nails correlate ring finger accents with engagement rings. This was the case with challenge participants who applied diamond patterns to their ring fingers and continued references to marriages and related norms.[61]

The term *nail art challenge* emphasizes women's attempts to represent a series of themes and produce successful nail art applications. However, participants seemed to be more challenged by conceptualizing femininity through such terms as "girly girl." They understood the challenges as ways of testing and rethinking their conceptions of self. Since StephanieLouise's blog does not have "loads of girly nail art," she thought it "would be a good challenge to branch out a bit."[62] Sam Fulton had not been a "very girly girl" so the challenge was a "stretch" but she was "up for it."[63] These women's understandings of the challenges as methods of thinking about their identities are related to the identification of blogging as a practice through which people have come to understand themselves.[64] However, in the case of the challenges, women often defined what they are not. They asserted that they are not girly girls or hyperfeminine and thereby established an unusual relationship to the purported focus of the challenges. For instance, ManisbyMoore does not identify as a "girly girl" but found the challenge to be viable because it "is just our nails."[65] ManisbyMoore associates nails with insignificant things. However, this coding of nails as trivial and a small part of the body enables women like ManisbyMoore to engage more freely with their nails. Interestingly, this conception of liberation allows nail polish bloggers, who have not identified with such positions as the girly girl, to explore more excessive forms of femininity.

Participants embraced the challenges and girlyness as opportunities to try something difficult. The focus was a "real challenge" for Mihaela Lacquerbuzz because she is "not a girly girl."[66] However, she likes "to be challenged" and did her "best to deliver some girly manicures." Through such comments, she and other bloggers emphasized the significant labor in being feminine. They also rendered women's relationship to femininity as constructed and negotiated rather than the more usual presumption that femininity is one of women's natural attributes. The challenges and related nail blog practices thus encourage women to consider their gender positions. Yet this undermining of stable gender has been coupled to women's pleasurable engagements with femininity. For instance, the challenge forced Cazzy Durcan, who is "not a girly girl" to "'think outside the box' a bit, which has been fun."[67] These women thus celebrate being someone other than their more typical gendered selves.

Afterword: The Gap as a Practice of Bodily Control and Fragmentation

Some popular writers conceptualize nails and nail polish applications as distinct from the controlling aspects of normative gender and beauty culture. This includes the ways bodies have been labeled and judged. For instance, Morrissey has argued that nail art transcends "body type. (Nobody ever says, 'I look fat in these nails.')." In a related manner, Bill Boraczek, who is senior vice president of Sally Hansen Global Marketing, has argued, "If you think you're too curvy or too straight, too young or too old, unattractive or not, it doesn't matter because you can still have beautifully groomed nails."[68] Boraczek has constructed a culture of bodily management while arguing that nail care and polish have enabled people to be equal. Yet nail polish bloggers like Megan suggest that some poses, application styles, and embodied features make nails look fat. Megan's "How To" about nail photography identifies the "death grip" where women hold the bottle so tightly that the "hand looks wrinkly and fat" and the "squeeze" where bloggers pull their fingers tightly against the palm so that the "fingers spread out and look super fat."[69] Through this commentary, Megan establishes women's "How To" knowledge and mandates certain forms of imaging and body, demonstrating one of the ways these blogs negotiate femininity. Bloggers also present photography and polish techniques that are designed to make nails look slimmer and more beautiful. They therefore propose that nails are an incomplete project and are deserving of labor.

Bloggers describe nails as canvases and changeable, which includes the ability to make nails look trimmer. Through these descriptions, these bloggers render the body as unfixed and available for transformation. While this can undermine expectations that women will always be the same and occupy set feminine gender positions, it also mandates women to maintain and improve their appearance. For instance, Michelle Mismas has included "Before" and "After" images that assert the ways bodies can be worked on and perfected.[70] She has written about being "saddled with short, wide nail beds." Mismas has emphasized the gendered aspects of this self-conception and asked, "[What is a] girl to do when she doesn't want the hassle of long nails but desires a slim, elongated look?" She has tips for "The Slimline Technique" that "really does thin the shape of the nail." This is the "equivalent of 'The Gap'" that a lot of nail bloggers have used to prevent flooding their cuticles with polish and drying out their skin. Rather than painting the nail "all the way to the sides," so that the polish touches the cuticle, you leave an unpainted "space" or gap to "create the illusion of a slimmer nail."

Mismas has also inquired, do her "nails look thinner and more elongated using The Slimline Technique?" This is the nail equivalent of the "Am I fat?" question. Jaime responds that she always creates a gap because it "makes fingers look slimmer."[71] Alice has given it a try because of her "fat short stubby fingers" but thinks that the gap between her painted nail and cuticle "is really obvious."[72] She associates fat with improper identity positions and indicates that the technique does not work and she needs to embrace her "man hands once again!!" These individuals suggest that all the parts of the body need to be assessed and controlled and should be a certain size and shape. They also intimate how such physiognomic and socially coded experiences render gender positions that are multiple, contradictory, and hyphenated (such as the female-male or female-masculine situation of Alice's "man hands").

The gap and the photographic aspects of nail polish blogging can be conceptualized through art historian Rosalind Krauss's theory of the photographic "cut" or "crop." Krauss has argued that these forms of photographic framing and production indicate that if "photography duplicates the world, it does so only in pieces."[73] Photographic cutting has gone "beyond simply ripping something out of a larger continuum; it charges the image in such a way that we feel it as something ripped away from us, as no longer the possible extension of our experience of our own physical occupation of the world that photographs had always seemed, dependably, to be."[74] Feminist media theorists have indicated that fragmentation is especially disturbing when the subject is female. The photographic "decapitation and dismemberment" of the female body in such genres as fashion photography has rendered a kind of violence against women.[75]

However, cropping, particularly when it has not aggressively severed the female body, also disturbs seamless conceptions of the world. It provides a different position from which to conceptualize women and femininity.

Nail blogging photographically and textually renders the body in pieces and parts. For instance, the nail is a canvas that is somewhat separate from the body but that women can still conceptualize and paint. Nail blog conventions encourage women to portray hands in such a manner that they seem detached from the rest of the body and from the surroundings. When nail bloggers crop hands and assert the gap between the painted nail and cuticle, they interrogate presumptions about the cohesion of the body and its cosmetic features. These hands, with their relationship to nail art activities and agency, may offer women a more assertive way of self-representing. Images of other female body parts have tended to render women as objects of the gaze. However, the gap and its rendering of a thinner nail and body has foregrounded the illusionistic aspects of beauty culture, distanced cosmetic practices from the body, and emphasized the canvaslike and constructed aspects of nails and nail polish. The gap, like the cultural association of nail polish with femininity, poses a splitting that leaves women to produce and conceptualize themselves from fragments rather than being coherently gendered or visually available bodies. The gap and nail polish bloggers worryingly indicate that women should engage with their bodies and nails as projects. Nonetheless, these women have also suggested that these forms can never be completely resolved and that femininity can never be fully articulated.

Many nail bloggers will not or cannot define femininity even though nail polish has been associated with the feminine. Given the overwhelming features of femininity, this is not surprising. Women's studies and gender scholars have defined its terms but there are still elements of femininity and feminine practices that remain amorphous. This is conveyed by Bordo's identification of "ever-changing" feminine ideals.[76] Women and other gendered subjects might use these instabilities to challenge and revise femininity and its political implications. While there are difficulties in researching and interrogating femininity, more detailed definitions of and alternative proposals for femininity are needed in order to change the limiting features of lived feminine experiences and cultures.

Notes

1. Polish or Perish, November 5, 2014, accessed January 2, 2015, http://polishorperish .blogspot.com. In the citations in this chapter, detailed information about website references is included. The constant reconfiguration of internet representations and changes in internet service providers make it difficult to find previously quoted material and important to chronicle the kinds of depictions that happen in these settings. Many internet

texts include typographical errors and unconventional forms of spelling, uppercase and lowercase typefaces, punctuation, and spacing. I have retained these formatting features in quotations and internet references, without such qualifications as "intentionally so written" or "*sic.*" The date listed before the URL is the "publication" date or the last time the site was viewed in the indicated format. When two dates are included, the first date points to when the current configuration of the site was initially available and the second date is the latest access date. Some versions of referenced sites can be viewed by using the Internet Archive's Wayback Machine. Internet Archive, "Internet Archive: Wayback Machine," accessed December 6, 2013, http://www.archive.org/web/web.php.

2. daydream222, "BB Couture Green Goblin," Polish or Perish, July 28, 2009, accessed December 6, 2013, http://polishorperish.blogspot.com/2009/07/bb-couture-green -goblin.html.

3. Megan, "About Me," Blondes Love Cupcakes, accessed November 4, 2013, http:// blondeslovecupcakes.wordpress.com/about/.

4. Pam Pastor, "Confessions of a Nail Polish Junkie," *Philippine Daily Inquirer*, September 26, 2010, accessed June 4, 2014, http://lifestyle.inquirer.net/sundaylifestyle /sundaylifestyle/view/20100926–294314/Confessions-of-a-nail-polish-junkie.

5. daydream222, "Thinking About Color . . . and a crazy NOTD," Polish or Perish, April 13, 2010, accessed June 4, 2014, http://polishorperish.blogspot.com/2010/04/thinking -about-colorand-crazy-notd.html.

6. B.Stone, "Thinking About Color . . . and a crazy NOTD," Polish or Perish, April 13, 2010, accessed June 4, 2014, http://polishorperish.blogspot.com/2010/04/thinking -about-colorand-crazy-notd.html.

7. Cindi, "Nail Polish Knows No Boundaries: Guest Post by Joanne Crandell," Vampy Varnish, January 9, 2010, accessed June 4, 2014, http://www.vampyvarnish.com/2010/01 /nail-polish-boundaries-guest-post-joanne-crandell.

8. Strawberrii Milk Nails, "Red nail polish . . . Classy or Trashy??" accessed June 26, 2014, http://strawberrymilknails.tumblr.com/post/53191065613/red-nail-polish -classy-or-trashy.

9. Michelle Mismas, All Lacquered Up, December 24, 2014, accessed December 28, 2014, http://www.alllacqueredup.com/; Hey, Nice Nails! December 24, 2014, accessed December 28, 2014, http://heynicenails.com/; Mihaela Lacquerbuzz, Lacquer Buzz, December 27, 2014, accessed December 28, 2014, http://www.lacquerbuzz.com/; Dori, Kiss My Acetone, January 19, 2011, accessed December 28, 2014, http://kissmyacetone.blogspot.com/.

10. Michelle Pratt, "Hit Me with Your Best Shot," *Nails Magazine*, July 3, 2013, accessed November 2, 2013, http://www.nailsmag.com/article/95236/hit-me-with-your-best -shot?page=3; Polish Etc., "Blogger Hand Positions," February 15, 2013, accessed November 4, 2013, http://www.polishetc.com/2013/02/blogger-hand-positions.html.

11. Susan Brownmiller, *Femininity* (New York: Simon and Schuster, 1984), 14.

12. Kathy Davis, "Remaking the She-Devil: A Critical Look at Feminist Approaches to Beauty," *Hypatia* 6, no. 2 (Summer 1991): 25.

13. Kathy Peiss, *Hope in a Jar: The Making of America's Beauty Culture* (Philadelphia: University of Pennsylvania Press, 2011), 135.

14. Sandra L. Bartky, "Foucault, Femininity, and the Modernization of Patriarchal Power," in *Feminism and Foucault*, ed. Irene Diamond and Lee Quinby (Boston: Northeastern University Press, 1988), 70.

15. Ibid.

16. Hannah Priest, "What's Wrong with Sparkly Vampires?" *The Gothic Imagination*, July 20, 2011, accessed January 14, 2014, http://www.gothic.stir.ac.uk/guestblog /whats-wrong-with-sparkly-vampires.

17. Davis, 25; Susan Bordo, "Beauty (Re)Discovers the Male Body," in *Beauty Matters*, ed. Peg Zeglin Brand (Bloomington: Indiana University Press, 2000), 112–154.

18. Tracie Egan Morrissey, "Nail Art, the Last Bastion of Female-Centric Beauty," Jezebel, August 7, 2012, accessed January 12, 2014, http://jezebel.com/5930229/nail-art-the -last-bastion-of-female+centric-beauty.

19. Sarah Hampson, "How Nail Art Is the New Unapologetic Emblem of Femininity," *Globe and Mail*, March 2, 2013, accessed August 30, 2013, http://www .theglobeandmail.com/life/fashion-and-beauty/beauty/how-nail-art-is-the-new -unapologetic-emblem-of-femininity/article9076963/.

20. Rosalind Gill, "Empowerment/Sexism: Figuring Female Sexual Agency in Contemporary Advertising," *Feminism and Psychology* 18, no. 1 (2008): 35–60; Angela McRobbie, *The Aftermath of Feminism: Gender, Culture and Social Change* (Los Angeles: Sage, 2009); Tania Modleski, *Feminism without Women: Culture and Criticism in a "Postfeminist" Age* (London: Routledge, 1991).

21. Jess Butler, "For White Girls Only?: Postfeminism and the Politics of Inclusion," *Feminist Formations* 25, no. 1 (Spring 2013): 35–58; Rosalind Gill, "Postfeminist Media Culture: Elements of Sensibility," *European Journal of Cultural Studies* 10, no. 2 (2007): 147–166.

22. D. Travers Scott, "The Postfeminist User," *Feminist Media Studies* 10, no. 4 (2010): 459.

23. Virginia Braun, "'The Women Are Doing It for Themselves': The Rhetoric of Choice and Agency around Female Genital 'Cosmetic Surgery,'" *Australian Feminist Studies*, 24, no. 60 (June 2009): 233–249.

24. Sophia Papadopoulos, "Nail Art: Small Canvas, Big Effect," Helium Magazine, December 2, 2009, accessed December 21, 2013, http://www.heliummagazine.com /nail-art-small-canvas-big-effect/.

25. Alaina, "About," The Little Canvas, accessed October 4, 2013, http://www .thelittlecanvas.com/p/about-me.html.

26. Mr. Kate, "DIY artist paint floral nail art," May 26, 2013, accessed October 5, 2013, http://www.mrkate.com/2013/05/26/diy-artist-paint-floral-nail-art/.

27. Lady Fancy Nails, as quoted in ashleyw, "Lady Fancy Nails at Trillectro," Miss KL Blog, accessed August 19, 2013, http://blog.misskl.com/index.php/2013/08/lady-fancy -nails-at-trillectro/#.UiegQ7xszeA.

28. Morrissey.

29. Olivia S., "Etude House Nail Polish Is Saving The Feminist Movement, Probably," xoVain, August 2, 2013, accessed December 28, 2014, http://www.xovain.com/nails/ etude-house-nail-polish.

30. Diane Naugler, "Credentials: Breast Slang and the Discourse of Femininity," *Atlantis* 34, no. 1 (2009): 101.

31. Sharon Murrell, "Hat Box Nail Art," July 5, 2013, accessed December 28, 2014, http://thenailinator.xyz/2013/06/hat-box-nail-art.html.

32. Ibid.

33. Mommy Loves Nail Polish, "Nail Stain Removal Experiment," November 17, 2012, accessed October 19, 2013, http://mommylovesnailpolish.com/2012/11/17/nail-stain-removal-experiment/.

34. Nail Art 101, "nail care," accessed October 19, 2013, http://www.nail-art-101.com/nail_care.html.

35. Bernadette Wegenstein, *The Cosmetic Gaze: Body Modification and the Construction of Beauty* (Cambridge: MIT Press, 2012).

36. Susan Bordo, *Unbearable Weight: Feminism, Western Culture, and the Body* (Berkeley: University of California Press, 2003).

37. McDiaz714, "Nail Hardeners—Nail Conditioning Treatments," loodie, loodie, loodie, June 15, 2011, accessed October 18, 2013, http://loodieloodieloodie.blogspot.com/2011/06/nail-hardeners-nail-conditioning.html.

38. Joy, "5 minutes nail polish removal tutorial," gingerbreadmanne, January 12, 2012, accessed October 18, 2013, http://gingerbreadmanne.blogspot.com/2010/09/5-minutes-nail-polish-removal-tutorial.html.

39. In-The-Red-Nails, "China Glaze Elephant Walk," Addicted to OPI-yum," November 6, 2012, accessed October 18, 2013, http://addictedtoopi-yum.blogspot.com/2012/11/china-glaze-elephant-walk.html.

40. Stylish Eve, "Easy Nail Art Designs Gallery Collection," accessed August 30, 2013, http://www.stylisheve.com/easy-nail-art-designs-gallery-collection/.

41. admin, "A Touch of Femininity at Your Fingertips with Girlish Nail Polish," Pink Zest, July 12, 2013, accessed December 28, 2014, http://thepinkzest.info/a-touch-of-femininity-at-your-fingertips-with-girlish-nail-polish/.

42. Amanda Brohman, "The Lazy Challenge!" October 31, 2012, accessed January 15, 2013, http://nailsinthemoonlight.blogspot.com/2012/10/the-lazy-challenge.html.

43. vicerimus, "The Lazy 15! Feminine Nails," November 17, 2012, accessed August 31, 2013, http://vicerimus.blogspot.com/2012/11/the-lazy-15-feminine-nails.html.

44. Cuti-CLUE-les, "The Lazy 15 Day Seven—Feminine Nails," November 16, 2012, accessed August 31, 2013, http://cuti-clue-les.blogspot.com/2012/11/the-lazy-15-day-seven-feminine-nails.html.

45. Fabby Nailed It, "Lazy 15 Day Seven: Feminine Nails," November 16, 2012, accessed August 31, 2013, http://fabbynailedit.blogspot.com/2012/11/lazy-15-day-seven-feminine-nails.html.

46. Priest.

47. Fitzy, "The Lazy 15 Challenge Day 7: 'Feminine' Nails," Lacquer Lad, November 16, 2012, accessed August 31, 2013, http://lacquerlad.blogspot.com/2012/11/the-lazy-15-challenge-day-7-feminine.html.

48. Sharra Farivar, "The Lazy 15 Challenge Day 7: 'Feminine' Nails," Lacquer Lad, November 16, 2012, accessed August 31, 2013, http://lacquerlad.blogspot.com/2012/11/the-lazy-15-challenge-day-7-feminine.html.

49. Fashion Footing, "The Lazy 15 Challenge: Feminine Nails," November 16, 2012, accessed August 31, 2013, http://fashionfooting.blogspot.com/2012/11/the-lazy-15-challenge-feminine-nails.html.

50. Kate, "The Lazy 15: Feminine Nails," LacquerCareFactor, November 17, 2012, accessed August 30, 2013, http://www.lacquercarefactor.com/2012/11/17/the-lazy-15-feminine-nails/.

51. Real_Girl_Fashion, "Girly Girls Are SO Annoying," Lovelyish, September 18, 2009, accessed December 27, 2013, http://www.lovelyish.com/2009/09/17/girly-girls-are-so-annoying/.

52. Elana Levine, *Buffy* and the "New Girl Order": Defining Feminism and Femininity," in *Undead TV: Essays on Buffy the Vampire Slayer*, eds. Elana Levine and Lisa Parks (Durham, N.C.: Duke University Press, 2007), 168–190.

53. LemonyEmily, "The girliest you will ever see me!" Emily's Nail Files, May 23, 2011, accessed December 7, 2013, http://emilysnailfiles.blogspot.com/2011/05/girliest-you-will-ever-see-me.html.

54. Holly, "Girly Nails," The Yummy Mummy's Beauty Blog, August 27, 2010, accessed November 7, 2013, http://www.ymbeautyblog.com/2010/08/girly-nails.html.

55. Lindsey, "Girly-Girl Challenge, Anyone?" Neverland Nail Blog, March 3, 2012, accessed January 1, 2014, http://www.neverlandnailblog.com/2012/03/girly-girl-challenge-anyone.html; ManisbyMoore, "Girly Girl Nail Art Challenge," Mani's by Moore, March 20, 2013, accessed January 1, 2014, http://manisbymoore.blogspot.com/2013/03/girly-girl-nail-art-challenge_20.html#comment-form.

56. Lindsey, "Girly-Girl Nail Art Challenge," Neverland Nail Blog, March 6, 2012, accessed December 7, 2013, http://www.neverlandnailblog.com/2012/03/girly-girl-challenge-think-pink.html.

57. Jessica, "Girly-Girl Nail Art Challenge Day 2," Luv My Lacquer, March 14, 2012, accessed November 17, 2013, http://luvmylacquer.blogspot.com/2012/03/girly-girl-nail-art-challenge-day-2.html.

58. Lauren M., "The Ring Finger of Mine," Utterly Engaged, accessed October 21, 2013, http://www.utterlyengaged.com/this-ring-finger-of-mine/.

59. Sarah Brown, "The Finger-Flagging Manicure for Ladies Who Are Into Ladies," Jezebel, September 28, 2012, accessed October 21, 2013, http://jezebel.com/5947301/the-finger+flagging-manicure-for-ladies-who-are-into-ladies.

60. Sarah Kane, "Let's Talk About Accent Nails," Hello Giggles, October 9, 2013, accessed January 2, 2015, http://hellogiggles.com/lets-talk-about-accent-nails.

61. Jessica, "Girly-Girl Nail Art Challenge Day 2," Luv My Lacquer, March 14, 2012, accessed November 3, 2013, http://luvmylacquer.blogspot.com/2012/03/girly-girl-nail-art-challenge-day-2.html.

62. StephanieLouise, "Girly Girl Nail Challenge Day #1: Michael Marcus Fuchsia Have This A Good Time + WnW Black Tips," All Things Beautiful, September 2, 2012, accessed

September 14, 2013, http://stephanielouiseatb.blogspot.com/2012/09/girly-girl-nail
-challenge-day-1-michael.html.

63. Sam Fulton, "Girly Girl Nail Art Challenge," Mani's by Moore, March 23, 2013,
accessed September 11, 2013, http://manisbymoore.blogspot.com/2013/03/girly-girl
-nail-art-challenge_20.html#comment-form.

64. Ignacio Siles, "Web Technologies of the Self: The Arising of the 'Blogger' Identity,"
Journal of Computer-Mediated Communication 17 (2012): 408–421.

65. ManisbyMoore, "Girly Girl Nail Art Challenge," Mani's by Moore, March 23, 2013,
accessed September 11, 2013, http://manisbymoore.blogspot.com/2013/03/girly-girl
-nail-art-challenge_20.html#comment-form.

66. Mihaela Lacquerbuzz, "Girly Girl Nail Art Challenge Day 1: Think Pink," Lacquer Buzz, September 2, 2012, accessed September 12, 2013, http://www.lacquerbuzz
.com/2012/09/girly-girl-nail-art-challenge-day-1.html.

67. Cazzy Durcan, "Girly Girl Nail Art Challenge Week 8 Girls Just Wanna Have Fun,"
May 17, 2013, accessed October 26, 2013, http://specialgirlnails.blogspot.com/2013/05
/girly-girl-nail-art-challenge-week-8.html.

68. Bill Boraczek, as quoted in Emanuella Grinberg, "On main street and the runway,
nail art is the new lipstick," CNN, February 12, 2012, accessed August 30, 2013, http://
www.cnn.com/2012/02/10/living/fashion-week-nail-art/index.html.

69. Megan, "How To: Take Nail Photos," Blondes Love Cupcakes, June 27, 2013,
accessed January 2, 2015, http://blondeslovecupcakes.wordpress.com/2013/06/27
/how-to-take-nail-photos/.

70. Michelle Mismas, "Nail Tip—The Slimline Technique," All Lacquered Up, April
12, 2010, accessed September 22, 2013, http://www.alllacqueredup.com/2010/04/nail
-tip-slimline-technique.html#.Uj-MlLxszeA.

71. Jaime, "Nail Tip—The Slimline Technique," All Lacquered Up, April 14, 2010,
accessed September 22, 2013, http://www.alllacqueredup.com/2010/04/nail-tip-slimline
-technique.html#.Uj-MlLxszeA.

72. Alice, "Nail Tip—The Slimline Technique," All Lacquered Up, April 13, 2010,
accessed September 22, 2013, http://www.alllacqueredup.com/2010/04/nail-tip-slimline
-technique.html#.Uj-MlLxszeA.

73. Rosaslind Krauss, "Stieglitz/'Equivalents,'" *October* 11 (Winter 1979): 133.

74. Ibid., 135.

75. Diana Fuss, "Fashion and the Homospectatorial Look," *Critical Inquiry* 18, no. 4
(Summer 1992): 718.

76. Susan R. Bordo, "The Body and the Reproduction of Femininity: A Feminist Appro-
priation of Foucault," in *Gender/Body/Knowledge: Feminist Reconstructions of Being and
Knowing*, ed. Alison M. Jaggar and Susan R. Bordo (New Brunswick, N.J.: Rutgers University Press, 1989), 14.

CHAPTER 8

Dance, Dance, Dance, Dance, Dance, Dance, Dance All Night!

Mediated Audiences and Black Women's Spirituality

BERETTA E. SMITH-SHOMADE

"When I think about Jesus, what he's done for me . . ." If you can finish this stanza, you'll be in good stead for the ground being addressed here. What accompanies these lyrics: The organ, the drums, the tambourine, and the exhortation, might provoke you to "shout right now," as Black gospel innovator Kirk Franklin often commands. Contemporary scholarship on religion and media deals mostly with three areas: God and capitalism (megachurches, big-time preachers, prosperity ministries); God and politics (religious right, nationhood and sovereignty, elections, public policy); and God and popular culture (Christian rappers, religious reality TV, Tim Tebow, new nonbelievers). Typically in mainstream news, derisive commentary reigns. Yet despite the deluge of coverage, media scholars enter unfamiliar territory within the realm of the Holy Spirit. Both a seemingly common sense understanding and a sense of "no clue" exist about what it actually means to deal with the spirit through media.

The confluence of media and religion has been both fortuitous and highly toxic from its earliest iterations: fortuitous inasmuch as proselytizing became much easier and more productive through radio, music, film, television, cable, and now web-based modes of communication; toxic in the fact that what Christianity or Islam or Judaism[1] means via media tends to cement a caustic notion of who believing folks are, what role they can and should play, and their worth to anything beyond that particular framework. This assessment fails to even consider the disparaging discourses around nontraditional religious practices.[2]

Every mediated realm shapes religiosity, or the performance of religion. For Black Christians, this performance gets visualized through the preacher, the choir, the work of the ushers, the parishioners (who become audience in a mediated context), and, critically, the viewers/users.

One of the most highly visible religious performances is the Holy Ghost run. In most Black Pentecostal and many Bapticostal churches, men and women run.[3] The Biblical admonition/justification for running lies in many books— both in the Bible's old and new testaments.[4] But there is something about a woman's run, a woman's tears, a woman's shouting, a woman's jumping that forges a connection, emotion, and a realization between the "what is" and the "what could be." In other words, women's visualized belief moves from acknowledgment to participation to performance and, in turn, transforms audiences. Moreover, "catching" the Holy Ghost can offer a freedom that people of color, and women even more, aren't often allowed to access. Psychologist Louis Hoffman talks about U.S. notions of freedom and its erroneous connection to only political freedom and individualism. He argues, "Choosing to be a part of a collective can be a profound expression of freedom. Choosing to embrace one's culture, its norms, and its rituals can be one experience of freedom."[5]

The Holy Ghost represents one of the three foundations of Christianity— the father, the son, and the Holy Spirit. The manifestation of spirit comes as God and from God through people, unplanned and certainly unmediated. Clergy and scholars characterize the Holy Ghost as "the Lord, the giver of life,"[6] "the divine presence in our lives,"[7] and as a "transformative power . . . a power felt both physically (the 'feeling' that penetrates from head to foot) and emotionally (the rapturous infusion of joy)."[8] This spiritual "gift" represents acceptance of Christian precepts and the activities thereof. It often also suggests a familiarity with particular Christian denominations that not only recognize but also ascribe to spiritual gifts such as these.

Mediation, in the context of this work, refers to the conduit, structuring, and transformation of what is electronically televised and webbed. Thus, to examine the mediation of black women's spirituality, I turn to two mediated praise breaks (as bodily expressions of the Holy Spirit are so often characterized): a 2010 performance on the BET network's gospel competition program *Sunday Best* featuring winner Leandria Johnson, and a 2007 performance by R&B singer Kelly Price, aired on BET's annual *Celebration of Gospel* in tribute to the deceased singer Gerald Levert. These national cable programs occupy central viewing opportunities for Black Christian communities. Performing in these spaces situates the performers in a particular arena of Black music and music traditions. I examine Black women's Christian performance via contemporary

158

television and the internet to gain insights into how screen audiences are invited to experience the Holy Spirit. In other words, I argue that in these moments, with Black women (and Black audience members and judges) performing, praising, and testifying, the Holy Spirit moves not only through the recorded, in-studio audience but also within screen audiences—both television viewers and internet users. And despite the justified rebuke of Black churches for their frequent dismissive dealings with women,[9] the manifestation of the Holy Spirit allows for an exaltation of women in the revelation of the spirit.

"What's the Buzz, Tell Me What's a-Happening"

In looking for ways to enter a discussion about the visceral impact of Black televisual religiosity, I employ the theoretical framework of phenomenology in its address of structures of feelings, emotions, and bodily experiences related to external stimuli. I am especially interested in employing a theory that allows for a consideration of mediation across and through embodied Black women. This type of theoretical framing is needed because something particularly tactile emerges for audiences when watching, for example, the clairvoyance and fortune-telling life work of Mozelle Batiste (Debbi Morgan) in *Eve's Bayou* (1997) or the remembrance of historical slave trauma in *Daughters of the Dust* (1991), in *Sankofa* (1993), and in *Beloved* (1998). Beyond these filmic narratives and the tactility they engender, examining television and internet texts encourages a particular grappling with race, gendered bodies, and religious practices, as shown in examples such as the HBO series *True Blood* (2008-) a la Tara (Rutina Wesley) and Lafayette (Nelsan Ellis) or in Toni Child's (Jill Marie Jones) redemption from past friendship failings in season two of *Girlfriends* (2000–2008). This encouragement is due, in some measure, to the immediacy and presumed connection of television to our real-life selves. Something in the confluence of the audio and image moves audiences, listeners, viewers, and users between active critical engagement and bodily response, as proscribed within Teshome Gabriel's theorization of memory, identity, gift, and culture.[10] Utilizing phenomenology as a methodological tool can instructively get at meanings and understandings of mediated raced and gendered bodies and their connection with the mind and spirit.

Marrying phenomenology and religious practices requires understanding key aspects of the phenomenological enterprise. The phenomenology of philosopher Edmund Husserl has been modified and continually retooled for useful contributions to several areas including media discourses. With both phenomenology and religious practices, visuality and viscerality are connected—when you watch something and are moved by it, the phenomenon is tied not only to a physiological response but also to a mind/body and, I argue, spirit connection. Hoffman suggests that, "Phenomenology and qualitative methods tend to assume one can better understand the experience of individuals through utilizing multiple ways of knowing."[11] In other words, phenomenology takes up and focuses on subjective experiences—experiences informed by cultural and personal elements that help shape meaning. A phenomenological inquiry takes account of philosophical criticality encountered with a phenomenon (the mind) in relation to its bodily manifestation. However, knowing the trajectory of a phenomenon is not enough. We must additionally grapple with mediation and its operations in order to understand how they work in relation.

In media scholarship, debates about the means, methods, and sometimes viability of phenomenological inquiry have continued since the late 1970s. For example, Vivian Sobchack wrote in her 1992 *The Address of the Eye*, "The cinema uses *modes of embodied existence* (seeing, hearing, physical and reflective movement) as the vehicle, the 'stuff,' the substance of its language. It also uses the *structures of direct experience* (the 'centering' and bodily situating of existence in relation to the world of objects and others) as the basis for the structures of language."[12] She directly compares the nature of film to human embodiment—arguing for their similar operation. While Harald Stadler in a *Quarterly Review of Film and Video* review contested many of her assertions (to which she responded in the next issue of that journal), their debates continue to be salient in twenty-first-century media discourses.

From film studies we know that cinema (and its cousins television and new media), do not exist as simply visual offerings. These media can produce in their audiences/users something tangibly felt. Cultural theorist Elizabeth Stephens argues, "Film is not simply a 'vision machine' . . . but a sensation machine, a technology for the stimulation and cultivation of all the senses."[13] To that end, new media scholar Michele White has amalgamated several women scholars' writings on the body (the conduit of the spirit) and media to suggest:

> Resonance and connective tissue provide a Merleau-Pontian means of understanding thought and methods for theorizing the kinds of communications that occur within one body, communications among individuals, the links between physicality and ideas, and connections involving self and the world . . . bodies, other people, and technologies are mediated and mediators. Phenomenological accounts, including the concept of flesh of the world and connective tissue, do not distinguish between the body and representation. The "medium that signifies the body, its representation" . . . is no longer distinct from the "raw material" of the body.[14]

160

Ostensibly, embracing these theoretical understandings allow us to consider viewers' ability to become a direct part of a spiritual/religious experience through media. Mediation not only does *not* hinder the relationship between text and audience, but it can help facilitate representation standing in for an actual being. As media apparatuses function in a similar way to humans' embodied selves, they pose no impediment to accessibility. In the case of my analysis of mediated spirituality, the Holy Spirit is not bound by flesh and thus can become actualized in the flesh of and for mediated audiences who believe.

Audiences' experiences are also shaped by generic knowledge of media and sometimes said audiences' responses to a certain genre. In particular, audiences know television genre constructions, even those of religious programming. Be it a game show, a physical challenge, or a singing competition such as *Sunday Best*, the basic aesthetics and production choices remain the same regardless of content. Music rising in climactic scenes, pauses for effect, close-ups, zooms, and other production and editing devices are all a part of the complete televisual experience, with online video employing those same techniques as well. While some scholars argue that spaces reserved for religious activity have a "distinctive character"—one that sets them apart from mere "profane" spaces,[15] I suggest that the "reality" of reality television is that audiences' familiarity with these types of program, religious or otherwise, sets standard expectations regardless of any higher purpose.

Moreover, many African-American audiences bring their cultural relationships to bear on mediated forms. Black audiences can be as comfortable talking with one another about what is being screened as they are to the nonresponsive screen itself. It stands to reason, then, that believin' folks would be able to access the spirit of God across platforms. In fact, argues sociologist Christian Smith, "In 'good worship,' Christians believe, the self opens up and mystically pours itself out to and unites with the transcendent source of all life, being, and truth. . . . Even rough approximations of such experiences can do things to people's bodies and spirits that are deeply emptying and fulfilling, challenging and affirming."[16]

The phenomenological approach forwarded by Stadler offers a way to deploy phenomenology for screens, especially television and the internet. Stadler argues for engaging a spectrum of experiences that involves the following: "1) [D]oing things as an active participant in events; 2) looking at events as a nonparticipant yet with an active evaluative attitude; 3) visualizing, in memory or imagination, things past or anticipated . . . ; 4) listening to representations . . . of actual events we missed seeing . . . ; and 5) listening to the telling of things that *might* happen."[17] Using this framing, I turn first to *Sunday Best* to explore deeper meanings and associations between the visual, the visceral, and the Spirit.

And the Word Became Flesh . . . *Sunday Best*

Beginning in fall 2007, BET's *Sunday's Best* became one of the network's most successful programs.[18] With recognized and loved contemporary gospel artist/host Kirk Franklin, judges (including singers Bebe Winans, Donnie McClurkin, Yolanda Adams, CeCe Winans, and the sisters of Mary, Mary), quality competitors, and high production values, it created a recipe for televisual (and ratings) success. More importantly, the program encouraged audiences to emote with it—to get up and clap, sing along, and empathize with the competitors. For twelve weeks, competitors perform always-evocative contemporary and traditional gospel musical selections. Coming from a network with a music video ethos, the program allows for audiences to really get to know the participants and to observe their holiness through outside-lives' vignettes and voice-overs. In the example used here, competitor Leandria Johnson sings the song, "I Love the Lord" as part of the finalists' round of season three in 2010.

The production practices employed for this series are commonplace for televised music competitions. A wide shot of the stage opens the performance and pushes in to the singer slowly. The audience follows through a cut to a close-up of her singing and then back out to a wide, moving shot. The audio mix includes sound from her microphone, the audience reaction, the piano, and, later, some of the organ, drums, and background singers. Shots are interchanged between singer, audience, musicians, the judges, and specifically Johnson's family (her mother, father, and brother) in the audience. While she performs the song powerfully and with in-studio audience support, what happens after the song provides the source of this phenomenological inquiry.

When Johnson finishes "I Love the Lord," she appears spent, exhausted. Her eyes are closed and head thrown back (see Figure 8.1). She seems overcome. She places her hands on her knees and then raises both hands in a praiselike position. She has "kilt it." On stage she waits for the judges' comments but with eyes filled with tears. Host Kirk Franklin celebrates how incredible she is and proceeds to ask the judges what they think of the performance. However, judge Yolanda Adams disrupts this continuance of the gospel competition proceedings and says to Franklin, "Kirk, let the child shout. Let her shout."

With this permission and invitation, Johnson's tears begin to fall, and she allows her belief in the manifestation of the Holy Ghost to flow through her

FIGURE 8.1. Contestant Leandria Johnson as she completes her performance on BET's gospel-performance competition, *Sunday Best,* in 2010.

body. We see this with the beginning of the dance. The organ, drums, and guitar begin to play in tandem, and the whole place erupts. The edits are rhythmic and match the bass lines of the drums and the guitar. Media audiences see, can actually feel, the beat as Johnson begins her characterized "Holy Ghost" dance. She backs up like a runner beginning a race and offers a combination of foot tapping and dance, arms akimbo and moving in time. Because of the palpable emotion of the performance, and the in-studio response, willing at-home audiences can feel the rush of the spirit in their hearts and spirits.

On his blog *Uppity Negro Network,* cultural critic Joshua Lazard characterizes praise breaks when he writes:

> What we see in the modern day church when it comes to a praise break is a result of the influence of Gospel music as a genre through the ages. Before when there was just a piano, and then drums were added and by the fifties there would be a whole band including guitars and bass guitars and also the ever influential Hammond organ, ... The sound that is associated with the shout is all based on the music—namely the organ. And much like the ring shout, a *true* praise break or shout is spontaneous. That is to say, often times a praise break'll happen after a song that the choir sang really stirred up the emotions of the congregation and the praise break acts as the cathartic release.[19]

Philosopher Gregory Currie maintains that in such cases,

> [M]embers of the audience come to play a dual role; they are both spectators of, and actors in, the production. They play, if they are willing, characters participating in the action, and may come to make-believe that they are those characters, bearing relations to the characters on stage and to each other. They are also members of the audience, and observe themselves playing these roles.[20]

When the music ends and Johnson stops to regain her breath, the judges begin to talk with her about the blessing she's going to be around the world.

In visualizing Johnson's presumed connection to God, through her dance, her tears, and the music of praise, audiences can forge their own personal connections. Starting with chest tightening and following with tears, that connection oftentimes provokes expressions of praise for television and/or internet audiences. Unlike the notion that this enthusiastic praise originates from the unacknowledged and involuntary impulses of a thoughtless mind—"excited utterances," if you will—a certain distinction and blend exists between cognition (thinking) and the visceral expressions of emotion during Johnson's break. These are the thoughtful, considered, and joined exhibitions of a mind-body-spirit connection that crystallize with the confluence of memory, recognition, and spirit. Articulated throughout the season for audiences, the combination of Johnson's history of loss (her memory), stellar performance nonetheless (recognition), and praise break (spirit) allow us to enter her head and heart space and replace it with our own narratives of loss, recognition, and redemption. Thus, at-home audiences can take up her praise as part of and prescriptive for their own challenges with and through the support of technology.

"For This I Give You Praise"

Unlike with Johnson's performance, screen audiences must get their praise on without the auditory support of the in-studio audience in the performance of R&B singer Kelly Price. The *Celebration of Gospel* audience is clearly moved, with Black women and some men crying, shouting, singing background, raising hands, rocking, and dancing. However, due to differences in what microphones get privileged for the performance, screen audiences are removed from the gravitas of the aural worship, only seeing the happenings and hearing Price and the choir's microphones until the performance ends.

The song Price sings, "For Every Mountain," was written by gospel singer and writer Kurt Carr and released on his 1997 album, *No One Else*. The album and song became enormously successful and a staple for gospel choirs nationally.[21]

Thus, the opening notes of this song alone produce an anticipated call of the spirit for those familiar with the world of gospel music. The context of this 2007 performance is BET's annual gospel celebration program with a special tribute for singer Gerald Levert, who died suddenly in 2006. It had the trappings of other similar tributes, including projected video of Levert singing with Price and renowned gospel singer Shirley Caesar on the same stage.

Before she sings, Price talks to the audience about being shocked by Levert's death but sums up with the reflection:

> The Bible does tell us, though, that there is a season for all things. There is a time to love; there's a time to laugh; there's a time to be born; and there's even a time to die. And even though we don't necessarily understand all the time, we know that God is sovereign, and we accept His will as being what it is. I would like to say that I count it a privilege and an honor, and I know that all of you do too, be you friend, family or fan, to have been blessed with the life and the gifts of Gerald Levert. So for this we give God praise.[22]

Her rendition of the selection begins as any other televised performance does, beautiful singing from a clear and strong mezzo-soprano. Dissolves to audience members (celebrity[23] and others) show them sitting in repose and prepared to enjoy the performance of a cherished song in reflection of Levert. The early part of the lyrics chronicles reasons why Price (and by extension all watching and listening) should be grateful to and praise God. Dissolves cut between Price, the choir (with smoke emanating from their silhouetted frames), and the audience. But "For Every Mountain" is not a song for repose.

The lyrics, organ, and voices of the choir begin to visually transform the space. The song itself changes rhythm. It slows and encourages a very deliberate call and response. But it also crescendos. The simple chorus becomes, "For every mountain, you brought me over. For every trial, you've seen me through. For every blessing, hallelujah! For this, I give you praise." By the second iteration of it, the onscreen audience members are clearly engaged with the singer, the song, the music, and their own personal narratives. Screened audiences see the intercuts of Price singing and auditorium audiences shaking their heads, raising their hands, singing, and beginning to stand.

By the third round of the chorus, the choir is enthusiastically worshipping, and the studio audience has become much more involved. While the preponderance of shots focus on Price, the choice of edits speak to the director's familiarity with the performance style of "Black church"—about the rhythm of expectation and the import of the repeated verbalization of the words and meanings to audiences both live and at home. In what should have been the final iteration of the chorus, the impact of what she sings seems to overcome

Price—so much so that she misses the arranged song out. And as the choir director and musicians reset the ending, she repeatedly asks the audience, "Has He ever brought you through anything?" For those who somehow missed the call of the spirit prior, this questioning invites audiences across platforms to make their own connections with God. Price asks audiences to remember. This direct appeal is unbounded and unfettered by tangible bodies.

Although sanitized, due to the aural exclusion of the in-studio audience, the familiarity and popularity of the song can help at-home audiences connect viscerally to Price and the feeling of the moment. The way she sings, "Hallelujah," throughout the song and shouts it as she walks off the stage after the song is over encourages audiences to respond with a shout to her and to God. "Hallelujah" means to praise God. And by the end, when the television director brings the house audio up for viewer consumption, the in-studio audience is participating in a praise party that continues to the television commercial.

The wonder of this song and its articulation in this context is its explicit connection to minds (memories, experiences), bodies (emotions), and spirit (God). Tapping into many Christians' Biblical interpretation of Jesus speaking in Matthew about two or three being gathered in the name of Jesus, so shall I be,[24] mediation makes a way for autonomous and singular home viewers to tangibly join with other believers in worship and prayer. Thus, the presence of God can move as easily in the live (recorded) body of worshippers as it can with those watching remotely. Moreover, as television tends to be a particularly audio-driven medium, not so much because of any acutely attuned attention to the sound but because so much of its articulation is dialogue-based, orality gets a further lift in this space—orality being central to African diasporic cultures.

The two praise breaks and their impact on televised and screen audiences are different for believers—one in response to a move of God as demonstrated by the singer, the other as a part of the singer's actual performance. In both cases, the spirit moves bodily across mediated spaces. The movement of the Holy Ghost in believing bodies makes visible what is ostensibly invisible. The combination of familiarity and knowledge, music, memory, sincerity, and spirit cut across space, time, and technology to touch believers where they are. That's why . . .

God Don't Need No Matches . . .

Black folks' Christianity often embodies performance. As noted by anthropologist Glenn Hinson, as early as the 1790s, African-American Christians have been articulating their faith in the language of experience.[25] Various expressions, movements, and ways of being exude a mark of religiosity. Getting/catching the Holy Spirit, lifting a finger up to move through church, the "You know you're a Black Christian if . . ." email, all mark a certain type of religious predisposition known to both participants and many outliers of the culture. With most churches' overpopulation of women, it seems almost commonsensical that the reflection of what "good church" looks like moves through their gendered presence. The *Sunday Best* judges affirm this transference through their praise of Leandria Johnson. Judge Tina Campbell tells her:

> The thing about you that gets me, you are honest. You are genuine. You are true. You are a real gospel singer because you have the heart of God. You ain't no fake. That stuff that be going on with you . . . that ain't for the stage, that ain't for the people, that ain't for entertainment. . . . I see it in your eyes. You so serious, so honest about it. Girl, you deserve to be here. God is all over you. You are anointed; You are real and people are going to be blessed and they goin' come to God watching you.[26]

While Campbell's comments certainly resonate with what I have described and discussed, they are not without naysayers. Some have argued that the Holy Ghost and phenomenological example can be incompatible, suggesting that when, "Spiritual sensations are prized for these reasons—because of their phenomenological feel or as a way of underwriting one's sense of one's own importance—then they will be religiously defective . . . and they are likely to be epistemically defective, because of the suspicion that the believer, whether consciously or not, is engineering the production of such experiences for the advantages that they confer in these respects."[27] Yet this rendering of the mind-body-spirit tie as "fake"—to make it plain, bears no weight on the audience/user who enjoys it. It is a particular interpretation that becomes the burden of the person who disbelieves (either in the practice or the person)—not the one caught up. Moreover, as film scholar Carol Clover postulates in a different context, in the same way in which women are supposed to be more "open" to the image, they may be "more open to the supernatural—and perhaps, ultimately for the same reason."[28] This attuned state, this phenomenological enterprise, is certainly a part of what at-home audiences are able to access and feel so concretely.

From a historical perspective, art historian Babatunde Lawal has talked about ways in which the visual is used for communication in certain parts of continental Africa. Specifically, he outlines two types of visual metaphors: 1) the exoteric—where meanings are accessible to adults of a given culture who pass that knowledge to young ones, and 2) the esoteric—metaphors that require intimate knowledge considered not for public consumption.[29] Most visual metaphors are coded folklore for spiritual beliefs, political ideology, and proverbs. These ideas are salient here inasmuch as both exoteric and esoteric visual modes of communication are in play with mediated offerings of the Holy Spirit. Similar to many people of color, Black folks frequently convey stories, histories, relationships, and spirit orally and visually. The body, the music, the voices, and the larger visual register foster a syncretic understanding—a code that, while public, is intimate; while accessible, can be highly unknown to nonbelievers.

While scholarship addressing the Holy Spirit consistently suggests that the tangibility of it cannot be measured nor necessarily put into words, it is this very inexplicability of the spirit that works for these praise break examples. As Hinson suggests, the "Essential untellability of holy experience, combined with the experiential prerequisite of 'membership' in the fellowship of saints . . . have led many to dismiss sanctified experience as 'emotionalism' . . . the emotion in this equation is *reaction* rather than *cause*. When the Spirit truly touches, emotion is the artifact of experience rather than the other way around."[30] In thinking about the various elements of this performance, social work scholar Rebecca Chaisson remarks, "I find it empowering to think about women as subject of something that is liberating and that we can be liberated from our living rooms. Dancing and singing with abandon resembles a kind of freedom of expression that occurs no where else. . . . If this leads to some kind of restoration from daily Microaggressions related to race and gender then television is making a contribution in invaluable ways."[31]

Can I Get a Witness?

Phenomenology allows/calls for adherents to employ multiple aspects of culture and sensibilities to assess a phenomenon. In other words, the framework embraces the articulated feelings of others as part of the theorist's memory and own experience. For example, I participated in a Facebook discussion about Johnson's break with several sistah-scholars around the country in September 2012. The audience commentaries from the online iteration of the break and a Facebook discussion support the assertions made and felt here:

> M.P. that's one of my favorite praise breaks!! i just looked at it too!!
> K.W. Mine too. It actually gives me chills. And the fact that Donnie can't hold his peace cracks me up.
> B.S.S. I look at the praise break regularly. I often have to get up and join her!!

K.W. I'm like that girl's mama making that rolling move with my arms!

B.S.S. HALLELUJAH!!!

K.W. I'm on my second run of the night.[32]

This closed dialogue flows between Black women scholars who demonstrate a collective relationship to and experience with this break and praise breaks in general. It operated with an understanding of what these breaks mean and their impact. But the discussion took place not only through the internet but also required the video to be reviewed repeatedly by the participants in order to tap into the power of what it can continually offer.

YouTube commentary primarily centers the blessing of the performances. People continue to find these video clips, watch them, and write about them. Early-twenty-first-century digital media allows for a global, on-demand, and repeated experience of these performances. Comments such as "SOME-BODY.....BRING ME MY TAMBOURINE !!!! YESSSSS_ LORD" (Valinda Jarmon); "like my post if you_ shouted or cried!!!!" (Arnella Flowers); and "Makes me wanna get_ saved!" (Charles King) pervade. One comment especially captured the feelings expressed by the more than 705,229 views for Johnson and 767,108 views for Kelly Price:[33]

> Oh my my my my my. WOWWEEEEE!!! I felt that through my phone so much so that the Spirit of God surely descended down into my car. She got me speaking in tongues. Glory to God, Praise Him. They just had church and I wanted to be there. But instead God met me where I was, in my car parked outside of work getting to go to work. What a amazing way to begin the day after prayer. 10 Thumbs Up!!! (JolynF)[34]

And for Price:

> Praise God! Six sessions of chemotherapy, bald, and still praising GOD! Kelly Price is a gift from God. I have listened to this version of For Every Mountain throughout my entire health challenge. Thank you Jesus, for every soul who has lifted my name up in prayer, thank you for covering me with your grace, strength, and endurance. Thank you for encouragement via the voice of Sister Kelly Price. Praise you Sister!" (Purple Green)[35]

Entries such as "anointed" and "blessed" reign—characterizing Price's singing, the song, and her ability to move people. Comparisons are made to Whitney Houston's version of the song and even Richard Smallwood's singers, who originated the selection. In a personal conversation about this break, one nonbeliever (a lapsed Catholic) remarked to me that this performance "makes you want to believe."

And Let the Church Say . . .

Praise breaks craft one of the few anointed spaces where Black women are allowed to "live and breathe, grieve and celebrate."[36] I have employed phenomenology to best capture the ways in which this particular believing group embodies, expresses, and then captures and is freed by the spirit within and outside of the screen. Some scholars, such as philosopher Erazim Kohák, argue, however, that when the divine presence functions in religiously resonant ways, "as to be rooted in certain experiences of the world," someone who lacks those experiences will not have the same idea of divine presence.[37] Or, as one anonymous reviewer of this work suggested, some may be "uncomfortable . . . with the positing of the Holy Spirit as a material reality . . . that can't be supported by analysis."[38] Yet English scholar Nghana Lewis disagrees, noting that something in Johnson's eyes, in the sincerity of her song and in her praise performance moves even unbelievers. It allows them to dabble a bit.[39] Said another way, Tina Campbell, judge on *Sunday Best*, ends her assessment of Johnson's performance with, "If I didn't know your God, I'd wanna know him."

As Black women, and women in general, are situated as the keepers of culture in families, in communities, and in nations, so too do they valiantly illustrate the power of God. Spirituality is an important aspect of many African-American women's belief systems. While it remains a highly contested term, scholar/pastor Carlyle Fielding Stewart writes that spirituality represents the "full matrix of beliefs, power, values and behaviors that shape people's consciousness, understanding, and capacity of themselves in relation to divine reality. [It is also] a process by which people interpret, disclose, formulate, adapt and innovate reality and their understandings of God within a specific context or culture."[40] And while Black and gendered bodies endure continued defaming, Black Christianity, surprisingly (patriarchal and homophobic as it can be), has allowed small avenues for women's whole being to be valued and validated.[41] It is why, when the spirit is manifest in praise, Black women are most often called upon to serve as the evidence. Mediation broadens this scope of being and perhaps can help forward progressive thought and action in larger sociocultural discourses surrounding the viability of visual media to impact lives, the visceral necessity of Black and female bodies, and the value of the Holy Ghost to believers and beyond. Amen.

Notes

The author thanks scholars Nghana Lewis, Katie Acosta, Rebecca Chaisson, Kristen Warner, and Miriam Petty for their valuable critique and insights in thinking through this work. As well, I thank editor Elana Levine and the two outside reviewers for their help in sharpening my insights and making them more accessible to nonbelievers.

1. Judaism is noted here in the context of religion and not necessarily the culture.

2. For example, I've conducted research on western representations of African traditional spiritual practices and found scholarship around this area shameful.

3. Pentecostalism forms a part of several Christian denominations that, among many things, calls for an expressive recognition of God's work in the lives of its believers and a relationship with Him. This relationship is evidenced through speaking in tongues, baptism by the Holy Spirit, prophecy, and healing. The term *Bapticostal* suggests the confluence of Black Baptist and Black Pentecostal traditions.

4. For example, Psalm 150:1–6 says, "Praise the Lord! Praise God in his sanctuary; praise him in his mighty heavens! Praise him for his mighty deeds; praise him according to his excellent greatness! Praise him with trumpet sound; praise him with lute and harp! Praise him with tambourine and dance; praise him with strings and pipe! Praise him with sounding symbols; praise him with loud clashing symbols! Let everything that has breath praise the Lord! Praise the Lord!" (*English Standard Version*). In the New Testament, Luke writes in Acts 4:31–32, "And they were all filled with the Holy Spirit and spoke the word of God boldly. All the believers were one in heart and mind" (*New International Version Bible*).

5. Louis Hoffman, "An Existential-Phenomenological Approach to the Psychology of Religion," *Pastoral Psychology* 61 (2012): 791.

6. "739 The Nicene Creed," *The Methodist Hymnal: Official Hymnal of the Methodist Church* (Nashville, Tenn.: The Methodist Publishing House, 1966).

7. "740 A Modern Affirmation," *The Methodist Hymnal: Official Hymnal of the Methodist Church* (Nashville, Tenn.: The Methodist Publishing House, 1966).

8. Glenn Hinson, *Fire in My Bones: Transcendence and the Holy Spirit in African American Gospel* (Philadelphia: University of Pennsylvania Press, 2000), 2.

9. See, for example, the 2013 Full Gospel calling for "movers and shakers of the kingdom" to revitalize the Black church—a call and room excluding all women. See Sinclair Grey III, "Black Church Leadership Gathering Excludes Women," http://allchristiannews.com/black-church-leadership-gathering-excludes-women/, December 14, 2013, accessed December 21, 2013.

10. For example, see Teshome Gabriel, "The Gift of Poetics: By Way of a Preface beyond Axum," *Emergences* 10.1 (2000): 5–7; "The Intolerable Gift," in *Home, Exile, Homeland: Film, Media and the Politics of Place*, ed. by Hamid Naficy (New York: Routledge, 1998), 75–84; and "Ruin and the Other: Towards a Language of Memory," in *Otherness and the Media* (Langhorne, Pa.: Harwood Academic Publishers, 1993), 211–220. Gabriel forces readers to embody their work, to consciously place themselves at the center of their critical interests and to move out from that space. He asks readers/writers/thinkers to take up elements and institutions of their lives to discover what the theoretical application may be within or outside of the subject.

11. Louis Hoffman, "An Existential-Phenomenological Approach to the Psychology of Religion," *Pastoral Psychology* 61 (2012): 785.

12. Vivian Sobchack, *The Address of the Eye: A Phenomenology of Film Experience* (Princeton, N.J.: Princeton University Press, 1992), 4–5.

13. Elizabeth Stephens, "Sensation Machine: Film, Phenomenology and the Training of the Senses," *Continuum: Journal of Media and Cultural Studies* 26.4 (August 2012): 529.

14. Michele White, "Networked Bodies and Extended Corporealities: Theorizing the Relationship between the Body, Embodiment, and Contemporary New Media," *Feminist Studies* 35.3 (Fall 2009): 603–624.

15. As found in the *Stanford Encyclopedia of Philosophy*. The entry cited Mircea Eliade, *Patterns in Comparative Religion* (London: Sheed and Ward, 1958).

16. Christian Smith, "Why Christianity Works: An Emotions-Focused Phenomenological Account," *Sociology of Religion* 68.2 (2007): 174.

17. Harald Stadler, "Film as Experience: Phenomenological Concepts in Cinema and Television Studies," *Quarterly Review of Film and Video* 12.3 (1990): 44. This outline of steps is very similar to the one offered in Don Ihde's *Experimental Phenomenology: An Introduction* (Albany: State University of New York Press, 1986), 29–54.

18. *Sunday Best* consistently ranks number one for its day and time part in African-American households. For more on BET and its pantheon of programs that target Black audiences, including religious ones, see my *Pimpin Ain't Easy: Selling Black Entertainment Television* (New York: Routledge, 2007).

19. Joshua Lazard, "This Is Why Folks Don't Take Church Seriously Pt. II: The Shout or Praise Breaks," on *Uppity Negro Network* blog, May 25, 2009, cited on October 13, 2012.

20. Gregory Currie, "Visual Fictions," in *Philosophical Quarterly* 41 (April 1991): 143.

21. The Brooklyn Tabernacle Choir won a Grammy Award for the 2000 CD, *Live-God Is Working*, which includes this song.

22. Quote from Kelly Price, *Celebration of Gospel*, BET, January 28, 2007.

23. A number of recognized audience members are featured, including actor Loretta Devine, singer Aretha Franklin, and producer/actor/writer Tyler Perry. This is significant to the telecast because it not only demonstrates and exploits other artists in attendance but, more importantly to this work, it validates the connection of potential Holy Ghost spirit moving as a part of these particular celebrities' brand as Christians.

24. This comes from Matthew 18:20. Scholars have argued that this verse actually references ideas of accountability and belief. However, it is commonplace in many Christian communities to invoke it as a testament to corporate prayer. See for example, http://www.reclaimingthemind.org/blog/2012/08/where-two-or-three-are-gathered-and-other-bad-interpretations/, accessed August 29, 2013.

25. Glenn Hinson, *Fire in My Bones: Transcendence and the Holy Spirit in African American Gospel* (Philadelphia: University of Pennsylvania Press, 2000), 15.

26. Tina Campbell, as taken from *Sunday Best*, season 3, original airdate June 2010, viewed on YouTube, November 1, 2012.

27. *Stanford Encyclopedia of Philosophy*, "Phenomenology of Religion," ed. Edward N. Zalta, http://plato.stanford.edu/entries/phenomenology-religion/, October 1, 2008, accessed October 11, 2012.

28. Carol J. Clover, *Men, Women, and Chainsaws* (Princeton: Princeton University Press, 1992), 74.

29. Babatunde Lawal, "The Use of Visual Metaphors for Mass Communication," talk, University of Arizona, January 26, 2002.

30. Hinson, 19–20.

31. Rebecca Chaisson, personal correspondence, October 25, 2012.

32. Facebook dialogue between Kristen Warner, Beretta E. Smith-Shomade, and Miriam Petty, September 6, 2012.

33. These are figures as of December 21, 2013. They continue to rise.

34. As found on YouTube comments for the video, posted in 2012, https://www.youtube.com/all_comments?v=eZoZ90GqBXM&page=1, accessed December 21, 2013.

35. As found on YouTube comments for video, posted March 2013, https://www.youtube.com/watch?v=jVKarYVYoIM&lc=vKHSg4Ixm8GpMmUZneEAb6NVAiaWS4JbYKh V6rtiUx4, accessed December 21, 2013.

36. Rebecca Chaisson offered this assessment so beautifully.

37. *Stanford Encyclopedia of Philosophy*, "Phenomenology of Religion," ed. Edward N. Zalta, http://plato.stanford.edu/entries/phenomenology-religion/, accessed December 22, 2013.

38. Anonymous reviewer comments for this chapter, June 2014.

39. Nghana Lewis, personal conversation, October 26, 2012.

40. Carlyle Fielding Stewart III, *Black Spirituality and Black Consciousness: Soul Force, Culture and Freedom in the African-American Experience* (Trenton, N.J.: Africa World Press, 1998), 1.

41. Clearly, examples of nonappreciation of these experiences come through spiritualized bodies, especially as articulated through nonmainstream spiritual practices. See for example, the films *Angel Heart* (1987), *The Serpent and the Rainbow* (1988), *The Skeleton Key* (2005), and on television, *Poltergeist, The Legacy* (1996–1999), and even *True Blood* (2008–2014).

PART III

Labors

CHAPTER 9

Working Girls

The Precariat of Chick Lit

SUZANNE FERRISS

Chick-lit novels have been criticized for glamorizing consumption and irresponsibly promoting unchecked consumerism in the young women presumed to be their audience. Critics have taken titles such as *Shopaholic* or *Bergdorf Blondes* as not only descriptive—that is, as accurate labels for their heroines—but as *prescriptive*, as advocating shopping as a sign of young women's success. As cultural commodities themselves, chick-lit novels are routinely dismissed as the literary equivalent of shoes or handbags, texts that package their disposable ideas within glossy covers and thus sustain American-style capitalism in both form and substance. And the image, so the prevailing argument goes, is relentlessly white: The typical chick-lit heroine—Caucasian, white-collar, armed with her credit card—defines postfeminist freedom as economic empowerment. Even texts credited with injecting color and/or ethnicity, such as *The Dirty Girls Social Club*, have been accused of packaging alternate forms of ethnic identity in a pleasing, homogenizing middle-class wrapper, muting cultural critique for fear of alienating mainstream readers and thus compromising sales.

Certainly chick lit, like all popular media, is inextricably entangled in the capitalist system, an inevitable consequence, it could be argued, of postmodern culture itself. But critics have taken its references to brand-name goods and status as an *endorsement* of global capitalism. Sustained, critical attention to the texts, however, suggests otherwise. As Caroline J. Smith argues in her book *Cosmopolitan Culture and Chick Lit*, the "novels question the 'consume and achieve' promise offered by . . . women's advice manuals and in doing so challenge the consumer industry to which they are closely linked."[1] Far from sanctioning aspirational spending or endorsing economic empowerment, prominent chick-lit examples dramatize the precarious economic and social position of young, college-educated, British and American women (of various classes and ethnicities) under late capitalism.

Chick Lit, Consumer Culture, and Postfeminism

Chick lit can be defined as contemporary fiction featuring identifiable, young heroines facing a series of romantic, professional, and cultural hurdles specific to their generation.[2] While its origins are Anglo-American, marked by the simultaneous appearance in 1996 of Helen Fielding's *Bridget Jones' Diary* in the U.K. and Candace Bushnell's *Sex and the City* in the United States, the genre has proved remarkably malleable, with specific varieties reflecting regional and national, racial and ethnic differences.[3] Ten years after chick lit hatched, Rachel Donadio announced a global "pandemic": "From Mumbai to Milan, Gdansk to Jakarta, regional varieties of chick lit have been sprouting, buoyed by the demographic that's both their subject and readership: 20- and 30-something women with full-time jobs, discretionary income, and a hunger for independence and glamour."[4] As novels reflecting contemporary young women's lives, they have found an avid international audience who find that their themes resonate with their own experiences.

It has become critical commonplace to consider chick-lit novels as part of postfeminist culture. As Stephanie Harzewski claims, chick lit is "the most culturally visible form of postfeminist fiction."[5] But little common agreement exists about the definition of postfeminism. Harzewski herself identifies three: positive, negative, and neutral.[6] On the negative side are those such as Yvonne Tasker and Diane Negra who perceive it as a backlash against second-wave feminism's collective, political agency.[7] Chris Holmlund points to "a white 'chick' backlash that denies class, avoids race, ignores (older) age, and 'straight'-jackets sexuality."[8] On the positive side are those who consider postfeminism the "third wave" of feminism, an extension rather than rejection of feminist ideas. Sarah Projansky has contended that it is "useful to approach postfeminism as a cultural *discourse*—an attitude, a reaction formation, . . . as a *cultural response to feminism*, one that seeks to rework—to steal rather than to supersede—feminism."[9] As Rosalind Gill has persuasively argued, *postfeminism* refers to a sensibility, rather than a set of political principles, a set of attitudes common to young, working women of the middle class (who are also predominantly white and urban, but not exclusively so). By contrast, in her view, the term *third-wave feminism* refers to an active, political project to develop and transform second-wave feminism.[10]

Regardless of differences in definition, all agree that postfeminism is complicit with consumer culture. Tasker and Negra contend that postfeminist culture valorizes an "emphatic individualism" that "tends to confuse self-interest with individuality and elevates consumption as a strategy for healing those dissatisfactions that might alternatively be understood in terms of social ills and discontents."[11] In other words, shopping substitutes for political action. They argue more broadly that "postfeminism is white and middle-class by default, anchored in consumption as a strategy (and leisure as a site) for the production of the self," that it "celebrates female agency and women's powers of consumption" and "is thoroughly integrated with the economic discourses of aspirational, niche-market Western societies."[12] In introducing their edited collection, Tasker and Negra fault all products of postfeminist culture—film, television, magazines, novels—for "celebrating," rather than rejecting or challenging, consumer culture. This not only fails to distinguish among the products of postfeminist culture (to recognize the inherent differences between film and literature, for instance) but simplistically considers fictional representation as endorsement. Can a novel or film not represent consumption to critique it? Does the mere mention of commodities lead audiences to buy? Does depicting shopping entice audiences to engage in the practice?

Singled out for their apparent realism, for their fidelity in representing the contemporary lives of young women,[13] chick-lit novels do highlight consumerism as an essential component of postmodern existence. As a result, the texts are inevitably imbricated with commodity culture, as Harzewski notes.[14] They reflect the economic advancement of women in the twentieth and twenty-first centuries: "[T]he chick lit genre's materialism reflects how the steep rise in single-women households has enabled women to engage in greater consumer activity, as women now account for about 90 percent of all apparel transactions and 80 percent of purchases overall in America."[15]

Women's enhanced purchasing power forms not only the subject of chick lit but fuels the "commercial tsunami"[16] that is chick-lit production. The novels themselves are commodities, packaged like other material goods, their covers decorated with the totemic icons of femininity: handbags, dresses, and shoes. They both announce the novels' preoccupations with consumerism and participate in commodity culture itself (see Figure 9.1). This neatly circular and knowing nod to economic reality under late capitalism has inspired further criticism. Jessica Jernigan has claimed that "the central role of consumption—whether of Cosmopolitans or Jimmy Choos—is one of chick lit's more pathological

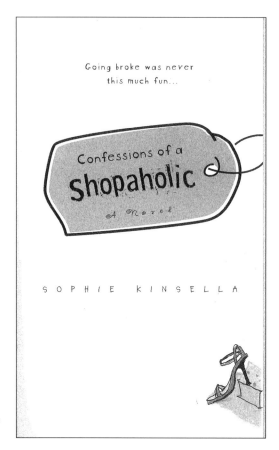

FIGURE 9.1. The price tag and shoes adorning the cover of Sophie Kinsella's *Confessions of a Shopaholic* typify the consumerist images of chick-lit covers.

features."[17] In *This Is Not Chick Lit*, Elizabeth Merrick dubbed chick lit the "stepsister to the fashion magazine," claiming "the genre's interest in glamour and goods is particularly suited to consumer-based media." She complained that "it became nearly impossible to enter a bookstore without tripping over a pile of pink books covered with truncated legs, shoes, or handbags."[18] But such criticism may have less to do with chick lit specifically and more to do with its status as popular fiction written by women. As Harzewski notes, "Chick lit's denigration stems in part from its gendered reclamation of the novel's commodity roots. Its covers and even its authors seem to court a consumerist ethos and thereby call attention to the novels' commercial origins."[19] As popular fiction, chick lit is suspect: If it attracts large audiences of reader-consumers, it must not be challenging or critical. Smith claims, "The assumption that novels such as these cannot challenge the consumer industry that they reference is . . . indicative of the deeply rooted, historical bias against popular fiction—a bias that exists against women's fiction as well."[20] An additional level of bias comes from the texts' association with consumerism, for, as Joanne Hollows has argued, consumption itself has been derided as aligned with "feminine" qualities—such as impulsiveness and passivity—and "femininity can be derided by aligning it with consumption." Myths about the female consumer, she further notes, equate consumption with leisure, failing to consider it a form of labor.[21]

Even if one assumes that the acquisition of goods is work, consumption is not solely the focus of chick-lit novels or the raison d'être of the genre.[22] Reflecting the economic realities of the contemporary era, the women of chick lit work—in jobs, not at shopping. While Tasker and Negra have argued that products of postfeminist culture feature "an affluent elite,"[23] little evidence in chick lit supports their assertion. Contrary to popular assumptions, chick-lit heroines do not routinely work in glamorous, high-paying careers in publishing that shower them with disposable income or afford them the luxury of leisure time in which to spend it. Most hold down demeaning dead-end jobs, often despite possessing college educations.[24] As such, they can more properly be classed among the precariat.

Chick Lit's Precariat

While the term *precariat* was first applied (by French sociologists) to describe temporary or seasonal workers,[25] it has come to refer broadly to "the conditions in which work is increasingly uncertain or short term, with weakened benefits or entirely without them (and, for an increasing set of interns, even without pay), where previously strong protections against firing and layoffs are eroded and where unemployment benefits are weakened or are more draconian than in the past."[26] The precariat is not a homogeneous group or identifiable class.[27] Instead, membership cuts across lines of race, gender, nationality, and socioeconomic class. The precariat includes, for example, poor, illegal immigrants providing temporary labor but also those in the service industry who perform jobs that are "dirty, unpleasant, and hazardous and entail low social esteem and low pay" such as "nurses' aids and orderlies, cleaners and custodians, busboys and kitchen workers."[28] The category includes not simply the Bangladeshi factory worker but the cleaning lady who buys the cheap T-shirts manufactured overseas.

Precarity is not a status but a condition, "less about your background or social identity than about the way you are able to think about your future," as one scholar put it.[29] The members of the precariat share a sense "that their labour is instrumental (to live), opportunistic (taking what comes), and precarious (insecure)."[30] And the condition of precarity may operate "on different levels (the job, the home, the bank account)."[31] The term, thus, captures not simply economic insecurity but the accompanying psychological consequences. As Simon During has argued, "it connotes a much more widely felt mood and condition of unease and groundlessness, characteristic of modernity as such."[32] Gary Standing describes this condition as being "precariatized": "to be subject to pressures and experiences that lead to a precariat existence, of living in the present, without a secure identity or sense of development achieved through work and lifestyle."[33] In both senses—economic and emotional—precariousness characterizes the lives of many of the young women featured in chick lit.

On the surface, it may seem nonsensical to apply the concept of precarity to the working women of chick lit, for, in terms of political agency, the precariat has been identified with Europe, rather than America or Britain (where chick lit originated),[34] and seemingly embraces those outside the middle class—not to mention that precarity affects real people, not fictional characters. While the working women of Anglo-American chick lit can hardly be described as living in poverty, it is worth noting that lower-class status is not a prerequisite for belonging to the precariat. As Mika LaVaque-Monty has noted, "Although the class background and, therefore, initial expectations of educated, middle-class, native youth might be different from those of the poor, the uneducated, and the immigrants, their qualitative conditions about their future are ultimately the same."[35] The precariat members tend also to be disproportionately young and female. And America and Britain clearly harbor their share. The American Occupy movement of the early 2010s drew attention to growing disparities between the haves and have-nots, while a contemporaneous study commissioned by the BBC identified the precariat as one of seven class positions in Bridget Jones's Britain. Over 160,000 respondents responded to questions devised to measure class not, as the BBC explained, "just by the job that you do, but by the different kinds of economic, cultural and social resources or 'capitals' that people possess."[36] Employing these measures, the researchers found that 15 percent of Britain's population belong to the precariat, "a significant group characterised by high amounts of insecurity on all of our measures of capital."[37]

In their depictions of the economic lives of young women, chick-lit novels highlight their precarious status. Many chick-lit heroines embody the new style and new identity Toby Miller identifies in the precariat who are educated in cultural, communication, and media studies: They are "young, female, mobile, international cultural workers" struggling against employment insecurity.[38] In

The Devil Wears Prada, for example, Andy Sachs works as a menial assistant to a magazine editor, even though she majored in English at Brown.[39] Bridget Jones lists "improve career and find new job with potential" as one of her diary's opening New Year's resolutions.[40] Although she too has a degree in English (26), when we first meet her at work she complains about her "obnoxious and bossy," "slightly senior" colleague Perpetua (17), while fielding weepy calls from her friends and engaging in email flirtations with her boss. In the first novel, Bridget fails at not one but two jobs. Her second job, as a researcher for the tabloid show *Good Afternoon!* was precarious from the start: She got it owing to her mother's connections and the lie that she has a degree in politics. Antonio Negri would class Bridget and Andy as among the *cognitariat*, those with "high levels of educational attainment, and great facility with cultural technologies and genres," who nonetheless occupy contingent positions.[41] As Andy explains, "Four years spent muddling around Providence in fleeces and hiking boots, learning about the French impressionists, and writing obnoxiously long-winded English papers did not—in any conceivable way—prepare me for my very first postcollege job" (11), which consists largely of fulfilling a set of capricious and demeaning demands from her editor-boss.

Chick lit's cognitariat members further introduce complications of sex and gender. Far from exuding postfeminist self-assurance, the heroines of these novels demonstrate the limits of women's presumed success based on enhanced access to education and the professions. The so-called "feminization" of labor means not only that more women are in jobs but that more jobs are of the "flexible type typically taken by women."[42] It does not mean women's incomes or working conditions are improving. "Gender-based wage and social income differentials [remain] inequitable" and "women have taken a disproportionate share of precarious jobs, being far more likely to have short-term contracts or no contracts at all."[43] While women in the early twenty-first century earn almost 60 percent of college degrees, they have tended to choose areas of study leading to "occupations that systematically pay less."[44]

Even *Shopaholic* can hardly be taken seriously as endorsing consumer spending as an index of women's economic power. The protagonist, another recent university graduate, faces bills from creditors and mounting student loan payments. Letters from banks are interleaved between chapters and they alternate between notices of overdrawn accounts and offers of easy credit. Becky Bloomwood receives two letters, dated the same day from the same clothing store, one seeking payment for an unpaid credit card bill, the other announcing, "There's never been a better time to spend!" and offering "EXTRA POINTS on all purchases" made with the same (overextended) card.[45] While many blame the novel's heroine for reckless spending, few have credited the book for convincingly depicting financial institutions' culpability in promoting personal fiscal irresponsibility and launching the global credit crisis. Smith has argued that, "Kinsella's narrative structure makes it clear that Becky's behavior is not one to be followed by readers. Rather, throughout the novel, Kinsella comments ironically on her behavior."[46] Attending to the distinction between the protagonist and the narrator, between the character and the novel she embodies, affords us the critical distance to recognize that the book highlights the precarious financial positions of contemporary workers.[47] In a neoliberal capitalist system, "growth is predicated on financial risk and indebtedness," so precarity is built in.[48]

While it may appear on the surface to be a joke that the "shopaholic" works for *Successful Savings* and fancies herself a "leading financial journalist" (93), we realize that she represents the market analysts and so-called economic experts guiding ordinary consumers—a shocking thought. And while this obvious irony could be dismissed as fictional exaggeration, two nonfiction books suggest otherwise. In *Pound Foolish*, Helaine Olen recounts that she received a call from an acquaintance asking if she would like to try writing for the *Los Angeles Times*'s Money Makeover series: "I was thirty years old and all I knew about personal finance was that writing about it paid more than the lifestyle features and breaking news coverage I'd been doing. So I accepted the gig eagerly. I figured I would write one sample, the editors would realize I had no idea what I was doing, there would be an uncomfortable confrontation, and they would issue me a check for double my usual fee and send me on my way. . . . In just a few months, I'd gone from money novice to personal finance expert."[49] Olen notes that she was not the only one to follow this career trajectory.[50] One woman with greater claim to being real-life Becky Bloomwood is Nancy Trejos. Her book, *Hot (Broke) Messes: How to Have Your Latte and Drink It Too*, details how, while working as the personal finance columnist for one of the nation's leading newspapers, the *Washington Post*, she descended into a financial crisis of her own.[51]

In fact, a spate of financial advice books, like Trejos's, take their cue from chick lit in form and title. Their covers in fluorescent pink and red feature the same totemic consumer goods that grace chick-lit covers: handbags, jewelry, and stilettos. To attract reader interest, their titles knowingly invoke luxury brands, as in *Shoo, Jimmy Choo!: The Modern Girl's Guide to Spending Less and Saving More*, or cheekily proffer puns, as in *A Purse of Your Own: An Easy Guide to Financial Security* or *The Frugalista Files: How One Woman Got out of Debt without Giving Up the Fabulous Life* (see Figures 9.2 and 9.3). These nonfiction books

FIGURES 9.2 and 9.3. Financial self-help literature targeted to women borrows the iconography of chick lit, as in the covers of *Shoo, Jimmy Choo!* and *The Frugalista Files.*

embrace the marketing techniques of their fictional counterparts to cultivate a popular audience of women readers. As a result, these advice manuals might also be dismissed as *Shopaholic* for sustaining the illusion of a "consumerist fantasy world in which reality never fully intrudes."[52] But—like chick lit—their glossy covers conceal warnings about succumbing to the lure of conspicuous consumption. In both cases—fictional and nonfictional—images of shoes and handbags may lure readers to purchase the text, but for a modest sum and to alert consumers to the traps inherent in the system itself. While this is an intentional strategy in the case of the advice manuals, it may well not be in the fictional texts. But, I would argue, serious attention to the novels exposes the same type of critique.

Certainly, chick-lit novels feature scenes of characters giddily snapping up scarves and stilettos, of "communing with . . . the god of shopping" (Kinsella 35). As Becky Bloomwood effuses, it's all about

> that moment. That instant when your fingers curl round the handles of a shiny, uncreased bag—and all the gorgeous new things inside it become yours. What's it like? It's like going hungry for days, then cramming your mouth full of warm buttered toast. It's like waking up and realizing it's the weekend. It's like the better moments of sex. Everything else is blocked out of your mind. It's pure, selfish pleasure. (30)

But it never lasts. In a later shopping spree, the same character, seeking to cheer herself up, finds she's not quite as happy as she should be:

> Every time I add something to my pile, I feel a little whoosh of pleasure, like a firework going off. And for a moment, everything's all right. But then, gradually, the light and sparkles disappear and I'm left with cold dark blackness again. So I look feverishly around for something else. (237)

The "whooshes" of pleasure get shorter and shorter: "Why won't the pleasure stay?" she asks. "Why don't I feel happier?" (237). By the end, Becky says she is faced with this: "A huge conspicuous pile of stuff. Stuff I don't need. Stuff I can't pay for. Suddenly the sight of it all makes me feel sick" (240). This can hardly be taken as an endorsement.

Novels featuring Latina and South Asian protagonists further complicate chick lit's relation to global capitalism and consumerism. Eva Chen, writing about chick lit's expansion into China, has argued broadly that it addresses "a global sisterhood of financially and sexually confident cosmopolitan women who are increasingly conforming to Western defined standards of what it means to be a liberated, confident and sexually attractive woman, a meaning predicated on a seemingly pervasive and universally shared consumerist discourse of freedom of choice and individual consumption."[53] Attention to the texts of "the global chick lit," as she terms it, reveals otherwise. In *Dirty Girls Social Club*, the characters' reverence for brand-name goods may be taken less as a sign of their capitulation to aspirational spending than an indictment of an American society where superficial displays of apparent wealth secure class and ethnic belonging. One of the *sucias*, the "dirty girls" of Alisa Valdes-Rodriguez's novel, Lauren Fernández, describes herself as wearing a "navy blue discount Barami suit and three-year-old pumps with a hole in the sole" during a job interview where she surrenders to stereotypical assumptions that, as a Latina, she must speak Spanish just to land a job.[54] With "$15.32 in her bank account and student loans due in a month" (6), she thinks, "Sí, sí *I will be your spicy Carmen Miranda. I will dance the* lambada *in your dismal gray broadsheet.... Just* hire *me. I'll learn Spanish later*" (7). Her appearance as a fashionista is as much an imposture as her lie that she speaks Spanish, all a desperate effort to fit into a capitalist culture.

As Pamela Butler and Jinga Desai have argued, in novels featuring South Asian protagonists, such as *The Village Bride of Beverly Hills*, the protagonist's "inability to consume properly marks her as an ignored and unrecognized female subject; it is only when she learns to consume and create an ethnicized feminine identity through consumption that she is recognized by the other characters as equal."[55] The novel's heroine Priya Sohni arrives from Delhi for her arranged marriage to a Los Angeles resident with a trousseau filled with silk saris. At her receptionist job, however, her dress only augments her precarious position in the workplace. She complains, "It wasn't too hard to feel invisible; all day long, people stood around me and chatted as if I wasn't there."[56] Wearing the "light-blue-with-black-trim *salwar kameez*, one of the nicest outfits from my trousseau," she hoped coworkers "might comment on the exotica of my dress sense, but they said nothing" (48). Only after she receives instruction on buying clothes from a coworker does she become visible: "Now you look like you belong here!" (85), she tells Priya. Far from endorsing neoliberal feminism or economics, such novels offer a potent critique of a consumer capitalist culture that equates recognition with consumption, and of particular, socially sanctioned goods.

Economic uncertainty is mirrored in the pervasive mood of unease and insecurity among chick-lit heroines.[57] Far from being the "helpless girls, drunken, worrying about their weight" that Doris Lessing dismissed,[58] chick-lit protagonists voice the contextlessness and groundlessness they feel as subjects of a consumption-driven culture. Simon During has argued that since "precarity is an interiorized or spiritual as well as material condition" this "means that the novel silently stakes a further claim, namely that literature's capacity to *imagine* and *suggest* private existential depression and disorientation is also a mode of *perceiving* and *knowing* opaque precarious life."[59] While During was referring to novels in general, his claim has particular relevance for chick lit, because the first-person narrative position typical of chick-lit novels offers readers unparalleled access to the interiorized condition of precarity During describes.

For instance, Lauren Fernández, the Cuban American "dirty girl" in Valdes-Rodriguez's novel, confesses her anxieties about being exposed as a fraud. "Whenever possible, I dress as though I sprang from a completely different and much more normal set of circumstances. Nothing thrills me more than when people who don't know me assume I'm from a typical, moneyed Cuban family in Miami" (7)—or, better yet, a financially ascendant generic Hispanic. Her position entails loss of her identity: She writes a column called "My Life" marketed to the growing demographic of Hispanics. It's not based on her experiences as a Cuban American, but pitched broadly to an expanding consumer group. In marketing materials, the promotions department darkens her complexion to make her "look more like what they probably think a Latina is *supposed* to look like" (9). Her appearance is shaped to conform to an ideal that sells—and is sold. Bridget Jones articulates the sense of helplessness induced by the consumerist pressures to conform to idealized constructions of femininity: "I am a child of *Cosmopolitan* culture, have been traumatized by supermodels and too many quizzes and know that neither my personality nor my body is up to it if left to its own devices" (52). It may be easy to dismiss Bridget as weak, as a "helpless girl," as Lessing did, but it is worth considering her comment in relation to Gary Standing's observation that "those in the precariat lack self-esteem and social worth in their work [and] must look elsewhere for that esteem, successfully or otherwise."[60] When that source of esteem—consumption—originates in the same capitalist culture that devalues their work, Bridget and her ilk can hardly be blamed for voicing their despair (or, for that matter, drinking too much wine to blot it out).

Chick lit's emphasis on individual experience has led many feminist and Marxist critics to presume the texts value individualism over collectivism. Tasker and Negra argue that postfeminist culture is compatible with the free market economy for they share "individualist, acquisitive and transformative values."[61] Angela McRobbie has similarly claimed that postfeminist culture offers young women "female individualization and the new meritocracy at the expense of feminist politics."[62] Such arguments overlook the novels' invocation of community, particularly their emphasis on female friendship. Miniature versions of the collective dominate chick lit, from Bridget Jones's "urban family" to the "dirty girls social club" of Valdes-Rodriguez's novel, which offers an excellent example. Lauren Fernández's column, "My Life," is about "real girls with real problems" (110). Her columns, snippets of which open each chapter, recount her experiences but consistently include references to the lives of her fellow "dirty girls": public relations representative Usnavys, magazine publisher Rebecca, stay-at-home mom Sara, musician Amber, and television cohost Elizabeth. While Lauren's column is the unifying thread, the novel consists of individual chapters narrated by one "dirty girl" at a time. The result is a collection of individual women voicing shared concerns—career, relationship, marriage, domestic violence, sexuality, sexual identity, and ethnicity. The same could be said of the chick-lit genre considered as a whole: Collectively, the novels offer a chorus of voices conveying young women's precarious status. Rather than speaking uncritically about and as a uniform collective of young women, the texts articulate the differences among individual women within a system of global capitalism. Again, Valdes-Rodriguez's text is exemplary not simply because it showcases the individual voices of the five women, but because it foregrounds their differences as Latinas. The women vary in national origin—from Colombia, Cuba, Mexico, Puerto Rico—and in their allegiances to their heritage. Amber refashions herself as Cuicatl, finding success by singing about indigenous traditions in Spanish and Nahuatl, while, as we've seen, Lauren accommodates herself to being "Miss Berlitz the Token Hispanic in the name of employability" (13). The "dirty girls" differ in sexual orientation, skin color, religious affiliation, class position, and more.

Attending to the specific literary dimensions of the texts further undermines critiques of chick lit's bias toward individualism. The same first-person narrative voice that affords access to the internal mental or emotional dimensions of precarious existence also fosters reader identification. The apparent spontaneity and candor of diary-style entries in *Bridget Jones's Diary* or the confessional style of *Shopaholic*, *Devil Wears Prada*, and *Village Bride* "craft the impression that the protagonist is speaking directly to readers."[63] This gives the texts an unparalleled authenticity, often cited as the source of chick lit's popularity. The texts appeal—in part—to an audience of women who see parallels to their own experiences and find emotional resonance in the protagonists' reactions.[64] The result is a virtual community of women—fictional and real—comforted by the knowledge that they are not alone in their insecurity and even isolation.[65] As chick-lit author Laura Zigman explained the effects of her own reading:

> In my heartbroken, urban, single, postfeminist mood I felt like there was a lot going on with women that no one was really talking about. . . . We had a lot of freedom and a lot of choices, but there was a price. People were lonely. . . .

But you would pick up these books and go, Okay, I am not mad, I am not the only loser in the world who feels lonely.[66]

The real women reading chick lit, however, may not share in the solutions afforded their fictional compatriots. Critics have charged that any cultural criticism postfeminist texts might offer is undermined by supplying narrative resolutions unique to their individual protagonists that simply support the status quo. "Weddings, birthings, and returns to the bosom of the family are all too often the substance of the endings of such novels," Imelda Whelehan concedes, "even when the implication of the rest of the novel has been that for young women with means and style there is an infinite number of possibilities beyond marital felicity and the nuclear family."[67] In *Village Bride*, for instance, Priya rejects a new opportunity for a job in cable television to resolve marital issues with her husband. Bridget Jones escapes another on-the-job disaster only with Mark Darcy's assistance. Fielding's novel ends with Darcy saving Bridget's family from possible financial ruin brought on by her mother's ill-fated romance and returning her to her husband before expressing his love for Bridget. Such examples would appear to support Whelehan's contention, but only by failing to attend to the literary dimensions of the texts. Fielding's novel not only revives the plot of Jane Austen's *Pride and Prejudice* but adheres to narrative conventions for a comedy: All ends happily. The resolutions of other chick-lit examples sustain the positive resolutions inherent to the genre without capitulating to traditionally feminine expectations for their protagonists. Unlike Bridget Jones, Lauren Fernández needs no career help from her boyfriend. Instead, she secures regular employment for him. At the end of *Devil Wears Prada*, Andy tells her overbearing boss off in a spectacularly satisfying rant and, nonetheless, secures a job as a writer for *The Buzz*. Her fairytale ending rests on finding a career, not romance. Becky Bloomwood finds both: As *Shopaholic* ends, she has a boyfriend and a new job on *Morning Coffee*. The final page of the novel is a letter from Endwich Bank thanking her for a recent deposit.

Ultimately, it is worth remembering that these are novels, not political primers. As Harzewski contends, "It is not fully fair to judge chick lit as a template for some twenty-first-century transnational feminist how-to guide."[68] Instead, these books offer fictional resolutions that provide temporary escape rather than actual solutions. Like Lauren Fernández, the working girl readers of chick lit turn to their imaginations for relief. In one confrontation with her "nervous twit of an editor" (103), Lauren fantasizes about "the buttery things in the windows of the Kenneth Cole store" (107). Chastised for being too opinionated and combative, in what she points out *is* an opinion column, she finds refuge in thoughts of "*New shoes. New comforter. Breathe*" (108). She does not act on her thoughts of shopping, any more than on her desire to sigh or roll her eyes (110). Confronted with her parents' marital difficulty, Bridget Jones imagines she's in a classic chick flick:

> "Couldn't we all talk this through together over lunch?" I said, as if this were *Sleepless in Seattle* and lunch was going to end up with Mum and Dad holding hands and me winking cutely at the camera, wearing a luminous rucksack. (47–48)

Note that Fielding acknowledges the shaping role of film on popular perception, while conveying Bridget's recognition that her life will never conform to its fictions. While, as she famously claims of the BBC's *Pride and Prejudice* miniseries, "the basis of my own addiction, I know, is my simple human need for Darcy to get off with Elizabeth" (246), Bridget has no desire to see their romance in real life: "I would hate to see Darcy and Elizabeth in bed, smoking a cigarette afterward. That would be unnatural and wrong and I would quickly lose interest" (247).[69] These words, voiced by a fictional character in a novel that takes its plot from Austen's, are cheekily and self-referentially directed at a knowing audience of chick-lit readers who are equally immersed in popular culture and equally cognizant of the difference between fiction and reality.

That is not to say, however, that chick-lit novels should be dismissed as escapist fantasies. To the contrary: Underneath the surface glitz and glamour of chick lit rests a provocative critique of consumer culture. The genre's naturalism means the novels, considered collectively, offer a rich portrait of the young, female precariat, one that provides the possibility for reflection on their condition, not simply by the working girls who read them but by all who consume them.

Notes

1. Caroline J. Smith, *Cosmopolitan Culture and Consumerism in Chick Lit* (New York: Routledge, 2008), 506.

2. See Suzanne Ferriss and Mallory Young, Introduction, *Chick Lit: The New Woman's Fiction*, ed. Suzanne Ferriss and Mallory Young (New York: Routledge, 2006), 1–16. Stephanie Harzewski offers a more detailed definition: "A characteristic chick-lit novel features a first-person narrative of a twenty- or thirty-something, white, middle- or upper-middle-class, never-married, childless, Anglo or American, urban, college-educated, heterosexual career woman engaged in a seriocomic romantic quest or dating spree." *Chick Lit and Postfeminism* (Charlottesville: University of Virginia Press, 2011), 29.

3. See Ferriss and Young, *Chick Lit*, as well as Harzewski, *Chick Lit and Postfeminism*, 3, and Smith, *Cosmopolitan Culture*, 2.

4. Rachel Donadio, "The Chick-Lit Pandemic," *New York Times* March 19, 2006, accessed March 19, 2006, http://www.nytimes.com/2006/03/19/books/review/19donadio.html?_r=1&ref=helenfielding.

5. Harzewski, *Chick Lit and Postfeminism*.

6. Ibid., 155.

7. Yvonne Tasker and Diane Negra, eds., *Interrogating Postfeminism: Gender and the Politics of Popular Culture* (Durham, N.C.: Duke University Press, 2007).

8. Chris Holmlund, "Postfeminism from A to G," *Cinema Journal* 44 (Winter 2005): 117.

9. Sarah Projansky, *Watching Rape: Film and Television in Postfeminist Culture* (New York: New York University Press, 2011), 88.

10. Rosalind Gill, "Postfeminist Media Culture: Elements of a Sensibility," *European Journal of Cultural Studies* 10 (2007): 147–166.

11. Tasker and Negra, *Interrogating Postfeminism*, 2. See also Diane Negra, *What a Girl Wants? Fantasizing the Reclamation of Self in Postfeminism* (New York: Routledge, 2009), 5–9.

12. Tasker and Negra, *Interrogating Postfeminism*, 2, 4, 7.

13. Ferriss and Young, *Chick Lit*, 4.

14. Harzewski, *Chick Lit and Postfeminism*, 51.

15. Ibid., 52.

16. Kate Zernike, "Oh, to Write a 'Bridget Jones' for Men: A Guy Can Dream," *New York Times* February 22, 2004, 9.1.

17. Jessica Jernigan, "Slingbacks and Arrows: Chick Lit Comes of Age," *Bitch* (Summer 2004): 71.

18. Elizabeth Merrick, Introduction, *This Is Not Chick Lit: Original Stories by America's Best Women Writers* (New York: Random House, 2006), vii–viii.

19. Harzewski, *Chick Lit and Postfeminism*, 50.

20. Smith, *Cosmopolitan Culture*, 15.

21. Joanne Hollows, *Feminism, Femininity and Popular Culture* (Manchester: Manchester University Press, 2000), 115. Such criticism further reflects common denigrations of consumption as materialistic or acquisitive, in opposition to production, overlooking the role of consuming goods in shaping identity and social relations. See Daniel Miller, *Material Culture and Mass Consumption* (Oxford, U.K.: Blackwell, 1987).

22. In fact, some chick-lit novels, including those of one of its most popular authors, Jennifer Weiner, make little overt reference to contemporary consumer culture.

23. Tasker and Negra, *Interrogating Postfeminism*, 2.

24. Elizabeth Hale has described this as "underling lit" or "assistant lit." See Elizabeth Hale, "Long-Suffering Professional Females: The Case of Nanny Lit," in Ferriss and Young, *Chick Lit*, 103.

25. Gary Standing, *The Precariat: The New Dangerous Class* (London: Bloomsbury Academic, 2011), 9.

26. Mika LaVaque-Monty, "Finding Theoretical Concepts in the Real World: The Case of the Precariat," in *New Waves in Political Philosophy*, ed. Boudewijn de Bruin and Christopher F. Zurn (New York: Palgrave Macmillan, 2009), 107. He offers a concise historical summary of the precariat's origins (106–109). Standing identifies May 1, 2001, as the date of their first "stirrings" in Italy and "EuroMayDay" 2005 as the first stirrings of the global movement (1). Standing stipulates a more precise definition of the precariat as people lacking seven forms of labor-related security (10–13).

27. Standing, *Precariat*, 13. Richard Seymour has taken Standing to task for describing the precariat as "the new dangerous class," as his book's subtitle announces, despite claiming in the text itself that its members cannot be identified with one class. Seymour traces the tendency to cast the group in class terms to the Marxist definition of classes as antagonistic. By contrast, he urges understanding the precariat as "a particular kind of populist interpellation which operates on a real, critical antagonism in today's capitalism." See Richard Seymour, "We Are All Precarious—On the Concept of the 'Precariat' and its Misuses," *New Left Project,* February 10, 2012, accessed November 8, 2012, http://www.newleftproject.org/index.php/site/article_comments/we_are_all_precarious_on_the_concept_of_the_precariat_and_its_misuses.

28. LaVaque-Monty, "Finding Theoretical Concepts," 107.

29. Ibid., 107–108.

30. Standing, *Precariat*, 14.

31. Seymour, "We Are All Precarious."

32. Simon During, "From the Subaltern to the Precariat," *2011 ELLAK International Conference Proceedings*: 128.

33. Standing, *Precariat*, 16.

34. LaVaque-Monty notes that while the precariat exists in America, and has for longer than in Europe, "there is nothing understood as the precariat in the United States, nor is there a collective actor—a social movement, say—we might understand as sufficiently similar to the European movement" ("Finding Theoretical Concepts," 113).

35. Ibid., 108.

36. BBC, "The Great British Class Survey: Results," BBC, April 3, 2013, accessed April 4, 2013, http://www.bbc.co.uk/science/0/21970879.

37. Mike Savage et al. "A New Model of Social Class? Findings from the BBC's Great British Class Survey Experiment," *Sociology* 47 (April 2013): 243, accessed April 4, 2013, http://soc.sagepub.com/content/47/2/219.

38. Toby Miller, "Culture+Labour=Precariat," *Communication and Critical/Cultural Studies* 7:1 (2010): 99.

39. Lauren Weisberger, *The Devil Wears Prada* (New York: Anchor Books, 2006) (hereafter cited in text).

40. Helen Fielding, *Bridget Jones's Diary* (London: Picador, 1996), 3 (hereafter cited in text).

41. Quoted in Miller, "Culture," 98.

42. Standing, *Precariat*, 60.

43. Ibid., 60–61.

44. Stephanie Coontz, "The Myth of Male Decline," *New York Times*, September 30, 2012, SR5.

45. Sophie Kinsella, *Confessions of a Shopaholic* (New York: Dell, 2001), 62–63 (hereafter cited in text).

46. Smith, *Cosmopolitan Culture*, 14.

47. In the transition from literature to film, such distinctions are lost, which may partly explain the film's dismal reception. Also note that the novel anticipates a spate of "recession-lit" offerings, such as Sarah Strohmeyer's *The Penny Pinchers Club* and Amy Silver's *Confessions of a Reluctant Recessionista*. See Harzewski, *Chick Lit and Postfeminism*, 22.

48. See Seymour, "We Are all Precarious." Tayyah Mahmud, applying Michel Foucault's construct of governmentality to debt, has argued, "The prescription of subjectivity to obtain interiorization of the market's goal in the context of precariatization of labor is accomplished through generalization of debt" (482). He adds that, "tying everyday practices," such as the purchase of goods, "to global financial networks . . . induces the self-fashioning of financial subject positions and identities" (484). Workers and consumers become entrepreneurial subjects responsible for managing their own human capital. See Tayyah Mahmud, "Debt and Discipline," *American Quarterly Special Issue: Race, Empire, and the Crisis of the Subprime*, ed. Paula Chakravartty and Denise Ferreira da Silva, 64 (September 2012): 469–494.

49. Helaine Olen, *Pound Foolish: Exposing the Dark Side of the Personal Finance Industry* (New York: Portfolio/Penguin, 2011), 1.

50. Olen further observes the dominant role of women writers in the personal finance field, citing Sylvia Porter's *Money Book*, Jane Bryant Quinn's *Making the Most of Your Money*, and Kathy Kristof's *Complete Guide to Dollars and Sense* (34).

51. Nancy Trejos, *Hot (Broke) Messes: How to Have Your Latte and Drink It Too* (New York: Hachette, 2010).

52. Jessica Lyn Van Slooten, "Fashionably Indebted: Conspicuous Consumption, Fashion and Romance in Sophie Kinsella's Shopaholic Trilogy," in Ferriss and Young, *Chick Lit*, 237.

53. Eva Chen, "Shanghai(ed) Babies: Geopolitics, Biopolitics and the Global Chick Lit," *Feminist Media Studies* 12.2 (2012): 221.

54. Alisa Valdes-Rodriguez, *The Dirty Girls Social Club* (New York: St. Martins, 2003), 7 (hereafter cited in text).

55. Pamela Butler and Jigna Desai, "Manolos, Marriage, and Mantras: Chick-Lit Criticism and Transnational Feminism," *Meridians* 8 (February 2008): 12.

56. Kavita Daswani, *The Village Bride of Beverly Hills* (New York: Plume, 2005), 47 (hereafter cited in text).

57. Imelda Whelehan notes the "almost palpable sense of anxiety emanating from many volumes of chick lit." See *The Feminist Bestseller* (New York: Palgrave Macmillan, 2005), 162.

58. "Bainbridge Denounces Chick-Lit as 'Froth,'" *Guardian Unlimited* August 23, 2001, accessed August 24, 2001, http://books.guardian.co.uk/bookerprize2001/story /0,1090,541335,00.html.

59. During, "Subaltern," 137.

60. Standing, *Precariat*, 21.

61. Tasker and Negra, *Interrogating Postfeminism*, 7.

62. Angela McRobbie, "Post-Feminism and Popular Culture," *Feminist Media Studies* 4 (2004): 258.

63. Ferriss and Young, *Chick Lit*, 4.

64. As novelist Jenny Colgan pointed out, however, lovelorn single women were not alone among the millions who purchased copies of *Bridget Jones's Diary*. See Fichara Gibbons, "Stop Rubbishing Chick Lit, Demands Novelist," *Guardian* August 21, 2003.

65. Whelehan sees this contemporary desire for community as echoing "the feelings of women in the 1960s and 1970s as communicated through popular feminism." She contends that reading chick lit to "feel part of a community suggests a longing for an inclusive female sphere of experience" (*Feminist Bestseller*, 177).

66. Quoted in Smith, *Cosmopolitan Culture*, 6.

67. Whelehan, *Feminist Bestseller*, 202. Jane Elliott defines the genre itself as "conservative," as "largely devoted to the easy narrative resolution of dilemmas familiar from earlier feminist fiction." See "Feminist Fiction," *The Cambridge Companion to American Fiction after 1945*, ed. John N. Duvall (Cambridge: Cambridge University Press, 2012), 152.

68. Harzewski, *Chick Lit and Postfeminism*, 192.

69. This sets chick-lit protagonists apart from the many readers who consume the apparently endless stream of contemporary "sequels" to *Pride and Prejudice* that imagine Mr. and Mrs. Darcy definitively coupled, with titles like *Mr. Darcy Presents His Bride: A Sequel to Jane Austen's Pride and Prejudice, Darcy and Elizabeth: Days and Nights at Pemberley*, and *Mr. Darcy's Daughters*. Unlike romance fiction, chick lit does not typically end in marriage, suggesting shifting attitudes among contemporary women about the inevitability—and desirability—of marriage. See Harzewski, *Chick Lit and Postfeminism*, 73.

CHAPTER 10

After Ever After

*Bethenny Frankel, Self-Branding,
and the "New Intimacy of Work"*

SUZANNE LEONARD AND DIANE NEGRA

At the helm of a dizzying array of ventures, reality television star cum lifestyle expert Bethenny Frankel has fomented an empire by lending her name to a constellation of products geared toward women. This output includes cookbooks; diet, exercise and lifestyle advice; chick lit; workout accessories; online personal training; four reality shows; a daytime talk show; and most famously Skinnygirl, a brand moniker attached to low-calorie alcoholic drinks, a daily cleanse, nonalcoholic drink mixes, nutrition bars, lotions, and shapewear. Frankel's tour-de-force economic position was perhaps best evidenced by her sale of Skinnygirl Margarita to Jim Beam in 2011 for a reported $100 million, a feat that landed her on the cover of *Forbes*. As this essay will explore, Frankel's stabilization as an icon coincided with a sharp increase in reality television's encouragement for stars to monetize their so-called "personal lives" and with a distinctive phase of capitalistic production where entrepreneurship of the self reaped a compelling combination of economic and affective reward. In this respect, what may appear as the rising stardom of a singular, idiosyncratic personality should instead be read as having particular ramifications for feminized media culture. Dovetailing with an early-twenty-first-century cultural moment dominated by a worldwide economic recession, Frankel's success illustrates that economies of self can be leveraged as platforms on which to model female self-actualization, a pathway that inevitably involves the accrual of monetary gain.

Frankel is thus a fitting subject of investigation for the dilemmas that typify this stage of capitalist self-production.

In addition to underscoring contemporary media's fascination with rags-to-riches stories, Frankel's trajectory illustrates reality television's aptitude for showcasing contemporary labor economies. As Heather Hendershot has postulated, "The vast majority of reality TV focuses in some way on work. . . . Work is work. Play is work. Banter is work. Sex is work."[1] Because Frankel's brand concretized itself through a circuit of successful television ventures—and became sharper, more distinctive, and more lucrative with each successive iteration—her story offers a primer on twenty-first-century branding cultures and the vagaries of marketing the self. Speaking to an increasingly prominent cultural phenomenon of female celebrity entrepreneurialism, Frankel typifies the dynamic identified by Alice E. Marwick: "The ideal of entrepreneurship expanded beyond the technology industry into other aspects of life, including our most personal understandings of selfhood, relationships, and the body."[2]

In her study of contemporary brand culture, Sarah Banet-Weiser notes that, "Postfeminism, in practice, is often individualized and constructed as personal choice rather than collective action; its ideal manifestation, in turn, is not struggle for social change, but rather capacity for entrepreneurship."[3] Frankel aptly embodied this tenet; yet, as a powerful female entrepreneur who willingly commercialized herself and lived many of her heartaches in the public eye, she simultaneously risked compromising intimacy for professionalism. This point was made particularly acutely in late 2012 when, after the reality show that had alternatively touted and queried Frankel's sanguine marital status featured a number of significant domestic fractures with husband Jason Hoppy, the couple announced their separation and intention to divorce. As this story line demonstrated, well-worn tropes such as that of the "woman who works too hard to find love" compete with Frankel's positioning as an autonomous corporate agent. Her performance of entrepreneurial zeal, coupled with her often fraught emotional life, thus engaged in the most modern of emotional economies, reflecting its terms of compromise and success. Treating Frankel as a case study reveals the sometimes hidden fissures that result from the commodification of intimate life. These points of fracture speak to the seemingly endless cycles of making and unmaking that animate an early-twenty-first-century postfeminist media culture fond of pairing stories of female financial vitality with punishment—reminders that the female lifestyle mogul must always be undeserving and flawed, even though (or because) her fortune is at least partially sourced by her personal life. Notably, Frankel is not subject to the same kinds of hagiographic conventions that structure the celebrity of a "moral entrepreneur" like Jamie Oliver or even potentially Facebook's Sheryl Sandberg, both of whom fortify discourses of public advocacy and value through exemplary personal lives.[4]

Reality Television and the Rise of the Self-Made Woman

Bethenny Frankel's status as a multiplatformed media megabrand was hardly assured by her appearance on the reality television circuit. While the promise that reality subjects will ascend from obscurity to celebrity is often attended by a fantasy of class mobility, in Frankel's case this narrative has been peppered with persistent reminders of her economic instability and troubled upbringing. Such stories nevertheless humanized Frankel and helped to constitute her lasting appeal as an "unlikely" millionaire. When giving accounts of her success, Frankel suggests that she fought the "planned obsolescence" endemic to reality stars, resisting the sort of flash-in-the-pan fame that is a hallmark of what Graeme Turner, et al., call the "celebrity commodity."[5] The nature and characters of the programs in which Frankel appeared since the start of her mid-2000s celebrity trajectory nevertheless offer an object lesson on how moving through the paces of reality celebrity denotes increased stature in terms of both fame and financial accumulation. Shifting from reality competition show to docu-soap to centering a cluster of series under her own name, Frankel's rise offers a glimpse into the labor economies of reality television, wherein the ability to successfully synergize the self represents the apotheosis of a branding effort. Frankel's distinctive personality, raw energy, and naked ambition clearly served her well in such economies, yet these traits paradoxically threatened to derail her progress in her first bid for recognition, as a contestant on *The Apprentice: Martha Stewart*.

In this 2005 spinoff of Donald Trump's popular reality competition, Martha Stewart judged a series of contestants vying for a job at Martha Stewart Living Omnimedia, a competition that Frankel—at that time a natural food chef running a company called Bethenny Bakes—almost won. (Her trademark work ethic already on display in the series' first monologue introduction, Frankel attests, "There's no one who wants to be here more than I do.") Stewart's successful corporatization of domestic labors would seem a natural model for Frankel. Yet, when faced with Frankel in the series, Stewart was mildly aghast at her exuberance. The competition ultimately pitted Frankel against Dawna Stone, a blond WASP-ish type who maintained that her primary virtue was her ability to stay composed and who repeatedly highlighted her difference from

Frankel, whom she called out for being "hyper" and "easily excitable." Whereas Stewart initially praised Frankel's "determination," this praise turned damning in the season finale, when the competition turned on the question of whether Frankel would "fit in" at Stewart's company. In explaining her rationale for dismissing Frankel in favor of Stone, Stewart said, "You feel you have to make a physical impression, which is really not terribly necessary at Martha Stewart Living Omnimedia." Stewart's characterization of Frankel's body and the dispositions it suggests was prescient in that embodiment came to represent a defining feature of Frankel's brand, as later indicated by her "Skinnygirl" label. More immediately, however, Stewart's comments betrayed her predilection for refined, reserved, upper-class white femininity and indicate how Stewart's wholly raced and classed brand was a poor fit for Frankel, an outspoken (if self-deprecating) careerist who is often read as Jewish.[6] Unlike Stewart, Frankel's image has not been that of a domestic maven but instead has demonstrated the attitudes and aptitudes that reality television formats tend to reward, which include "authenticity," "ordinariness," and "drive."[7] Stewart's critique of Frankel points out the anachronism of relying on notions of gentility and reserve as the preferred terms for normative female self-presentation and, in hindsight, position Stewart as out of touch with a zeitgeist in which unabashed ambition, peppered with a can-do ethic, represent foundational tenets of neoliberal entrepreneurialism.

Outspoken displays of personality like Frankel's have, in fact, subsequently come to dominate feminized popular culture in the twenty-first century, a recognition that Frankel capitalized on with the publication of her first novel, the 2012 chick-lit offering, *Skinnydipping*, a thinly veiled roman à clef about her experiences with Stewart. Sporting a cover photo that features Frankel's torso and the bottom half of her face, the book's prominent story line focuses on a female protagonist whose "loud mouth and tell-it-like-it-is style," gets her into trouble when she appears on a reality show hosted by a "domestic goddess." (In yet another iteration of brand synergy, the title of the novel coyly calls on Frankel's lucrative marketing of the "skinny" label; see Figure 10.1).

Drive and desire likewise constitute the hallmarks of the NBC-owned Bravo network where Frankel saw her star rise when she was cast, in 2008, in *The Real Housewives of New York*. As the 2003 originator of *Queer Eye for the Straight Guy*, wherein a group of gay men lend fashion and grooming advice to ill-attired and domestically challenged straight men, Bravo built its brand around unscripted lifestyle programming intended to appeal to upwardly mobile consumers it dubbed "affluencers." The brain child of former Bravo president Lauren Zalaznik, the affluencer has been, as Erin Copple-Smith explains, "viewed

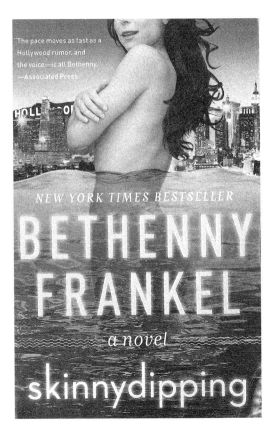

FIGURE 10.1. *Skinnydipping* is Bethenny Frankel's roman à clef, her contribution to the genre of chick lit.

as an audience member with a great deal of cultural capital," a heavy consumer of upscale lifestyle products with the capacity to "influence culture as a taste maker."[8]

Since the success of *Queer Eye*, the network has gravitated to programming that features professionally successful women who corporatize domestic, aesthetic, and affective labors and simultaneously manage taste cultures, as evidenced for example by *Kathy Griffin: My Life on the D List* (2006–2010), *Tabitha Takes Over* (2008–2013), *The Millionaire Matchmaker* (2008–), and *The Rachel Zoe Project* (2008–). Bravo's dominance in programming content for women in the 18–49 range should likewise be credited to its savvy use of cross-promotion, and its adept use of social media to build brand awareness through multiplatformed markets. In addition to the blogs, tweets, and public appearances that have come to be mainstays of reality celebrity, "Bravolebrities" have made guest appearances on one another's shows, as well as routinely appearing on *Watch What Happens Live* with Andy Cohen, the chatty, five-night-a-week sit-down that extended viewer access to Bravo's stars.

Frankel's successful tenure with the Bravo network, which included the spinoff series *Bethenny Getting Married?* (2010) and *Bethenny Ever After* (2011–2012), can be attributed in part to the synergy between her lifestyle brand and the sort of educated, upwardly mobile, cosmopolitan consumer that Bravo marketed itself toward. Frankel's brash and unabashed self-presentation, in other words, perfectly matched Bravo's brand identity, and Bravo's alliance with Frankel had a sort of airtight corporate logic insofar as Frankel herself would come to represent a media empire that is, like Bravo, highly proficient at cross-promoting various lifestyle products across multiple platforms.[9] The rewarding of Frankel with her own show(s) speaks to the dictates of niche marketing in the early-twenty-first-century television economy, as well as to Frankel's appeal to female consumers. According to publicity reports, during the initial seasons of *The Real Housewives of New York*, Bravo asked viewers which network personalities they wanted to see more of, and what story lines they were eager to see them in, and Frankel's single-girl story line scored highly in both categories.[10]

Brand Logics and Tie-In Products

Frankel's appearance for three seasons (2008–2010) as the token single girl in *The Real Housewives of New York City*, her stint as a prospective bride on *Bethenny Getting Married?* and her trials as a new wife, mother, and mega businesswoman in *Bethenny Ever After* worked synergistically with the Bravo brand in terms of its market logic, emotional tenor, and attempt to corporatize and cross-promote its stars. Tracing this trajectory, it bears mentioning that *The Real Housewives of New York City* was the second installation of the *Real Housewives* franchise but arguably the first one to foreground product development, an innovation for which Frankel and her handlers should be given significant credit. On the show, Frankel navigated a rocky love life, worked as a natural foods chef, and plotted the branding and release of the Skinnygirl margarita, while participating in the competitive intrafemale dynamics that have now come to define the series at large. Because Frankel's initial appearances on *The Real Housewives of New York* were framed by her career ambitions and dating travails, her flavor of product development was apt in terms of her characterization. Thanks to iconic series such as *Sex and the City* (1998–2004), the scenario of single women drinking cocktails in a bar has served as a hallmark for postfeminist culture. Frankel's object choice—a low-calorie, ready-to-serve alcoholic beverage marketed to women—thus fit squarely not only with her persona but also in a postfeminist moment that read such products as a metonym for sophisticated and urbane femininity.[11]

Frankel's solo career likewise capitalized on recognizable postfeminist trends. Unexpectedly pregnant and planning a quickie wedding, Frankel earned her own show, *Bethenny Getting Married?* a development that further confirms the stronghold that marriage programming has had in glutted markets, where it has remained a lucrative subgenre and staple of reality television specifically, and women's media culture more broadly. Much like any stereotypical chick-lit heroine, Frankel was a self-deprecating urbanite at the time, a media professional aspiring to greater material wealth and status. Making adept use of postfeminist media predecessors, the depiction of Frankel's station in New York as a prospective bride and rising media celebrity mimicked the narrative pleasures of chick lit and the visual fantasies of the chick flick, wherein access to the glamour of commodity culture sets the terms for visions of romance and femininity. Marked by a revelry in consumerism and participation in a lifestyle culture grounded in the belief in self-fashioning, Frankel's marital and domestic narrative existed in accordance with the principles of "late heterosexuality," which literary critic Stephanie Harzewski identifies as a condition of late capitalism wherein business-based calculations inform the most intimate arenas of everyday life. As Harzewski writes, "It is not quite hyperbole to say that the chick-lit protagonist can only experience romance, desire, or self-esteem through commodities,"[12] a characterization that similarly applies to Frankel.

Frankel's most famed commodity is her signature initiative Skinnygirl, a brand that explicitly calls attention to the female body and in so doing perfectly encapsulates the pressures and potentials of posfeminist subjecthood. As Rosalind Gill writes, "The body is presented simultaneously as women's source of power, and as always already unruly and requiring constant monitoring, surveillance, disciplining, and remodeling (and consumer spending) in order to conform to ever narrower judgments of female attractiveness."[13] As a moniker, "Skinnygirl" flaunts *and* disciplines the body, reminding women that the body's shape is paramount in defining participation in feminine citizenship. The product positions drinking as a measured indulgence, hence establishing an obvious syllogism where thinness not only equals success and self-control, but also establishes one's worth *as* a postfeminist subject, entitled to participate in lifestyle events like having cocktails, dining out with friends, and going on dates. (Such activities were mainstays of *Real Housewives* series content as well as featured prominently in Frankel's solo ventures).

On a broader scale, Skinnygirl set the terms for subsequent *Real Housewives* iterations in that product tie-ins would come to be a defining feature of the franchise writ large. According to a 2012 *Huffington Post* article that reviewed all seven of the housewives' shows, 42 percent of the housewives launched their own product lines and brands, which include clothing, makeup, shoes, handbags, beauty products, advice books, foods and drinks, fashion lines, vacation sites, and real estate agencies.[14] Housewives' products are touted on the shows and reinforced in other social media venues including blogs and personal websites. Despite this crowded commodity field, Frankel's seamless alignment of her product with her larger lifestyle nonetheless has been instructive in the broader branding landscape. No other Housewife who initiated product development while on the series has approached Frankel's level of success, likely because Skinnygirl invoked *the* key affective keynotes of postfeminist womanhood—namely girlishness, consumption, and aspirationalism in relation to love and career—and tied them directly to Frankel's life. In this way, the brand helped to establish the legitimacy of Frankel herself and the legitimacy of her brand. In short, Frankel both created and *was* the "Skinnygirl," a feedback loop that masterfully associated her brand identity with the affective qualities and class positioning that came to be associated with her as a person.

Relatedly, Frankel's introduction of a light cocktail proved prescient insofar as it complied with a trending national attention to obesity prevention. Though thinness has been a mandate for women for years, the Obama administration's explicit focus on health attempted to democratize this pursuit, an effort that also made its way into the spirits market. In fact, industry observers noted that Skinnygirl cocktails spawned a nationwide low-calorie liquor and dining trend, with mentions of the term "skinny" on menus at leading restaurant chains jumping 44 percent from 2012 to 2013.[15]

The dominance of Skinnygirl also throws into stark relief the attempts of other housewives to use their televised personas to shape product development. Personality-themed commodities from the original New York cast have included: manners advice (Luann de Lesseps's *Class with the Countess: How to Live with Elegance and Flair*), shapewear (Jill Zarin's "Skweez Couture") and parenting tips (Alex McCord and Simon van Kampen's *Little Kids, Big City: Tales from a Real House in New York City (With Lessons on Life and Love for Your Own Concrete Jungle)*). Yet, the failure to establish a legitimate association between the persona and the product stalled a number of these marketing efforts. For example, according to Jorie Lagerwey, New York housewife Ramona Singer's difficulties in branding can be traced to the lack of continuity in her product line (which has included offerings in domains as varied as skin care, jewelry, and wine), the perception that Singer is crazy, and the sense that her products are both tasteless and cheap.[16] Similarly, when *Real Housewives of New Jersey* star Teresa Giudice attempted to launch the "Fabellini," a sparkling wine, in 2012, she sought to brand herself with a hairpin differentiation from Frankel, writing on her blog that, "My drink of choice has always been the bellini, which is just sparkling wine and fruit nectar. It's naturally low in calories so you don't have to do anything to it or change the taste. You saw me drinking bellinis on the show before Bethenny ever did alcohol, when she was making her all-natural cookies."[17] While attempting to invoke her personal consumption habits as justification for going head to head with Frankel, and thus complying with contemporary branding norms whereby "real life" interests authenticate corporate identities and products, Giudice's efforts nevertheless read as both desperate and forced.

In contrast, Frankel's concomitant emergence as a celebrity, a health and lifestyle expert, and a powerful businesswoman corroborates Sarah Banet-Weiser's claim that successfully branding the self has become the means by which to successfully access the self. As Banet-Weiser writes, "In the contemporary context, the creation of the authentic self continues to be understood as a kind of moral achievement, but moralism itself has metamorphosed . . . where to truly understand and experience the authentic self is to 'brand the self.'"[18] Such understandings, in turn, have fueled the rhetoric of empowerment that has surrounded Frankel since Skinnygirl's rise and her own marriage and motherhood, milestones heralded as indicative that, having found a commercially viable "fit" between her interests and public demands, Frankel also successfully realized her "true self." Nowhere is this sentiment more evident than in her 2011 book, *A Place of Yes: 10 Rules for Getting Everything You Want out of Life*, where Frankel explained, "A place of yes is an 'It-will-happen-because-I'll-make-it-happen' kind of an attitude." It is the place you "always go back to. The real you."[19] (This "real you" mantra is also common in dieting and makeover discourse, where the objective is to release the self from the tyranny of a body that does not match the person's "true self.")

Like much postfeminist self-help, *A Place of Yes* employs an ethos of unabashed neoliberalism couched in pop psychology, a bootstrap narrative that perfectly accords with the sort of affective economies that confer moral or spiritual authority on women when they align financial success with compliance to heteronormative life stages. Adhering to such ideologies while also reinforcing them, Frankel garnered publicity for the book by embarking on a bus tour where she sat on a stage in front of large groups of women, had a Skinnygirl cocktail, and dished about her career, her marriage, and her child. Because, as Banet-Weiser explains, "work on the self, affect, and emotion"[20] constitutes the primary form of labor within early-twenty-first-century branding cultures, Frankel's celebrity dominance was also easily read in affective terms, a string of associations that lump psychological and spiritual well being in with purchasing power.

The tremendous advantage accrued to Frankel in such competitive economies reminds us that, paradoxically enough, having an accessible persona serves as its own form of superiority. By touting "on the go" products—which tend to emphasize versatility and affordability rather than fussy specialty items, commonsense eating habits rather than extreme diets or workout regimens, and shapewear rather than high fashion—Frankel positioned herself in solidarity with average women, an affiliation that suggests the extent to which populist rhetoric conveniently serves as a twenty-first-century tool to advantage the corporate businesswoman. As the cover model for *Self*'s 2012 "Summer Confidence Special," Frankel balanced authority with vulnerability, sharing advice on topics such as food, sex, fashion, exercise, and business: "Sometimes I go too far in being honest, but I don't know how to be any other way."[21] Her relatability to women similarly helped to establish Frankel's fitness as a talk show host. During *Bethenny*'s trial run on FOX in six cities during the summer of 2012, the offering brought in twice the number of female viewers than the time slot had in the previous summer, numbers that spoke to her wide appeal.[22] The democratizing aspects of Frankel's celebrity have in turn been underlined by her affiliation with other likeable women—Frankel's talk show was coproduced by American favorite Ellen DeGeneres, and the women's friendship was on particularly strong display in the months following Frankel's divorce announcement, when she made numerous appearances on *Ellen*. During these (sometimes tearful) conversations, Frankel plugged her own talk show as affording female guests and audience members an outlet to discuss similarly difficult topics.

Marriage and Motherhood as (Always Insecure) Postfeminist Milestones

Frankel's romantic and maternal trajectory undeniably incorporated the revered celebrity culture tenets of disclosure and transparency; she met and married Hoppy on camera, gave birth, negotiated marriage and motherhood, and played her divorce and its proceedings out in the public eye. Frankel's narrative was thus as much a story about her entrepreneurial successes as it was a testament to her sequencing through heteronormative life stages and willingness to paint these in recognizable postfeminist terms.[23] In this way, her story aligns with popular culture's consistent and singular narrative about privileged American women's lives, namely that their primary concerns include finding a suitable partner, securing self-actualizing work, and becoming a mother, as well as serving as a reminder of the tenuous quality of such milestones, particularly for driven professional women who are rendered as always at risk of losing "it all." In these ways, Frankel strikingly complies with Angela McRobbie's identification of an emergent "repertoire of woman-centered positions which will confirm and enhance the core values of the neoliberal project."[24]

The quest to "have it all" in the Frankel narrative inevitably included a high-profile wedding and a display of "working through" the mastery of emotional health in order to be "fit" for marriage, an issue of particular relevance for Frankel, whose aversion to commitment and skittishness about marriage have informed her characterization. Charting higher marriage rates among well-educated women, sociologist Andrew J. Cherlin noted in 2013 that the institution of marriage in the United States was in the midst of a status shift whereby its preeminent function became the corroboration of a classist and consumerist positioning. He explained that, "Today, marriage is more discretionary than ever, and also more distinctive. . . . It has become the capstone experience of personal life—the last brick put in place after everything is set. People marry to show their family and friends how well their lives are going, even if deep down they are unsure whether their partnership will last a lifetime."[25] In short, according to Cherlin, "Marriage has become a status symbol—a highly regarded marker of a successful personal life."[26] Frankel's use of marriage to shore up her psychological profile was necessitated by her previously unstable romantic trajectory. With a host of fears and anxieties about having been "damaged" by her own unhappy childhood, one failed marriage, and a string of broken engagements behind her, Frankel's personal life offered tensions and intrigues typical of commercialized femininity. As if to underline (and frankly, market) this instability, the title of Frankel's reality series, *Bethenny Getting Married?* openly invited speculation on its impossible premise, an impossibility that was realized when the marriage ultimately dissolved.

The conceptualization and depiction of marriage in Frankel's reality oeuvre has vividly borne out Cherlin's assessment that marriage serves as a social marker, since marriage and motherhood exist as part of a larger plotline of the therapeutic discovery of self-actualization. In this formulation, wifehood and motherhood serve merely as additional tasks to be completed in the pursuit of a "realized" life. In the pilot episode of *Bethenny Ever After?* Frankel frets about the travails of a later-in-life pregnancy but most significantly about her workload: "I have an obscene amount of things going on right now. I got engaged, got pregnant, have to plan a wedding. Just finished a month-long book tour. Launched Skinnygirl margarita. . . . It's not like I'm twenty-two and all this is happening. I'm thirty-nine."[27] As these comments attest, Frankel's romantic identities and affective bonds collapsed into her professional aspirations, an interlocking that was further reinforced when her participation in New York's Fashion Week was the first featured event on a television show supposedly devoted to her impending nuptials. Walking the runway in a benefit for heart health (its red theme a convenient tie-in with the signature color of the Skinnygirl brand) Frankel was shown surrounded by celebrities, paparazzi, and an adoring fiancé.

Frankel's televised offerings also centralized the most regularized of tropes pertaining to modern femininity, those of the supposed "work-life" balance. In a typical episode of *Bethenny Getting Married?* wedding planning competes with Frankel's myriad other obligations, including the hiring and training of a new assistant, public appearances to promote her books and Skinnygirl, and visits to her therapist. Additionally, in an attempt to get married before giving birth, Frankel's wedding is planned in four short weeks, an effort that coincides with the requirement that Frankel edit and rewrite *A Place of Yes* in the same time period. These pressures only intensified in *Bethenny Ever After*, where Frankel attempted to negotiate her rising celebrity, which demanded an ever-increasing number of public appearances. Added to these stresses were mounting tensions in her marriage, insecurities over being a new mother, navigations of fraught relations with her in-laws, and the difficulties of managing a media empire, while her entire staff worked out of her cramped Tribeca apartment. With classic postfeminist emphasis on the precarious nature of female achievement, the series illustrated such commitments as potentially destabilizing, with Frankel's high stress levels and frayed nerves threatening to erode her mental health.

One particularly rich story line in this vein, which likewise emphasized the transmedia potentials of reality television stardom, was Frankel's participation in the ABC reality competition show *Skating with the Stars* (2011) during the filming of season one of *Bethenny Ever After*. A requisite part of Frankel's work-life balance was then, literally, managing work on two reality shows simultaneously. Frankel multitasked even her reality television persona since grueling choreography and skating practice sessions functioned as the backstory to *Skating with the Stars* but comprised significant content for *Bethenny Ever After* as well. Frankel and her skating partner made it to the finals of *Skating with the Stars*, and the penultimate episode of her own series focused on the skating competition's finale in Malibu.

While this story line was presented in triumphant terms, Frankel's manic accumulation/work was nevertheless often pathologized, to the point that the relentless commodification of her identity became the source of always-imminent breakdown. That her class privilege is fraught with personal and professional panic was vividly demonstrated in the 2012 season of *Bethenny Ever After*, which showcased her failing marriage and the resignation of her longtime assistant, Julie, and included allusions to a lawsuit filed against Frankel by her ex-manager in the wake of her Jim Beam sale. Moreover, as in the previous season, Frankel remained dangerously thin (perhaps literalizing the pressures of being the "skinny girl" that her brand name touts). The self-branding of Frankel's identity and the pressure to maintain the postfeminist work-life balance on which the brand was built hence continually threatened to rupture. Frankel divulged in a January 2013 episode of *Ellen*, shortly after her divorce announcement, "I feel like a failure. . . . I wanted the fairytale. I thought I had it."[28]

The Female Mogul and the Marketization of Intimacy

A cluster of studies by Michael Sandel, Arlie Hochschild, and Melissa Gregg have sought to explore how rationalization, market logic, and work obligations inflect spheres once thought to be immune from such calculations.[29] In such a labor economy, there is scant distinction between labor and leisure, a conjunction literalized by the fact that the Skinnygirl company was for years housed in Frankel's apartment. In Frankel's mediated world, market concerns saturate literal and symbolic spaces, and all experiences are monetized as brand-making endeavors. Frankel's reality selfhood has maintained a conspicuously fine line between production and consumption, as is illustrated in the third episode of *Bethenny Getting Married?* when Frankel goes to an outer-borough Costco to sign books. When hardly anyone appears she begins shopping with gusto, appreciative of all the bargains.

In the Frankel reality oeuvre, conflations of market and intimacy realms were myriad: Frankel's assistant was her best friend, her baby allowed her to expand her brand identity, and her husband, while a necessary figure in the marital and maternal narratives of her celebrity, was also depicted as a potential liability to her efficiency and productivity (and further scripted as such during their lengthy divorce proceedings). Illustrating this conflation between emotion and profit, in the second episode of *Bethenny Getting Married?* Frankel repeatedly used the phrase "in love" to describe whether she thinks well of someone and can work with them in a business sense. In the series pilot Frankel even tells her dog, "You need to be a team player."

Maria Pramaggiore and Diane Negra read the Kardashian television empire (a significant antecedent to Frankel's reality oeuvre and one whose various series were often copromoted with Frankel's in international syndication on the E! Network) as balancing female unruliness with conservative ideation about the monetization of "family values."[30] While a full exploration of the many interconnections between the belabored female selves of these franchises is beyond our scope, we would observe that while the reality series associated with the Kardashian family and with Frankel trumpet the pleasures of unruly female speech and sexuality in a bid to appear unconstrained by social norms and taboos, there are also rigid affective rules in play in these domains. An unyielding devotion to marketplace labor is matched in such series by a strong social prohibition on "negativity," which interrelates with the celebration of wealth and privilege and diminishes the likelihood of any conceptual alternatives to neoliberal selfhood. In the 2010s, terms such as *haters* have emerged in public discourse, often working to police class resentment and insulate the privileged from it. These series' frequent use of such terms is part of a relentlessly affirmative discourse (a "place of yes," to cite the title of Frankel's autobiography) that positions Frankel and other reality moguls as having achieved a state of exemplary, transcendent selfhood that implicitly stands in contrast to the petty, primitive emotions of the lower orders. Frankel's brand instantiates the way that, as Barbara Ehrenreich has pointed out, positive thinking "has entered into a kind of symbiotic relationship with American capitalism."[31] However, it also endows that long-standing formulation with new energies that serve particular ends in a climate of dramatically escalating economic inequality. Indeed, the presentation of a ferocious work ethic alongside exceptional entitlement has become the hallmark attribute of a range of early-twenty-first-century female stars from Beyoncé to Gwyneth Paltrow.

Arlie Hochschild has noted that, "In the marketization of personal life, acts that were once intuitive and ordinary . . . now require the help of paid experts."[32] Frankel models a selfhood in compliance with the terms of Hochschild's account. Vividly illustrating the marketing of personal life, Frankel performed outsourcing to such figures as assistants, wedding planners, therapists, baby nurses, and nannies, while demonstrating an aggressive assertion of consumer entitlement to good service from such figures. Frankel's constant declarations of her right to such service modeled the exceptionalism of the privileged in an era of diminished service in which the figure of the embattled average consumer has come to achieve a certain ubiquity and is frequently juxtaposed to the "VIP" who purchases consumer dignity and staff attentiveness in such locations as airports, hotels, and department stores. "Customer service," as Emily Yellin has noted, "is a prolific contributor to the tone of our public life."[33]

Frankel's reliance on staff members and frequently expressed disappointment with their performance is thus a significant part of how her celebrity offers a means of measuring nebulous changes in American public culture. She claims to have fired assistant Max Meisel for asking for a condom from husband Jason Hoppy at a Skinnygirl event (a request she cites as inappropriate) yet Meisel was nevertheless routinely featured on *Bethenny Getting Married?* handling Frankel's personal business—Meisel's tasks included going shopping for "I just had a baby" underwear for Frankel and building a crib for daughter Bryn. As she staged a virtuoso performance of the outsourcing of the self, Frankel's brand also proliferated as a provider of services to the self for dieting and fashion-conscious women.

While epitomizing the aggressive self-branding that characterizes much early-twenty-first-century convergent media, a figure like Frankel illustrates an ambivalent neoliberalism and an anxious postfeminism. As exemplars of potent new forms of self-branding, affluent female moguls like Kim Kardashian and Frankel are nevertheless consistently threatened by suggestions that they are at risk of failing at femininity, unable to secure the concomitant professional and domestic achievements stereotypically formulated as "having it all." As female celebrities in an era of hypervisibility, they are closely tracked for signs of hypocrisy, and their activities are raked over for proof that their intimate lives are contaminated by market concerns. The most significant elements of their public personae turn on this particular issue, foregrounding specula-tion about Kardashian's short-lived "stunt" wedding to basketball player Kris Humphries and the perceived precarious state of Frankel's marriage as a result of her overdedication to work. Viewers have been regularly prompted to read Frankel as a self-involved "Type A" mogul whose emotional neglect of her spouse is literalized in recurrent paparazzi and tabloid images (see Figure 10.2).

The contrast between Frankel's pulled-together, expensively accessorized, yet casual appearance and gritty urban signifiers in the background of the shot illustrates another aspect of her persona—its urbanized/regionalized charac-ter. One of the preexisting typologies to which Frankel conforms is that of the "New York Broad," a well-established, semisanctioned exception to normative rules of female conduct.[34] In this formulation, New York is a "proving ground" for female "Type A's" but also the site of intimacy challenges for privileged and achieving women always under threat for neurosis. Frankel's "hustle" is thus always regionally inscribed and justified and this is one of the ways in which her self-presentation has been differentiated from other celebrities whose personae also focus on food and the body, such as Martha Stewart or Gwyneth Paltrow.

The rhetoric of dogged determination and propulsive self-will that marks Frankel's persona is typified by her assertion in *A Place of Yes* that, "It doesn't matter what anybody else thinks of your life. All that matters is what you think of it, and what you decide to make of it."[35] In many ways, Frankel's unapolo-getic statements of self-interest shade into a postfeminist solipsism, sentiments that starkly embody George Packer's account of the nature of contemporary

FIGURE 10.2. Typical
paparazzi photo of Bethenny
Frankel and Jason Hoppy,
emphasizing her "Type A"
identity. Used with permission of
Bauer-Griffin.

celebrity in a period of dramatically increasing inequality: "These new celebrities are all more or less start-up entrepreneurs, and they live by the hacker's code: ask forgiveness, not permission."[36]

Conclusion

Bethenny Frankel's endurance and format versatility give the lie to the notion that reality celebrity is always ephemeral. Her lucrative celebrity represents the (sometimes awkward) fusion of postfeminist romance narratives and their associated credos of partner scarcity for privileged white women with the marketization of intimacy. In the complex self-branding work that marks this celebrity category we can see evidence of the ambivalence that surrounds female entrepreneurialism in convergence culture.[37] Bethenny Frankel's carefully wrought commercial synergism consistently emerges as a threat to her domestic identities and in turn to the brand itself, paradoxically generating the ongoing dramatic tension that fuels her reality oeuvre. (Notably, in the

2012 phase of coverage relating to Frankel's divorce from Hoppy, talking points focused less on her marriage than it did on her amassed wealth. The split was consistently referred to as her "$100 million divorce," a phrase indicative of material rather than emotional cost.) Yet, the fact that she was undergoing such a period of tumult—and willing to reveal these struggles in female-oriented formats such as women's magazines and daytime talk shows—seemed to humanize Frankel as a worthy confidante for feminine audiences.[38] Frankel's presentation in reality and celebrity tabloid media stresses her hyper-entrepreneurial selfhood in deeply ambivalent ways, most consistently conveying the notion of self-branding as lucrative but dangerously so, a hazardous exercise with unpredictable costs.

Notes

1. Heather Hendershot, "Belabored Reality: Making It Work on *The Simple Life* and *Project Runway*," *Reality TV: Remaking Television Culture*, ed. Susan Murray and Laurie Ouellette (New York: New York University Press, 2009), 243–259.

2. Alice E. Marwick, *Status Update: Celebrity, Publicity and Branding in the Social Media Age* (New Haven: Yale University Press, 2014).

3. Sarah Banet-Weiser, *Authentic: The Politics of Ambivalence in a Brand Culture* (New York: New York University Press, 2012), 56.

4. See Joanne Hollows and Steve Jones, "'At Least He's Doing Something': Moral Entrepreneurship and Individual Responsibility in *Jamie's Ministry of Food*," *European Journal of Cultural Studies* 13(3) (2010): 307–322.

5. Graeme Turner, Frances Bonner, and P. David Marshall, *Fame Games: The Production of Celebrity in Australia* (Melbourne: Cambridge University Press, 2000).

6. Though Frankel's biological father was Jewish and her mother converted to the faith as a result of their marriage, the couple divorced when Frankel was a young child. Frankel does not self-identify as Jewish, though her fans occasionally refer to her as such.

7. Indeed, as if to emphasize her exasperation with normative domesticity, Frankel was represented as a reluctant hostess. In episode 2 of *Bethenny Getting Married?* she expresses concern about adding coffee cups to her wedding gift registry for fear that offering coffee after dinner would be an incentive for guests to stay too long.

8. Erin Copple-Smith, "'Affluencers' by Bravo: Defining an Audience through Cross Promotion," *Popular Communication: The International Journal of Media and Culture* 10:4 (2012): 291.

9. Further indication of such logics and the lengths to which industrial cross-promotion can go in the age of mega conglomeration was a passing reference to Frankel in the fourth season opener of the sitcom *Parks and Recreation*, in which the hyper-entrepreneurial Tom Haverford is questioned about the value of his frenetic efforts to network and merchandise on behalf of Entertainment 7Twenty, the corporation he has started with the equally jejune Jean-Ralphio Saperstein. In response he asks, "You think Bethenny Frankel sits behind a desk all day? She makes a hundred million dollars a year." Since NBC Universal

owns both Bravo and the network on which *Parks and Recreation* appears such a reference appears to be an in-house joke of a very particular kind.

10. Stephanie Clifford, "We'll Make You a Star (if the Web Agrees)," *New York Times,* June 5, 2010, BU1.

11. Skinnygirl was also part of a recasting of a once pejorative term as an accolade. "Skinny" is an aspirational target not just in Frankel's brand domain but also in the best-selling diet book *Skinny Bitch* (published in 2005, it achieved its peak success a few years later) and the trend toward naming clothing after this body ideal, notably "skinny jeans."

12. Stephanie Harzewski, *Chick Lit and Postfeminism* (Charlottesville: University of Virginia Press, 2011), 12.

13. Rosalind Gill, *Gender and the Media* (Cambridge, U.K.: Polity Press, 2007), 255.

14. Youyoung Lee and Liat Kornowski, "*The Real Housewives* of Bankruptcies, Businesses and Divorces by the Numbers," *Huffington Post,* January 25, 2013.

15. Ed Shultz and Maureen Morrison, "Restaurants Slim Down Cocktail Calorie Counts," *Advertising Age,* May 21, 2013. That these mass-market restaurant chains are also notorious for selling large portions of extraordinarily high-fat food speaks to the paradoxical logics of calorie counting and gorging in contemporary U.S. food culture.

16. Jorie Lagerwey, "*The Real Housewives'* Ramona Singer: Crazy, Offensive, and Feminist?" Paper Delivered at Society for Cinema and Media Studies Conference, Chicago, Ill., 2013.

17. Bravo Website, http://www.bravotv.com/the-real-housewives-of-new-jersey/season-4/blogs/teresa-giudice/the-knitting-circle?page=0,4, accessed May 27, 2013.

18. Banet-Weiser, 61.

19. Bethenny Frankel, *A Place of Yes: 10 Rules for Getting Everything You Want out of Life* (New York: Touchstone, 2011).

20. Ibid., 78.

21. "Frankly, Bethenny," *Self,* May 2012, 48–50.

22. Elizabeth McNeil, "Something to Talk About," *People,* July 30, 2012, 57.

23. Such personal milestones worked in tandem with branding imperatives in each of these phases. Frankel appeared on the covers of *Engagement 101* (before her wedding); *Parenting* and *People* (after the birth of her daughter); *Self* (while juggling marriage and motherhood); and *People* and *Redbook* (during her divorce proceedings).

24. Angela McRobbie, "Feminism, The Family and the New 'Mediated' Maternalism," *New Formations* 80/81 (2013): 121.

25. Andrew J. Cherlin, "In the Season of Marriage, A Question. Why Bother?" *New York Times,* April 27, 2013, SR7.

26. Ibid.

27. Although it is not our focus here, Frankel's consistent discursive emphasis on her age works to situate her within a postfeminist framework that highlights (always precarious) mastery of the female aging process. In this respect, her celebrity vividly bears out the notion of postfeminist "time crisis" discussed by Negra in *What a Girl Wants?: Fantasizing the Reclamation of Self in Postfeminism* (London: Routledge, 2008).

28. *The Ellen DeGeneres Show,* January 8, 2013.

29. See Melissa Gregg, *Work's Intimacy* (Cambridge, U.K.: Polity Press, 2011); Arlie Russell Hochschild, *The Outsourced Self: Intimate Life in Market Times* (New York: Metropolitan Books, 2012); Michael Sandel, *What Money Can't Buy: The Moral Limits of Markets* (New York: Farrar, Straus and Giroux, 2012).

30. Maria Pramaggiore and Diane Negra, "Keeping Up with the Aspirations: Commercial Family Values, Second Generation Celebrity and the Kardashian Family Brand," in *Reality Gendervision: Decoding Gender in Transatlantic Reality TV*, ed. Brenda Weber (Durham, N.C.: Duke University Press, 2014).

31. Barbara Ehrenreich, *Bright-Sided: How the Relentless Promotion of Positive Thinking Has Undermined America* (New York: Metropolitan, 2009), 7.

32. Hochschild, 12.

33. Emily Yellin, *Your Call Is (Not That) Important to Us: Customer Service and What It Reveals about Our World and Our Lives* (New York: Free Press), 2010, xii.

34. Previous iterations of the type range from the financially enterprising golddiggers of 1930s cinema to the cartoonish Fran Drescher and the despised female real estate mogul Leona Helmsley, and it informs, if in a more modulated way, the ambition and tenacity of more recent fictional characters ranging from Carrie Bradshaw to Liz Lemon.

35. Frankel, *A Place of Yes*.

36. George Packer, "Celebrating Inequality," *New York Times*, May 19, 2013, A21.

37. Similar ambivalent treatment has been accorded to actress Gwyneth Paltrow, nearly simultaneously voted *People*'s Most Beautiful Woman in the World and *Star* magazine's Most Hated Celebrity in 2013. Paltrow is Frankel's doppelganger and inverse; her website, celebrity appearances, and cookbooks position her as a comparable figure of brand synergism, yet she presents in a nearly opposite affective register, which has been characterized as elitist and preachy, thanks to her website Goop's breezy treatment of the sometimes exorbitant costs of the organic foods and other commodities she avows.

38. It was seemingly on this basis that Fox green-lighted the Frankel-hosted daytime talk show *Bethenny* in 2013. The subsequent cancelation of the series in February 2014 represented a rare commercial misstep for her though it should be noted that that particular genre and day part have proved treacherous in the post–*Oprah Winfrey Show* era, generating no truly successful new series and proving inhospitable for such established broadcast stars as Katie Couric in addition to Frankel. Nevertheless, we might speculate that with a persona so strongly associated with romantic decision making and the arduous work of relationships Frankel may have proved a problematic fit with a daytime talk genre that currently skews toward lighter approaches and concerns as exemplified in its most conspicuously enduring star, Ellen DeGeneres (who was herself a coproducer of *Bethenny*). Furthermore, the "tooth-and-nail" elements of Frankel's celebrity biography and demeanor may be as affectively out of sync with the empathy required of a talk show host. As if to rehearse the fact that reality venues provide the best accommodation for her celebrity, it was announced in October 2014 that Frankel would reprise her role on *The Real Housewives of New York*.

CHAPTER 11

Keeping Up with the Kardashians

Fame-Work and the Production
of Entrepreneurial Sisterhood

ALICE LEPPERT

The Kardashian family vaulted to stardom on a litany of reality shows beginning in 2007 and airing on E!—the U.S. cable channel focused on entertainment culture. These programs have molded sisters Kourtney, Kim, and Khloé into complex feminine ideals for a postfeminist consumer-audience. As Rosalind Gill suggests, postfeminism is a sensibility that privileges individual empowerment alongside pressure for women to "choose" to live up to sexualized ideals of femininity through careful consumption and self-monitoring.[1] To this end, the Kardashian sisters are exotically hypersexualized, yet family-oriented; they are shrewd businesswomen who love to clean house. Capitalizing on this image, the Kardashian sisters have promoted an array of products intended for feminine self-fashioning, including clothing, perfume, makeup, nail polish, and diet systems, and their younger half-sisters Kendall and Kylie Jenner have been groomed to follow in their footsteps and usher in the next generation, offering style and beauty tips to *Seventeen Magazine* readers and helming a clothing line of their own for the juniors market.

Contrary to earlier modes of reality TV celebrity (which separated "real" people desiring fame from "real" celebrities exposing their everyday lives), the prized early-twenty-first-century mode of reality celebrity has become self-branding, wealthy, and entrepreneurial, epitomized by the Kardashians and several of Bravo's *Real Housewives*. When the show debuted, Kim was the only semifamous sister, thanks to her red carpet appearances with socialite Paris

Hilton, her dates with newly divorced singer Nick Lachey, and her leaked sex tape with ex–boyfriend/musician, Ray J. However, the Kardashian name was familiar to viewers old enough to remember the 1995 O. J. Simpson murder trial, where Kim's father Robert Kardashian made up part of the famed defense "Dream Team." Since then, the Kardashians have come to occupy a liminal space of reality celebrity—between ordinary fame-seekers and "real" celebrities showing that they're "just like us." Icons for postfeminist self-entrepreneurship, the Kardashians capitalize on and brand their most intimate moments—Kim's sex tape, the births of Kourtney's children, even Khloé's ob-gyn appointments.

The Kardashians have become models for young women seeking success through self-branding, a practice Alison Hearn describes as "involving an outer-directed process of highly stylized self-construction, directly tied to the promotional mechanisms of the post-Fordist market."[2] With its emphasis on style and self-fashioning, self-branding is a deeply gendered process; as Julie Wilson claims, following Angela McRobbie, "In the postfeminist, neoliberal milieu women must perform as self-entrepreneurial, self-promotional workers on equal footing with their male colleagues yet still be invested in and appear willing to perform traditional gender roles."[3] While engaging in aggressive branding and self-promotion, the Kardashians simultaneously have avowed their devotion to heterosexual love and motherhood, with Kim and Khloé both desperate to provide Kourtney's children with cousins. Indeed, the very structure of the Kardashian-Jenner family as represented on *Keeping Up with the Kardashians* mirrors the postfeminist life cycle that Diane Negra identifies, with Kendall and Kylie, ages 12 and 10 when the series began, representing the "accelerated consumerist maturity of girls," Kim, Khloé, and Kourtney representing "the necessity of marriage for young women and the glorification of pregnancy," and their mother Kris Jenner representing "midlife women often cast as desperate to retain or recover their value as postfeminist subjects."[4]

Although the themes of self-branding and self-entrepreneurship saturate much early-twenty-first-century reality television targeted at young women, the Kardashian empire incorporates a novel twist—sister-branding and sister-entrepreneurship. This twist provides some relief from the social costs of entrepreneurial individualism, which, according to Anita Harris, brings with it "a sense of change, insecurity, fragmentation, and discontinuity within communities and nations, as well as a new emphasis on the responsibilities of individuals."[5] In contrast to the potentially alienating individual empowerment ideal of postfeminist neoliberal culture, wherein Sarah Banet-Weiser claims, "feminism fades from vision, the individual entrepreneur takes its place," the Kardashians privilege sisterhood, a fact that might account for their massive popularity among young women and girls.[6] Though the Kardashians clearly exemplify postfeminist culture, they also fill in some of its shortcomings, which may be central to their appeal. Whereas postfeminist entrepreneurial culture tells young women they don't need to build connections with other women, the overwhelming popularity of the Kardashians' investment in sisterhood suggests that young women do value and desire bonds with each other, even though those bonds may be in the name of a brand. While many postfeminist texts suggest that bonds between women can be emotionally fulfilling (e.g., *Sex and the City, Desperate Housewives*), *Keeping Up with the Kardashians* positions sisterhood as a vital part of career success. Rather than simply providing women with a supportive social circle, the Kardashians model sisterhood as entrepreneurial and productive—an antidote to the potentially alienating culture of neoliberalism that demands enterprising individualism. The intimacy that the sisters share not only nourishes them emotionally, it also plays a central role in their professional ambitions.

Much of the Kardashians' appeal lies in the virtual extended sisterhood they have fostered by establishing intimacy with female fans not only through their televisual omnipresence and array of self-fashioning products, but through social media. In contrast to earlier postfeminist texts focused on sisterhood, the Kardashians invite fans to participate in their sisterhood in a variety of ways, for instance, addressing fans as "dolls" on Twitter, just as the sisters address each other on the shows. Of course, the primary goal of this extended sisterhood is profit, but nevertheless, the practice suggests that connections among women are valuable, emotionally and financially. As of late 2013, Kim had over 18 million followers on Twitter, and 9 million followers on Instagram, where she promotes her media empire, rendering even her most diminutive musings worthy of monetary value. Although Kourtney and Khloé have half as many Twitter followers, the three sisters often tweet among themselves and other family members, at once shoring up their brand and extending their sisterhood to millions. As Alice Marwick and danah boyd point out, "If we accept that Twitter creates a sense of ongoing connection with one's real-life acquaintances and friends, following a famous person's tweets over a period of time may create an equally valid feeling of 'knowing' them."[7] Kim in particular takes the "performative intimacy" that social media fosters seriously.[8] Her devotion to Twitter was a rumored catalyst of her divorce from NBA player Kris Humphries, as his reluctance to tweet and garner followers was incommensurate with Kim's brand-building.

Such doomed efforts to combine work and family define each sister, despite, or perhaps because of, how carefully their brand has been built on their familial bonds. Kourtney has had a tumultuous relationship with her boyfriend, yet achieved blissful motherhood, Khloé achieved heterosexual matrimony, yet has struggled to conceive and keep her marriage together, and Kim has found herself twice divorced, yet finally started to raise the family she had long desired. These intimate struggles make the Kardashians exemplars of postfeminist celebrity brand culture, where successful professional women are set up to fail in the realms of love and family. Yet these same struggles make them compelling points of identification for young women who want to "have it all," but fear they can't—in this way, the Kardashians function as a fantasy sisterly support network, suggesting the importance of sisterhood in a neoliberal entrepreneurial culture preoccupied with self-branding.

Their meticulously maintained brand depends upon the seamless combination of entrepreneurship and family, best exemplified in Kris Jenner's now trademarked title, "momager." Thus, familial tensions threaten the brand as much as they threaten to upend the sisters' so-called work-life balance, and so family members often resolve squabbles through business deals. At the same time, the Kardashians point to one way out of the work-life conflict in combining the two—their work is precisely to maintain their branded family, and the sisters support each other by sharing both familial and professional labor. The narrative of *Keeping Up with the Kardashians* and its spin-offs mirrors the postfeminist lifecycle, with early seasons focusing on work (primarily Kim's), followed by weddings (Khloé's and Kim's), child-rearing (Kourtney's), and failing marriages (Kim's and Khloé's). The thread that remains constant, and which distinguishes the Kardashian programs from other postfeminist media texts, is their insistence on the primacy of sisterhood as a means to both personal *and* professional success. Whereas the sisters may struggle to combine their careers with romantic relationships and children, their sisterhood, which is the basis of their collective career, remains intact. For young women who have been sold the postfeminist ideal of individual empowerment over collective political action, the Kardashians reconcile a continued desire for connections between women with the pressures of neoliberal postfeminist culture, promoting not a self-brand, but a sister-brand.

Kim's Work-Life Balance

Keeping Up with the Kardashians carries the process Melissa Gregg describes as *presence bleed* to the extreme. Here, work "invade[s] spaces and times that were once less susceptible to its presence. . . . firm boundaries between personal and professional identities no longer apply."[9] For the Kardashians, virtually

218

every minute of every day could be constituted as work, and Kris laments in her memoir and to *Us Weekly* the difficulties of relating to her children as both their mother and their manager.[10] The most intimate, private moments become work: When Kourtney prepares to go to the hospital to give birth to son Mason, E! cameras capture the puddle of amniotic fluid on the floor of her bedroom. When her boyfriend Scott Disick inquires why she is putting on makeup to give birth, she explains, "There's pictures involved!" Likewise, *Us Weekly* described the birth of Kourtney's daughter Penelope as a "red carpet event." As Leigh Edwards notes,

> Many Kardashian series stories [have become] meta-commentaries on reality stardom. Kris worries about her appearance in front of cameras and gets plastic surgery, Kim and Khloé fight about who is more famous or more jealous of the other, Kourtney's boyfriend Scott Disick grows weary of always being placed in the villain role on TV.... By engaging with the meta-narrative of the family's media celebrity, these plotlines allow the series further to market themselves and the family brand, engaging in saturation and excessive branding.[11]

While Edwards frames this as a newer phenomenon in the series, *Keeping Up with the Kardashians* has always narrativized fame-work, with its pilot episode revolving around Kim debating how much to reveal about her sex tape in her first television interview with Tyra Banks and the second episode focusing on Kris struggling to manage all of Kim's work commitments. Kim's ambitions threaten her romantic relationships, with the program using her as a cautionary tale of the ill-fated work-life balance.

In the fourth season, Kris and Kim debate the presence bleed, as Kris had turned down a party-hosting gig on Kim's behalf so that Kim would not have to work on her birthday. However, Kim is shocked to hear of this development, and explains to the viewer, "I've always worked on my birthday in Vegas. This is work—I'm not going to turn it down." When Kim confronts Kris, demanding that she reinstate the booking, Kris remarks, "Kim makes it sound like I've cancelled her birthday celebration, when in fact, it's an appearance. She's gotta be on schedule, she's gotta do a red carpet, she's gotta do a meet and greet, she's gotta stay for a certain amount of time, and Kim has been working *so* hard, 24 hours a day, 365 days a year." When the whole family goes to Las Vegas, their intention is both to celebrate Kim's birthday and to work—Scott and Rob Kardashian get extremely drunk and belligerent, and Kris struggles to contain them, exasperatedly telling the viewer, "This is a *major* business dinner, and I'm trying to get our products sold across the country." Once she believes she has sent them up to sleep it off, she rejoices, "Finally, we can just have our business meeting, and celebrate Kim's birthday." For her part, Kim is exhausted the whole day, flopping on the couch of her suite upon entering and proclaiming, "I literally just want like ten minutes" (see Figure 11.1). Just as she curls up with a pillow, the hotel's public relations director comes in and runs down her schedule. As the public relations director leaves Kim to squeeze in a nap, the episode cuts to Scott and Rob at a bar, where they down multiple beers and tequila shots at two o'clock in the afternoon (see Figure 11.2). As if the constant dialogue about how hard Kim works were not sufficient, the episode's structure of crosscutting between Kim working and Scott and Rob overindulging in leisure activities emphasizes Kim's work ethic while implicitly critiquing Scott and Rob's freeloading, speaking to women viewers who might feel as though they have to work much harder than their male colleagues to get ahead and be taken seriously.

More than Kourtney or Khloé, the first few seasons of *Keeping Up With the Kardashians* showcase Kim's gender-specific struggles to combine success in business and in love. Throughout the third and fourth seasons, Kim's devotion to her work begins to drive a wedge between her and then-boyfriend, NFL player Reggie Bush. Kim narrates a montage of her many business undertakings, telling the viewer,

> So much is going on, my life is so crazy busy. I'm doing everything from great photo shoots to magazines, another calendar, my shoe company with Robert Shapiro, ShoeDazzle, I just finished filming a movie, my career is just on the up and up and I've got this momentum going, so no matter what it is in my life, Reggie, my friends, right now everyone's gonna have to understand

FIGURE 11.1. Kim Kardashian, exhausted from her nonstop work schedule. *Keeping Up with the Kardashians*, "Blame It on the Alcohol," season 4, episode 10, E!

FIGURE 11.2. Scott Disick and Rob Kardashian drink at a Las Vegas bar mid-afternoon, as juxtaposed with Kim's overworked exhaustion. *Keeping Up with the Kardashians*, "Blame It on the Alcohol," season 4, episode 10, E!

that I am on this train that's not gonna stop, and I need to be dedicated and focus on my career right now.

As soon as she speaks these words, her comanager asks to book her on the same day as Bush's first game, setting up a literal work/love conflict. Kim tells her manager to book it, because, "Work comes first," only to have Bush tell her later, "That's not cool." When Kris convinces Kim to take time for her personal life, Kim flies to New Orleans, but as she spends time with Bush and makes "I Heart Reggie" signs in preparation for his game, her voice-over belies her anxiety over missing work, as she worries about "burning bridges" as a result of backing out of her contract. Still, at the end of the episode, Kim comes to the revelation that she needs to "switch gears a little bit, and balance everything out," and make Bush her "number one priority."

This choice appears bound to fail, however, as Kim lovingly cuddles up to Bush and tells him about all the sacrifices she's prepared to make to be with him while he stares at the television. Despite her devotion to Bush, this episode marks his last appearance on the show, and early in the next season, Kim deals with their breakup, at first blaming her career, but then reclaiming it, remarking, "I don't need a relationship to define who I am." Kim's subordination of her own career to Bush's undoubtedly speaks to many women who find themselves pressured to support their partners' careers at the expense of their own. The episode sets up this conflict by juxtaposing Kim's hectic schedule and obvious passion for her work with Kris lamenting the fact that Kim takes little time for her personal life and Bush being disappointed by Kim's inability to spend time with him. The viewer feels the same pressure that Kim does, thanks to fast-paced montages that underscore her hectic life and the slow-paced, uncomfortable scenes that emphasize her guilt and desire to spend time with Bush.

The doomed E! special, *Kim's Fairytale Wedding*, exposed the inherent contradictions of postfeminist female celebrity by positioning Kim's dedication to her fame-work as jeopardizing her commitment to marriage. Susan Douglas suggests that celebrity culture's "ideal women" "are independent—they have their own professions, money, and sources of success—and yet are completely reliant on the love and approval of men. And they get that approval because their economic independence is tempered by their hyperfemininity."[12] Though Kim has the hyperfemininity bit down pat, the backlash she endured after the divorce suggests her economic imperatives were not properly mitigated by a feminine commitment to marriage. Throughout the wedding special, Kim focuses more on bolstering her brand through excessive displays of wealth than she does on cultivating "fairytale" romance.

One central source of conflict in the wedding special is the issue of whether or not Kim will change her last name upon marrying Kris Humphries. Though Kim makes all the clichéd remarks about Humphries being traditional, and wanting to change her name to make him happy, she seems most excited about the prospect of her new initials enhancing her own brand, through conspicuous additions to her Hermès collection. She delights in all Hermès apparel that sports an H logo, registers for Hermès china, and totes several Birkin bags, suggesting her consideration of changing her last name has as much to do with further marking her connection to luxury brands as it does with pleasing Humphries. Kris Jenner is distraught over the possibility of Kim changing her last name, primarily due to the challenges it poses to the Kardashian brand. Her exclamation, repeated over and over in previews and at ad-break teasers, "You are *incorporated*, Kim Kardashian, Inc.," reinforces the threat Humphries poses to the brand and privileges Kardashian as a businesswoman over her status as a soon-to-be wife. Jenner further flexes her momager muscle, telling the viewer in a direct address interview, "I can't believe Kim is talking about how she's going to change her name to Humphries. She needs to be Kim Kardashian. There is no way that I'm letting Kim change her name."

To seal the deal, Jenner brings Kim into her office to show her the branding hurdles she faces if she were to change her name. Pitching the couple's branded identity as "Hump," Jenner unveils product mock-ups of the "Hump Rope," a fragrance called "Hump" and butt pads. Interestingly enough, all of these products reference Kardashian's famous butt in their design, thus the shift in branding appears more seamless than Jenner lets on. Yet Jenner's presentation of this overtly sexualized branding suggests that the lifestyle brand she has worked to establish is a departure from Kim's original claim to fame. She thrusts the portfolio at Kim, telling her, "I want you to take this with you, and show it to your hubby, with an H, and then think about what you've given me to work with!" In the end, Kim decides that for business documents, she needs to be able to sign "Kardashian," thus she retains her last name not as a feminist statement, but as a postfeminist entrepreneurial necessity. At the same time, Kim's decision also maintains her primary bond with her sisters, choosing to share a last name with them and their collective brand instead of with her future husband, putting sister-entrepreneurship above all else.

In the reality show narrative, Kim's commitment to her postfeminist lifestyle brand and fame-work presents the most obvious rift between herself and Humphries. Humphries grows increasingly weary of being mobbed by the paparazzi and, following a sequence of the couple wading through a crowd of photographers on their way into a restaurant, Humphries voices his discomfort with Kim's work and lifestyle. He tells her their lives would be different if they moved to Minnesota and started "pumping out babies," pointing to an image of factory-style domestic motherhood obviously out of step with Kim's glamorous workaholic image. Kim counters his vision, telling him, "I think the reason I fell in love with you was 'cause you could handle my career, like my career wasn't an issue for you." When she says, "career," he starts laughing, and the camera zooms in, pointing to his refusal to take Kim's fame-work seriously. When they fight again later, Kim tells Humphries that he knew what he was getting into. When he asks, "With what?" Kim replies, "with my work ethic, with everything that I do," and he parrots back sarcastically, "my work ethic," and laughs, again ridiculing Kim's commitment to her career. Though Humphries's jabs may appeal to a viewer who has animosity toward the Kardashians and their success, the wedding special carefully guides the sympathetic, aspirational Kardashian fan to support Kim. Although Humphries plays for the NBA and comes from a wealthy family, *Kim's Fairytale Wedding* works hard to define Kim and the rest of the Kardashians against him. Instead of the exterior shots of L.A. traffic and high-end shops that scream Kardashian, the program signifies Minnesota, and by extension, Humphries, with establishing images of quiet streets and close-ups of a cobweb. When they head to the grocery store, Kardashian opines, "Even the grocery carts in Minnesota are weird."

Humphries's refusal to take Kim's career seriously came back to bite him as the Kardashian publicity machine dealt with the fallout from their divorce. Though he continued to mock her fame, notoriously telling her in an episode of *Kourtney and Kim Take New York* that by the time she has kids, no one will care about her anymore, gossip magazines like *Us Weekly* and *Star* quickly moved to Kim's defense, accusing Humphries not only of being a lazy freeloader but also of verbally abusing Kim. *Us Weekly*'s December 5, 2011, cover screamed, "Husband from Hell," with the subtitle, "He called Kim FAT and mocked her family" (see Figure 11.3). The accompanying article claims, "It had become a familiar pattern in their short-lived marriage: Kim Kardashian hung back at home or worked, while Kris Humphries and his friends enjoyed his newfound VIP status, including free meals and booze at the trendiest hot spots. . . . When Kim's unemployed husband returned to her $4.8 million Beverly Hills mansion after a night out with buddies at pricey restaurant STK, the newlyweds had a huge blowup."[13] Numerous articles note the cost of Kim's home (notably not referred to as "theirs"), alongside the disparity in her and Humphries's earnings, but perhaps most egregiously, *Us Weekly* quotes "a Kardashian insider" as relaying that, "'He would say truly terrible things. One time, he said she had no talent and her fame wouldn't last.'"[14] While *Us Weekly* has long been

FIGURE 11.3. *US Weekly*'s cover documenting the disintegration of the Kardashian/Humphries marriage, December 5, 2011. Copyright © *Us Weekly* LLC 2011. All Rights Reserved. Reprinted by Permission.

sympathetic to the Kardashians, its coverage of the divorce helped E! shift the popular discourse from outrage over whether or not the marriage was a sham to sympathy for unlucky-in-love Kim.

According to Su Holmes and Diane Negra, "Female celebrity models for managing the (feminized) 'work-life balance' are often positioned as only precariously and temporarily stabilized; we are invited to play a 'waiting game' to see when their hard-won achievements will collapse under the simultaneous weight of relationships, family, and career."[15] Indeed, the aftermath of Kim's failed marriage, as well as the wedding special that barely preceded it, has become a cautionary tale that is an integral part of her working-girl persona. Just one year prior to her divorce announcement, Kim appeared on the cover of *People* looking wistful, with the headline, "I thought I'd be married by now."[16] In the season finale of *Kourtney and Kim Take New York*, during which Kim's marriage to Humphries unravels, Kim cries to Kourtney, "At 30 years old, I thought I'd be married with kids, and I'm not. I failed at this." Kim's failure to succeed in love (later magnified by tabloid reports that Kanye West spent most of her pregnancy overseas), combined with her eminently successful self-branding career, could easily vilify her as a cold, calculated businesswoman, one who would turn her own wedding into an opportunity for profit. Yet the fact that Kim's sisters repeatedly expressed their doubts about Humphries both before and during their marriage has helped recuperate Kim's image, while validating their sisterhood.

The Intimacy of Can-Do Sisters

Kourtney, Kim, and Khloé all embody what Anita Harris has termed "can-do girls," who "are identifiable by their commitment to exceptional careers and career planning, their belief in their capacity to invent themselves and succeed, and their display of a consumer lifestyle. They are also distinguished by a desire to put off childbearing until 'later.'"[17] Delayed childbearing, of course, brings with it a postfeminist "biological clock" panic, or what Yvonne Tasker and Diane Negra refer to as a "temporal crisis."[18] Despite the fact that Khloé is the youngest of the three eldest sisters, and would thus seem to be the least implicated in the postfeminist temporal crisis, her narrative on the shows and in gossip media was defined throughout her marriage by a struggle to conceive. In the seventh season of *Keeping Up With the Kardashians*, Khloé and Kim visit a fertility clinic, and the episode includes a flashback to previous footage of Khloé undergoing a pelvic exam. Khloé explains to the viewer that she would rather be at the doctor with Kim than with her husband Lamar Odom, which places the viewer in the position of surrogate sister, learning the details of Khloé's fertility before she even tells her husband. The end of the episode goes one step further, showing ultrasound images of Khloé's ovary (see Figure 11.4). The camera zooms in on the ultrasound image as the doctor moves a cursor to show Khloé (and the viewer) that she may not be ovulating. Khloé

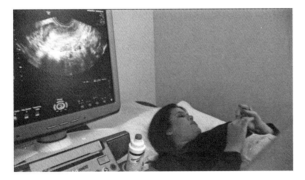

FIGURE 11.4. Khloé Kardashian, getting an ultrasound of her ovaries in her quest for fertility. *Keeping Up with the Kardashians*, "Cuts Both Ways," season 7, episode 17, E!

takes this news very hard, seemingly seeing it as a challenge to her femininity and helplessly sobbing to the viewer in a direct address interview, "Who doesn't ovulate!?" The narrative parallel between Khloé's struggle with infertility and Kourtney's multiple pregnancies embodies both the anxieties produced by the postfeminist work-life balance, and the ideal of the can-do girl, with Kim positioned squarely between the two.

At age 32, Kim is also already feeling the pressure of the postfeminist temporal crisis. She undergoes an ovary ultrasound as well, in order to begin the process of freezing her eggs. In a later episode, we see her injecting herself with hormones to further the process, the camera providing extreme close-ups of the needle penetrating her flesh. Though the Kardashians' bodies have long defined them and their fame outside of their television programs, Kim, Kourtney, and Khloé appear throughout the run of their E! shows in various states of undress not so much for an erotic male gaze, but for an intimate, sisterly one. Kourtney and Khloé have both taken home pregnancy tests on the show, complete with images of them sitting on the toilet and afterward brandishing the pee stick. Not only has each sister appeared naked (albeit blurred out) at one time or another on the series, but the viewer has accompanied each of them to the doctor's office on multiple occasions—an intimate space most often reserved for immediate family. By providing the viewer with access to these intimate moments and spaces, the series addresses the viewer as another sister, who anticipates and experiences deeply personal moments along with the Kardashians.

Kim's decision to freeze her eggs, alongside Khloé's long-standing fertility struggles, speaks to postfeminist concerns about delaying pregnancy in favor of work, while the show celebrates Kourtney's pregnancies, accompanying her to multiple ultrasound appointments. In one such episode, a close-up of the ultrasound monitor reveals Mason's penis in utero to the viewer and every family member with the exception of Khloé, as the family cheers. Seeing Kourtney's fetus at multiple stages of development cements viewer interest in and connection with a new Kardashian generation, while branding Kourtney's familial, reproductive life. Kourtney's successful transition to blissful motherhood further marks her as an exemplary "can-do girl," because

> [c]hildren are important accessories to the successful can-do life. . . . Can-do girls are thus encouraged to delay motherhood until their careers are established; then they can treat it as both an essentially feminine moment of fulfillment and a consumer lifestyle experience that enhances an image of success.[19]

Indeed, several episodes revolve around baby showers and shopping excursions for nursery decorations and baby supplies. *Us Weekly* delighted in reporting Kim's expenditures for daughter North, listing a $4,000 crib and $1,170 stroller to add to her shopping spree at a Paris children's boutique.[20] Yet many of the baby-themed episodes are also tinged with a sense of empathy and even pity for Khloé, as in a season eight episode that revolves around Kourtney and Kim bonding over baby purchases, which leaves Khloé feeling left out.

The siblings are often jealous of each other, and Kris is constantly under attack for favoring Kim, with Khloé referring to Kim as Kris's "prized possession." Yet, as Kris reminds them during a fight over the name of Kim's perfume, "You guys have to stay united and realize that anything that either one of you does builds the whole Kardashian brand." When Kim tells Khloé and Kourtney that she has an opportunity to do a lingerie line in the Philippines, she meets resistance for her desire to be an individual entrepreneur unbridled by the sisterhood. Kourtney tells Kim, "It's rewarding if we're all there together to experience it," and Khloé agrees, saying she could also work alone, but would rather work together. In a season three episode of *Kourtney and Kim Take Miami*, Kourtney tells Kim and Khloé that she's scheduled to appear on QVC, but she feels like flying there with two kids is too much of a hassle and wants to cancel. Khloé and Kim are aghast at that suggestion, and Kim agrees to go, since it's her day off. In the same episode, Kourtney leaves a photo shoot early, and Kim tells Khloé, "Maybe I'll have a baby and then I won't have to do as much work."

The conflict explodes when Kim's friend Jonathan accuses Kourtney of "collecting Kim's money as it falls out of her ass," and being "pregnant and doing nothing" while Kim works "365 days a year for the last four years." While this particular fight speaks to the postfeminist trials of the work-life balance, in fact, Jonathan is wrong, as Kourtney's motherhood and willingness to film her pregnancies, births, and children's lives for the shows became a major part of the Kardashian brand, epitomized by an *OK! Magazine* collector's issue cover story and 10-page spread titled, "Growing Up Kardashian," revolving around Mason and Penelope.[21] Even if Kourtney did reduce the amount of time she spent shilling products, the contours of the Kardashian brand are such that she is constantly working. In fact, the presence and visibility of Kourtney's children may be even more important to *Keeping Up with the Kardashians* since Kim and husband Kanye West have claimed that they will not allow their daughter North to appear on any of the shows. This pledge is particularly dubious, however, given the intimate nature of the Kardashian brand. After all, as West noted of Kim's rise to fame via sex tape, "My girl famous all from a home movie."

Extending the Sister-Brand

The Kardashians reveal the secrets of the sisterhood in their 2011 bestseller, *Kardashian Konfidential*, and invite the reader to become a part of it, telling her, "You're pretty much just like us."[22] Despite the jealousy-fueled feuds that provide narrative tension on *Keeping Up with the Kardashians*, the sisters declare, "Our attitude is, there's plenty to go around, we say, 'Yay!' when something good happens to one of us, because it's kind of like something good happens to all of us."[23] This attitude pervades both work and family life. In addition to reminding the sisters that each of their individual endeavors builds their collective brand, Kris also announces when Kourtney and Khloé attend Kim's ultrasound, "If one of you are [*sic*] pregnant, you're all kinda pregnant. We're all in this together," a sentiment Kourtney takes to heart when she announces that she wants to join Kim in eating the placenta after North's birth. Just as the Kardashians' media empire has worked to extend their sisterhood to include female fans, in later seasons, Kourtney, Kim, and Khloé have expanded their sister-brand to include Kendall and Kylie, thus promoting their branded sisterhood to an even broader audience.

A season eight episode of *Keeping Up With the Kardashians* finds Kourtney and Khloé passing on their sisterly affirmation to their younger sisters, who spend much of the episode at odds with each other. Kendall and Kylie appear to be off on the right foot in building their own entrepreneurial sisterhood, as the episode shows them attending a meeting for their clothing line and modeling at a photo shoot together. When Khloé has to break up an argument between her younger siblings and remind them that they should "be on each other's teams," she schemes to help them repair their relationship, bringing them together with Kourtney and Kim for a sisterly pep talk. Khloé tells the next generation of entrepreneurial sisters, "Just 'cause you're sisters doesn't mean you have to be friends, but we've all *chosen* to be best friends 'cause we respect, envy, love, and honor one another, just like you two do, deep down. There'll be no other friend like your sister." A few scenes later, Kendall and Kylie mark their reconciliation through scouring family photo albums and helping each other post old snapshots to social media sites, thus healing the rift in their branded sisterhood by extending it to their fans. Although postfeminist culture has often encouraged young women to eschew connections to other women, this episode offers an appealing affirmation of sisterly bonds, while entrepreneurializing them through social media sister promotion.

As the younger Jenner sisters have grown up, they have come to occupy a more prominent position in the family brand and have begun to infiltrate Kim, Kourtney, and Khloé's primary entrepreneurial sisterhood. In a season eight episode, pregnant Kim frets over "losing her cool" and fawns over Kylie, who, she tells Khloé, is "the end all, be all of cool." Setting Kylie up for the viewer as the last up-and-coming member of the sisterhood (that is, at least until Penelope and North enter their tween years), Kim explains in a direct address interview, "Kylie has this amazing Tumblr that just like is such an expression of who she is. She'll post these fashion pictures and the style that she's into, and I just know that, like, she's really cool." Halfway through this utterance, the episode cuts away from Kim's interview to a montage of images from Kylie's Tumblr, introducing this personal "expression" directly to the viewer, and inviting her to check out Kylie's mediated persona as Kim's most recent endorsement. Kim's obsession with Kylie continues throughout the episode, as she interrupts a clothing design meeting to recommend changes to a garment based on what Kylie would wear. She refers the designers to Kylie's blog, promising, "It's just like so her soul, and it's what I want our line to be."

Kim even seeks Khloé's advice for becoming more prominently featured on Kylie's Tumblr. When Khloé wonders if Kylie posts pictures of her older sisters out of sympathy, Kim snaps, "No! She doesn't do anything out of sympathy. She only does what's cool, that's why I love her, 'cause she, like, is so authentic, she's like the real deal." To further validate her claim to Kylie's authentic cool, Kim reveals that Kanye West seeks Kylie's opinion on his album artwork. Whereas the rest of the Kardashian family has long faced criticism for the calculated nature of their personas, Kim attempts to set Kylie apart. Yet Kim also seeks to participate in and commodify Kylie's (already) commodified authenticity. As Sarah Banet-Weiser argues, "Rather than representing the loss of authentic humanity, the authentic and commodity self are intertwined within brand culture, where authenticity is itself a brand."[24] While up to this point, Kim's authenticity has largely resided in her body, as that body changes during her pregnancy, Kim seeks a different, more holistic authenticity, which, the episode suggests, can be found in her younger sister.[25] As with every Kardashian endeavor, branding the next generation is both hard work and a family affair.

Diane Negra and Maria Pramaggiore argue that *Keeping Up With the Kardashians* is "Dedicated to repairing the contradictions between a neoliberal economic structure and idealized family life," seeking to "reassure us that the intense, relentless commodification of identity need not threaten family solidarity and intimacy."[26] While this dynamic is undoubtedly a large part of the Kardashian television narrative, it is also a dynamic that attracts wide derision. *Us Weekly* is by and large sympathetic toward the Kardashians, but it regularly slips in jabs about the commingling of business and family, as when an article notes that Kris Jenner is "the mother of six brands, er, children,"[27] or refers to North as Kim's "little spin-off,"[28] and her prospective marriage to

Kanye West as a "West-Kardashian merger."[29] The promotional extravaganza that was *Kim's Fairytale Wedding*, and the scorn Kim briefly experienced when she announced the divorce, exemplifies the limits of public tolerance for the Kardashians' monetization of their "private" lives. Despite this backlash, the Kardashians have retained millions of young female fans who idolize them and aspirationally identify with them. Kim, Kourtney, and Khloé have all experienced setbacks in their attempts to successfully navigate the so-called work-life balance. The fact that their personal lives are interwoven with their work lives has both helped and hurt, but what has remained consistent throughout the years that their lives have been televised is their sisterly bond. As they tell their readers in *Kardashian Konfidential*, "The most important thing about being the Kardashian sisters . . . is being sisters."[30] Kourtney and Khloé helped Kim through her divorce, Khloé and Kim helped Kourtney through multiple breakups and reconciliations with Scott, and despite an *Us Weekly* story that reported that Khloé broke the "first rule of the Kardashian sisterhood" by lying about Lamar Odom's drug use,[31] two weeks later, the magazine ran a photo of Khloé and Kourtney holding hands in sisterly solidarity.[32] This emphasis on family, and, more importantly sisterhood, as a vehicle for both professional and personal success sets the Kardashians apart from some of the confines of neoliberal postfeminism. While each sister has her own branded identity, the greater Kardashian brand is built upon the close relationships the sisters (and to a lesser extent, the rest of the family) have with each other. Postfeminist culture sells female viewers an image of can-do individualism dependent upon each going it alone, apart from any literal or figurative sisters, and especially when it comes to their professional success. Yet even as they serve as brand ambassadors for postfeminist entrepreneurialism, the Kardashian sisterhood highlights and depends upon bonds between women that appear essential to both their personal well-being and their professional accomplishments.

Notes

1. Rosalind Gill, "Postfeminist Media Culture: Elements of a Sensibility," *European Journal of Cultural Studies* 10.2 (2007): 147–166.

2. Alison Hearn, " 'Meat, Mask, Burden': Probing the Contours of the Branded 'Self,'" *Journal of Consumer Culture* 8.2 (2008): 201.

3. Julie A. Wilson, "Star Testing: The Emerging Politics of Celebrity Gossip," *Velvet Light Trap* 65 (2010): 25–38.

4. Diane Negra, *What a Girls Wants?: Fantasizing the Reclamation of Self in Postfeminism* (London: Routledge, 2009), 47.

5. Anita Harris, *Future Girl: Young Women in the Twenty-First Century* (New York: Routledge, 2004), 4.

6. Sarah Banet-Weiser, *Authentic: The Politics of Ambivalence in a Brand Culture* (New York: New York University Press, 2012), 61.

7. Alice Marwick and danah boyd, "To See and Be Seen: Celebrity Practice on Twitter," *Convergence: The International Journal of Research into New Media Technologies* 17. 2 (2011): 147–148.

8. Ibid.

9. Melissa Gregg, *Work's Intimacy* (Cambridge, U.K.: Polity, 2011), 2.

10. Kris Jenner, *Kris Jenner . . . and All Things Kardashian* (New York: Gallery Books, 2011); Kevin O'Leary, "My Mistakes as a Mom," *Us Weekly*, Mar. 4, 2013, 38–41.

11. Leigh Edwards, "Transmedia Storytelling, Corporate Synergy, and Audience Expression," *Global Media Journal* 12 (Spring 2012): 5.

12. Susan Douglas, *Enlightened Sexism* (New York: Times Books, 2010), 255.

13. Eric Andersson, "Husband from Hell!" *Us Weekly*, Dec. 5, 2011, 54.

14. Ibid., 56.

15. Su Holmes and Diane Negra, Introduction, in *In the Limelight and under the Microscope*, eds. Su Holmes and Diane Negra (New York: Continuum, 2011), 2.

16. *People Magazine*, Nov. 22, 2010.

17. Harris, *Future Girl*, 14.

18. Yvonne Tasker and Diane Negra, "Feminist Politics and Postfeminist Culture," in *Interrogating Postfeminism*, eds. Yvonne Tasker and Diane Negra (Durham, N.C.: Duke University Press, 2007), 10.

19. Harris, *Future Girl*, 25.

20. Eric Andersson, "Kim Kardashian: Splurging for Nursery," *Us Weekly*, June 10, 2013, 41.

21. "Growing Up Kardashian!" *OK! Magazine* Collector's Issue: Hollywood's Cutest Kids 2013, 14–23.

22. Kourtney, Kim, and Khloé Kardashian, *Kardashian Konfidential* (New York: St. Martin's Press, 2011), 7.

23. Ibid., 103.

24. Banet-Weiser, *Authentic*, 13–14.

25. Jessalynn Keller attributes the location of authenticity in the body to female celebrity at large. Jessalynn Marie Keller, "Fiercely Real?: Tyra Banks and the Making of New Media Celebrity," *Feminist Media Studies* (2012): 5.

26. Maria Pramaggiore and Diane Negra, "Keeping Up with the Aspirations," in *Reality Gendervision*, ed. Brenda Weber (Durham, N.C.: Duke University Press, 2014).

27. O'Leary, "My Mistakes as a Mom," 39.

28. Kevin O'Leary, "Why Kim's in Hiding," *Us Weekly*, July 22, 2013, 61.

29. Sarah Grossbart, "Kanye and Kim: Ready to Wed!" *Us Weekly*, Aug. 19, 2013, 62.

30. Kardashian et al., *Kardashian Konfidential*, 237.

31. Kevin O'Leary, "Khloé Kicks Lamar Out," *Us Weekly*, Sept. 9, 2013, 64.

32. Kevin O'Leary, "Khloé's Private Hell," *Us Weekly*, Sept. 23, 201: 64–69.

CHAPTER 12

Pinning Happiness

Affect, Social Media, and the Work of Mothers

JULIE WILSON AND EMILY CHIVERS YOCHIM

From Facebook status updates offering mothering advice to Instagrammed images of a family's summertime fun to lifestyle blogs that can make kitchen sinks look elegant, social media overflow with images of domestic bliss. This world, known around the web as the mamasphere, is never-ending and constantly changing, highly customized and produced by a community of everyday women and the corporate marketplace. While women traveling through the mamasphere are clearly exposed to deeply traditional and gendered discourses about women's work in the home, what makes these sites hard to pin down is their incessant, customized flow of content and their unruly network form, which perpetually expands and contracts in conjunction with users' online travels and real world pursuits and passions. In this chapter, we unpack the cultural power of the mamasphere, drawing on network theory and affect theory to explore what happens to the work of mothering in this environment, where the labors of domesticity and child-rearing are continuously and constantly shared, put on display, and narrated through digital packets of information. Circulating mediated happy family scenes into complicated and difficult everyday lives, the mamasphere distributes happiness, bolstering the family in a world that feels increasingly precarious. By thinking through the affective potential unlocked when online worlds meet everyday life, we demonstrate how the mamasphere works to stabilize the family as a "happy object," Sara Ahmed's term for objects that point toward happiness.[1]

In the early twenty-first century, the social networking and bookmarking site Pinterest has been a primary entryway into this online world, and its content and form usefully encapsulate how women operate around the mamasphere. "A tool for collecting and organizing things you love," Pinterest brags that it has "helped millions of people . . . plan life's important projects."[2] Originally launched in March of 2010, Pinterest quickly amassed a dedicated user base, and, by early 2013, the scrapbooking site was approaching 50 million users globally and valued at 2.5 billion dollars.[3] Pinterest has been organized as a virtual inspiration board where a social network of "pinners"—the vast majority of whom are white, upper- and middle-class women—develop highly organized boards populated by "pins," images pulled from around the web and described in brief captions written by pinners. Pins could be virtually anything, but typical examples include images of modern kitchens, snapshots of toddlers creating crafts, and photos of common household items captioned with "genius" uses for those items. Boards, which categorize the pins, might be conceived narrowly or broadly: "Beautify Nails," "Elf on a Shelf," "Cleaning and Organization," and "Words to Live By" are just a few examples. On this social network, pinners follow one another's boards, "repin" others' pins to their own boards, and "like" or comment on pins.

We might think of Pinterest as organizing happy objects. Indeed, as its tagline announces, the cheerful site houses "A few (million) of your favorite things." A highly feminized digital platform where certain women share recipes, fitness tips, crafting projects, party ideas, toddler activities, decorating advice, and much, much more, Pinterest has been intimately bound up in the everyday lives of its users, and the happiness it promises often intersects with women's work as homemakers and mothers. Indeed, with its glossy images and neatly organized boards, Pinterest has made the mundane labors of domesticity professional, artistic, and inspiring. Domestic labor, which is invisible, monotonous, quite physical, and never complete, becomes beautiful, promising, even fun and happy, when deemed a "21 Day Organization Challenge" or depicted as a series of peacefully performed acts of motherly love.

While Pinterest relentlessly reinforces gendered ideologies and norms—as the "good" mom on Pinterest is ever-crafting, ever-cooking, ever-teaching— here, we push beyond ideological critique to suggest a different starting point for analyses of social media platforms like Pinterest that seem so bent on enhancing and optimizing women's work. Critically important about feminized digital media is the way that its endless streams of content might enter into, punctuate, and impact women's daily lives, tweaking, exacerbating, or revising how women move through and feel everyday experiences. For, we argue, it is at the meeting point between pockets of everyday life and packets of online data that digital media are imbued with power.

The digital world of mothering media is one that thrives on "pinning" happiness, that is, on the displaying, archiving, detailing, and sharing of happy family lives. Pinning is a key practice for popular social media that involves the selection and sharing of content. It is best, and most obviously, exemplified on Pinterest by pinners who cull images and curate boards, but it also occurs on many platforms where users are enabled and encouraged to produce, post, and/ or share content with each other, including Facebook, Twitter, Instagram, and blogs. Specifically, the practice of pinning happiness is posting and sharing content that points toward the possibility of happiness: happy scenes, good habits and best practices, fun activities, and thoughtful ruminations on the meaning of life. Happy families are pinned down—put on display and stabilized—through pinning. While in the midst of everyday family life, happiness can be elusive, pinning happiness serves as a constant reminder of the potential and promise of family happiness. Indeed, pinning happiness is a powerful media practice endemic to the lived realities of early-twenty-first-century neoliberalism, where family life feels increasingly precarious and mothers are responsible for managing threats to their families' economic, emotional, and physical well-being. In these precarious times, what often gets pinned on feminized sites like Pinterest are not simply ideological messages about gendered domesticity but also broader affective structures that shape how mothers invest in, desire, and orient themselves to family life.

Women's Work and Mediated Domesticity

Liberal democratic capitalist societies have long depended on women's work, that is, on the affective, caring labor performed by women in the domestic sphere. Political theorist Wendy Brown argues that liberal rule was in fact premised on a tripartite social order—where state, economy/civil society, and family were posited to exist as distinct realms.[4] The work of mothers, in turn, was always already less visible as "work" because it happened in the "separate sphere" of family and private life, where the requisite social bonds of love and obligation were to be forged. A "naturalized haven in a heartless world," the family—and, in particular, the autonomous white, nuclear family—has been held out as the "anchor" for civil society and public life, as the "seat of moral restraint in an immoral world."[5] According to Brown, a generalized gender division of labor was axiomatic to liberal capitalism; care work was privatized and relegated to the domestic sphere, while men's work, enacted outside of the home, was increasingly socialized.[6]

As many feminist scholars have pointed out, popular media have played a crucial role in sustaining liberal social order and its gendered (as well as raced and classed) division of labor. For example, Mary Beth Haralovich has examined how family sitcoms like *Father Knows Best* and *Leave It to Beaver* participated in the postwar economy by mediating the broader social repositioning of the housewife vis-a-vis her domestic labor for the burgeoning suburban consumer culture.[7] As Lynn Spigel has documented, the early television industry worked vigorously to shape women's reception by constituting the act of television viewing itself as integral to women's work as housewives: The goal was not "to fit its programming into the viewer's rhythms of reception" but rather "to change those rhythms by making the activity of television viewing into a new daily habit."[8] The postfeminist media milieu certainly has offered new and relatively diverse images of women and work in both public and private spheres. However, most agree that these updated discourses of gender subjectivity and social life tend to sustain liberalism's gendered division of labor by articulating white, upper- and middle-class women—their desires and pleasures—to the feminized, privatized social spheres of domesticity and consumption.[9]

At least since the postwar rise of the mediated "happy housewife," women's domestic labors have been oriented toward maintaining family happiness. While traditional domestic labors like cooking, cleaning, and household shopping maintain the home as a "haven," the documentation of family life also puts happy families on display and solidifies the potential for families to be happy. As Susan Sontag has argued, "Through photographs, each family constructs a portrait-chronicle of itself—a portable kit of images that bears witness to its connectedness. It hardly matters what activities are photographed so long as photographs get taken and are cherished."[10] Photographs and captured memories have long circulated through the domestic sphere in the form of family photo albums and scrapbooks, but with the rise of digital media, these images flow through networks, becoming readily accessible to online communities.

In the early twenty-first century, online discourses of domesticity are collectively produced, boundless, and customized for individual consumption. Domestic work online, then, is paradoxically privatized and socialized: Women produce content collectively, for both themselves and their followers (e.g., creating boards, pinning ideas), while their consumption of content and the broader reception context is highly individualized (following specific boards, searching out particular content specific to the needs and whims of everyday life). The multiple potential modes of engagement with Pinterest offer different digital pathways to content: Women might scroll through the latest pins on their Pinterest home page or app (thus viewing a random assortment of images); they might click through one particular pinner's boards (thus viewing a still random but highly curated assortment); or, they might search for pins related to a specific theme (thus actively limiting their individual experience with the platform). Reception of social media is clearly far more individualized and customized than in the case of niche magazines or DVR'd television shows; but, at the same time, it is also far more open and linked up to a vast community of users.

Pinterest thus has done more than extend and reinforce dominant discourses of women's work: It also has constituted mothers and their engagement with popular media as a network. In this network, content is ever-flowing, as women both produce and consume pins in conjunction with the rhythms of their everyday lives and constant labors as mothers. Social media appear as a kind of perpetual flow, where content shoots along customized paths paved by algorithms and protocols, in and out of inboxes, and across newsfeeds and boards in conjunction with the dynamics of the network and its users. These networked flows of content configure communities, providing a space for sharing and socializing and transforming the privatized domain of domesticity into an ongoing, mediated, collective endeavor. Digital content flows through the mamasphere, shaping the work of mothers with continuous and constant affective punches that come to matter only as they open, fit into, and shape the feelings and potentialities of everyday life.

Packets and Pockets

In digital culture, power must be seen as constantly cycling through media flows and everyday life, as packets of content have the potential to open up pockets of experience: affective moments in the course of the mundane rhythms of life when "a space opens up"—a "pocket"—where it feels that some thing is going to happen.[11] For affect theorist Kathleen Stewart, structural forces (e.g., the primacy of the nuclear family, the dual-income economy, the rise of intensive mothering) are lived, experienced, and suffered most acutely in the pockets of everyday life, at the level of what she calls "ordinary affects." Stewart elaborates ordinary affects as "the varied, surging capacities to affect and to be affected that give everyday life the quality of a continual motion of relations, scenes, contingencies, and emergences.... They happen in impulses, sensations, expectations, daydreams, encounters, and habits of relating ... in publics and social worlds of all kinds that catch people up in something that feels like something."[12] With this theory, Stewart is trying to capture how big forces get folded into minute life-worlds in multiple, shifting ways. As such, they are "a kind of contact zone" where events, strategies for living, politics, and "flows of power" meet and are enacted.[13] And as Stewart insists, "Their significance lies in the intensities they build and in what thoughts and feelings they make possible."[14]

The cultural powers of social media—and specifically, the feminized flows of content across social media networks—become most legible when thought in relationship to the pockets and ordinary affects of everyday life. In digital culture, made up of kinetic platforms and communities of users, popular content exists as a pulsating sea of packets. As theorist Tiziana Terranova suggests, the internet, a network of networks, is "continuously although unevenly agitated, constrained and transformed by the movement of packets;"[15] packets of data (e.g., a perfectly decorated birthday cake posted to a Pinterest board) and their relentless and customized, yet erratic, flow only come to matter, only become powerful, in relation to the affective contexts of everyday life.

Commenters on the popular blog Momastery, written by Glennon Doyle Melton, a mother of three young children and a recovering alcoholic and bulimic, frequently thank Glennon for "speaking" to them at the moment when they most needed it. For example, commenting on a May 30, 2013, post suggesting that what children need most, and most simply, is their parents' love, reader Caitlin commented, "Was having one of those mornings. Feeling like I am not enough, I never get it all done, all of that. And I found this and read it. Twice. Crying. You're totally right, and I know it, but I forget it. Thank you for reminding me and giving me some perspective back." Reader Mandi echoed Caitlin's words: "I love this- ABSOLUTELY big fat crocodile tears this morning- I needed this . . . SO BADLY today- thank you thank you thank you to Rachel and Glennon- this post. . . . THIS morning . . . so needed in the world's worst way . . . I am enough . . . my love for my daughter is enough. . . . and I don't have to be, or do, or compete with anyone else . . . Love this!!!! thank you."[16] "One of those mornings" is a pocket where things could go this way or that; in this case, a moment when these women were feeling unmoored and uncertain, and a single blog post from Momastery felt profoundly stabilizing. The power of this post, just one packet sent out among millions, becomes legible in its deeply felt relationship to the lived pockets of everyday life. And its power was felt most deeply at the level of ordinary affect: While it did push on women's ideological understanding of the "good mom," its critical impact was affective, creating "big fat crocodile tears" and a sense that "I am enough."

Social media's intimate relationship to everyday life—a relationship exemplified by the example above and crystallized neatly by Pinterest and its close correspondence with women's work—can be conceptualized in terms of the interaction of packets and pockets. Digital packets come into contact with and work to develop pockets, opening up space where one feels that some thing might happen. Packets may offer information about that thing; provide images of that thing happening; suggest what to do to avoid that thing or how to manage that thing; and so on. So, a mother deeply frustrated with constantly cleaning up her children's messes might check into Pinterest one morning to find a beautifully lit image of a modern wooden bowl filled with ping pong balls and captioned, "Here's a great tip for getting the house picked up family style! Clutter Busting game using ping pong balls."[17] The mother might put that pin into action, using the strategy successfully and thus feeling like a "good mom" for an hour, or she might follow the pin's link to the *Better Homes and Gardens* website, offering that site her digital data and her time, or she might close the pin, perhaps finding it too silly or feeling bad for not turning every household chore into a fun game. The mother's frustrations are a site of affective potential; the pin becomes consequential only as it moves into this space of potential and is shaped by and works to shape it. What matters most, then, are not the customized flows and the ideologies they carry, but rather the affective structures of everyday life, which help to prestructure which pins become power-full. Certainly, which particular pins come to matter has as much to do with algorithms and protocols as it does with the rhythms, concerns, feelings, and power plays that make up everyday life.

Simply put, pins are packets that carry the potential to produce and shape pockets. As social media become more central to everyday life, packets and pockets become more significant for theorizing the cultural power of popular media. New forms of cultural power shape motherhood in digital media environments, transforming women's work and affective labor. Indeed, across the digital landscape, mothers use social media to curate and document pockets in daily life through the production and consumption of packets. Pinterest functions in part to generate sites of potential happiness: images of happy families, tools for enhancing home life, and meditations on caring for the self and one's family. These digital packets package up the family as happy and bring that potential onto digital screens and into pockets of experience.

Affective Labor and the Values of Feminized Contribution

The digital networks where family packets circulate only come into being and thrive through the perpetual production, sharing, and consumption of content by members of the community. These contributions are a form of affective labor, and the fruits of this labor are valuable to both mamas and marketers. On the one hand, corporate entities often maintain platforms designed to encourage mothers to contribute to online communities, but they of course use these communities primarily to gather data. For example, BabyCenter, the popular website for would-be, expecting, and new moms, offers an assortment of digital "calculators, calendars, checklists, and worksheets [that] can help take the stress out of pregnancy and parenting."[18] The site also hosts online communities and message boards, providing a space to share photos, meet other moms, find support and advice, and foster an online community of mothers, an active network of individual BabyCenter users. BabyCenter promises marketers: "We know what moms are saying, who they are listening to, what they are buying, and when. Our innovative blend of marketing solutions connects brands with moms in powerful ways, at key decision making moments throughout the journey—from preconception to big kid."[19] The site claims to know that, at 32 weeks into their pregnancy, moms are likely to start financial planning, and that, 6 months after their baby is born, they are likely to be interested in new beauty routines.[20]

Still, individual mothers find decidedly more social forms of value in the community provided by networks. BabyCenter is, after all, just one powerful hub within the vast online networks of mothers; in 2012, it was widely reported that there are 3.9 million so-called "mommy blogs" in North America.[21] In this mamasphere, mothering is often about creating community, solidarity, and systems of support.[22] Glennon's Momastery, mentioned previously, for example, is a community of "monkees," of "truth tellers" and "hope spreaders." As the site explains:

> The third rule of Momastery is that we are not just mothers, we are Mothers, with a capital M. A Mother with a capital M knows that the children under her roof are not her only children. A Mother knows that All God's children are her children and all God's mamas are her sisters. Here we remind each other that we are ALL family.
>
> We do that through loving and encouraging each other on this blog.[23]

In Spring 2013, Glennon began to solicit "Momastories" from her readers and from other bloggers. In these stories, women offered up their own experiences as mothers and articulated how Momastery has impacted their lives. Reader Jaime Fitch-Jenett's deeply moving Momastory details her life as the mother of a young son with a life-threatening illness and the life-saving role that Momastery played:

> Without people, we might be another tragic story of a couple whose kid got sick and their lives were ruined and they went bankrupt and divorced. But that's not our story. We're not buried. Our lives aren't ruined. They're just different. With our community, including our family and friends and

Momastery, we have managed to grow big, sprawling, tangled up, thriving, joy-filled lives.[24]

Running on contributions and the interactions of packets and pockets in everyday life, BabyCenter and Momastery can be seen as catalyzers of what Terranova calls free labor.[25] By free labor, Terranova has in mind the unpaid, freely exchanged contributions that users make to networks—for example, producing content to share, providing feedback and comments on pins, or helping the network to expand by bringing in new members. Critically, as Terranova is keen to point out, free labor, such as Jaime's Momastory, is a gift that is volunteered in a spirit of community building. Networked mothers reach out to each other through blogs and other social media platforms, offering affective care and connection through shared moments of family life. Free labor, then, is also a form of affective labor, what we might think of as a digital form of caring labor where what is cared for and tended to is the network, in our case, the networks of mothers. Indeed, Momastery is nothing else if not a mobilizer of free, caring labor for mothers. However, as the BabyCenter case makes clear, the free affective labor of contribution is a gift that is not only nurtured and sustained by social media but also readily exhausted and exploited by corporations and marketers.[26]

The free affective labor of contribution that fuels the mamasphere suggests that what ultimately circulates on and through networks like BabyCenter and Momastery is ordinary maternal affect itself. Put differently, social media do not merely spread content and attendant ideologies; they also amass and distribute affect. As Jodi Dean describes:

> Blogs, social networks, Twitter, YouTube: they produce and circulate affect as a binding technique. Affect . . . is what accrues from reflexive communication . . . from the endless circular movement of commenting, adding notes and links, bringing in new friends and followers, layering and interconnecting myriad communications platforms and devices. Every little tweet or comment, every forwarded image or petition, accrues a tiny affective nugget, a little surplus enjoyment, a smidgen of attention that attaches to it, making it stand out from the larger flow before it blends back in.[27]

For Dean, these affective networks cohere and fuel the new forms of exploitation specific to communicative capitalism.[28] Of course, women's caring and reproductive work in the domestic realm has always been affective in nature and exploited without pay. Following Dean though, mothering in the network has intensified the scene of affective exploitation for women, as the pleasures mothers take in—as well as the digital women's work they perform by contributing their family packets to popular sites like Pinterest, BabyCenter, and online communities like Momastery—has become a new site for capitalist valorization.

However, as Jaime's Momastory attests, affective networks do more than fill corporate coffers. The cultural powers of contribution concern how free labor cycles affect through everyday life, distributing it into, and thereby shaping, pockets of experience. In other words, when it comes to the cultural power of family content being shared and circulated online, we need to think seriously about what Terranova theorizes as the "power of affection" and "the kind of affect it packs."[29] Why and how might one pin come to "stand out from the larger flow," and what happens "before it blends back in"? The remainder of this chapter takes up these questions by honing in on the pervasive practice of curating images germane to family life and domesticity. This is an affective practice where what gets pinned is not only an idea, an image, or a moment, but also a particular affective structure—in this case, the affective structure of happiness. In the early twenty-first century, curating family packets is often about pinning the family as a site of potential happiness in neoliberal times, when social security webs are weak, threats both local and global abound, and 'the good life' is increasingly unattainable.

Pinning Happiness

Pinning is a form of free labor and contribution with its own peculiar cultural dimensions and politics. For mothers, it is a form of digital care work that involves not simply contributing to a network but also curating one's family life and displaying one's women's work. As Alexander Galloway and Eugene Thacker point out, such curation is fraught:[30] The very act of selecting, sharing, and thus stabilizing a pin—of trying to make it "stand out from the larger flow"—opens the curator and the curated up to the contingencies of consumption and reception, as well as to the contingencies of ordinary affects. Pinning may yield support and community, but it may also result in misinterpretations and harmful comments. Pins may go viral, interacting with pockets near and far, while others may "blend back in" without ever going noticed. As mothers curate family packets on social media sites, they both contribute and open themselves up to the uncertain sharing and circulation of affect. Indeed, moving through the pinned world of feminized social media is an experience rife with affective potentiality, for participating in this curated space perpetually promises to collide with everyday life in unexpected ways. What is more, what is often at stake in the care work of curation is their own women's work, and, more pointedly, the happiness of their family.

Indeed, Pinterest is littered with "happy objects,"[31] as pinners curate objects that point to and hold the promise of happiness: inspirational or funny quotes, books one loved or hopes to love, recipes one plans to try, and so on. It is a social network that thrives off and capitalizes on the contribution of happy packets and the free labor of promoting "a few (million) of your favorite things." Thus, what so often circulates across the affective networks of Pinterest is happiness, or rather the promise of happiness. For Ahmed, happiness is not simply an emotion, but a rather powerful affective structure, as it is "an orientation toward the objects we come into contact with. We move toward and away from objects through how we are affected by them."[32] In other words, happiness carves out social worlds, prestructuring how objects come to affect us and thus what objects will be valued and how. In this way, happiness forms our "near sphere, the world that take shapes around us,"[33] for it is via happiness that we "come to have our likes, which might even establish what we are like.[34]

The feminized character of Pinterest is owed in part to the fact that, in liberal capitalist societies that rest on unpaid caring labor in the domestic sphere, the family becomes the ultimate happy object. According to Ahmed, it is a cultural scene drenched in the promise of happiness: "We hear the term 'happy families' and we register the connection of these words with the familiarity of their affective resonance. Happy families: a card game, a title of a children's book, a government discourse; a promise, a hope, dream, an aspiration."[35] Happiness is routinely posited as the end, the telos, of family life; adopting happiness as a goal shapes ordinary affects in the domestic sphere, including how mothers value the objects that populate it and experience the labors it demands. For Ahmed, the happy family is "a myth of happiness, of where and how happiness takes place," as well as an inheritance. As such, happiness becomes a duty to the extent that mothers feel obligated to aim for it, to advocate for those things that promise it, and to help themselves and others achieve it.

As Ahmed suggests, "We can think of gendered scripts as 'happiness scripts' providing a set of instructions for what women and men must do in order to be happy, whereby happiness is what follows being natural or good."[36] These scripts are upheld as paths to the good life, even if, and when, they do not result in happiness. Put differently, the affective structure of happiness asks mothers to see women's work as both holding and preserving the potential for happiness. However, if happiness is the point of family life, it is an elusive point, hard to pin down in the muck of endlessly packing lunches, wiping off tables, and coordinating busy schedules. Calling and experiencing this labor as "happy" undoubtedly takes some affective effort. Crucially, it is in opening up and revealing pockets in everyday life—spaces that hold potential for happiness—that the family can maintain its status as happy.

And here is where social media sites like Pinterest step in: They allow happy family objects to be regularly displayed and readily accessed, priming the promise of happiness to materialize. On Pinterest boards, mothers curate the minutia of everyday life, pinning ideas for birthday cakes, strategies for stimulating babies' brains, exercises to do at home, and activities to keep toddlers occupied. The quest for happiness in women's work is documented here, thought through here, promised here, and held near here. And women's inherited duties to happiness are performed here. For example, on a pin displaying rainbow-colored cupcakes, Marie G. commented, "My mom made me cupcakes like that for my 10th birthday. . . . I still remember it 20+ years later so totally worth the effort!"[37] Pinned here is the potential to recreate the moment this commenter remembers so fondly—a promise to return to childhood happiness bound immediately with the family, and more importantly, with the mother and her labor.

Indeed, Pinterest's platforms actively incite mothers to participate in the affective structure of family happiness, to document, display, and organize a "horizon of likes"[38] through curating boards and pins. Consider, for example, the popular parenting blog Modern Parents Messy Kids's Pinterest page. It hosts 45 boards, all of which promise to enhance women's work as mothers by "providing you with the best ideas for raising engaged kids and simplifying your life in style." Board titles include: "Playtime," "Art and Craft," "Design with Kids in Mind," "Clean Eating Recipes," "Busy Bags," "Playroom Ideas," and "Words to Live By."[39] Each board hosts a variety of pins, each of which packages up an object, an idea, a technique of happiness. One pin offers "20 Ways to Get Closer to Your Child Today," another suggests "Wake Up Happy: Starting a Child's Day with JOY," and another lists "8 Simple Ideas for Making Meal Time Meaningful." While these happy packets may not actually bring happiness, because they have been already established as a cause of or means to happiness, they are held near, displayed, and shared. Images of mother/son and father/daughter "date nights," promises of "perfect mornings with your kids," and countless strategies for making birthdays meaningful all promise that family life can be joyful and purposeful. In making these promises, these boards and pins help to strip everyday family living of banality and uncertainty by infusing pockets with potential happiness. The affective networks of Pinterest can thus be seen as passing the potential for happiness around. The platform provides a hub where mothers seek out, preserve, and share happy objects, for it is a place where the expectation of happiness abounds.

From this perspective, what is most politically problematic about the curating of family happiness via Pinterest boards like Modern Parents Messy Kids is not necessarily the exploitation of contributions by corporations and marketers, but rather the ways in which the site and the practices it mobilizes sustain social structures at the level of affect and affective networks. In particular, Ahmed is interested in how desire for, pleasure taken in, and ideas of the good life are bound up with the affective structure of happiness; as she puts it, "Happiness allows us to line up with things in the right way."[40] In other words, the pursuit of a happy family—that is, living with the family as the primary site of potential happiness—signals one's capacity for desiring well and rightly. Pinterest can be thought of as an affective network for curating and sharing the good life, for displaying that one desires the right kind of things and takes pleasure in the right kind of ways. Thus, it is also a site of social and cultural privilege: Its happiness is primarily reserved for those who are already invested in, and have access to, a particular raced, gendered, and classed conception of the good life for those who already have a taste for it. Put differently, Pinterest makes mothering social, collective, and shared for only those mothers who already have been oriented to find happiness there.

In this way, the affective communities configured by sites like Modern Parents Messy Kids are affectively structured to most readily benefit those members whose pockets seem to be already aligned with its templates for potential happiness. For example, under a pin titled "5 Lessons from Great-Playing Dads," one pinner commented, "And if your [sic] a single parent does this still apply? Do single parents still find the time to enjoy and fun in parenting whilst working, supermarket/dog runs, raising teenagers with toddlers and so forth? I don't see my son play with his father- we are separated. I am parenting almost full time on my own, do you have any advice for types like me? So far my son (2.5 yrs) likes to clean, cook and wear make up?!!! :^) help!!"[41] Here Pinterest's happy packets only open, exacerbate, and intensify pockets already rife with the stress and anxiety of not having that "great-playing dad."

The fraught practice of pinning happiness extends far beyond the well-furnished walls of Pinterest pages like Modern Parents Messy Kids to encompass a broader array of activities that fuel the online networks of mothers. From corporate sites like BabyCenter to Glennon's community of "monkees," pinning happiness is about sharing content and affect germane to family life, women's work, and their potentiality. Technically, pinning happiness is an act of contribution, of curation, and of free labor. Culturally and socially, it is an affective practice of women's work, one that involves the production and consumption of happy family packets and is aimed toward the opening of pockets in everyday life where women might feel as though the labor they relentlessly perform might carry the promise for family happiness.

For mothers, the work of creating happiness in everyday life—that is, the affective labor demanded by happiness scripts—is unrelenting, especially in the early twenty-first century. In this context, the work of keeping the family happy has become increasingly fraught, as it has been overdetermined by larger political and economic structures bent on dismantling the very social glue that makes family fantasies of the good life possible in the first place. Most notably, neoliberalism has rendered all of life precarious. Social safety webs continue to erode as states pursue austerity. Individuals and families have been left with little other than their own enterprise to confront the immense challenges of health, environmental degradation, declining opportunity, and rising inequality.[42] Considered within the context of the affective structure of happiness, then, mothers' pinning practices can be seen as a volatile form of care work, not only because of the paradox entailed in the free labor of curation, but also because of the precarity that perpetually threatens to upset the family's promise as a site of happiness. Feminized social media sites and, more specifically, the practice of pinning happiness, garner much of their cultural power in the affective context of precarity. In such precarious times, the affective structure of happiness and its gendered happiness scripts are evermore key to sustaining neoliberal social order. Indeed, perhaps the most important cultural work that pinning happiness does is to stabilize the happy family, as a myth, an inheritance, and a duty. Lauren Berlant might recognize this stabilizing work as "cruel optimism": The happiness of the good life is increasingly out of reach, rendering the optimistic work of affective investment in it decidedly cruel.[43]

Sharing domestic life via the affective networks of mothers on social media can be seen as a way to stabilize the precarious happiness of the family. This stabilization happens in a number of different ways, though on two primary levels. First, the production of family packets, the pinning of one's own happy objects and scenes to Facebook, Pinterest, and blogs is a means to narrativize the work of happiness. It is about taking notes on where happiness might live and thereby inscribing happiness' elusive potential into everyday life. Taking note is a process of opening up or revealing pockets in the ordinary, moments where some things might and do happen. Part of the reason for opening these pockets, it seems, is that the promise of happiness requires them. If happiness is the end goal, the telos of family life, but exists only when one feels its potential, taking note becomes vital affective labor, especially in the context of precarity. Social media then provide a readily accessible mechanism to take note of pockets that point toward and ultimately guarantee the happiness of the family. What is more, they allow this vital affective labor to be shared and socialized, as well as perpetuated. Happiness may be impossible but its potential can be readily and continuously documented, displayed, and passed around online for others to see and share.

Second, consuming family packets—taking notes on others' notes and following their narratives of happiness—may enable everyday lives, animated by precarity, to feel full of potential on the horizon, both for the self and for others in one's near sphere and network. One mother's packet becomes another's pocket: This is the cultural power of social media and the free affective labor it mobilizes. As women capture moments of happiness and share them online— by uploading photos of smiling children to Facebook, detailing themed birthday parties on blogs, or offering advice on Pinterest—they inscribe happiness as a potential for other mothers, and perhaps more importantly, they suggest that happiness truly can be captured, won, and achieved, even in a world that constantly feels scary and uncertain. In this way, pinning happiness is an affective practice of individual and community stabilization.

Pinning happiness is about pointing to and thereby inscribing moments when kids might be optimized, families connected, and mothers fulfilled. Pinning these moments becomes a way of stabilizing the uncertain happiness of the family, as well as one's purpose to keep the family happy. The ones who profit from feminized social media are, of course, the marketers who peddle in—and have long peddled in—the promise of happiness. Also rewarded are the millions of mothers who take pleasure in—and find hope in—the volatile affective practice of passing family happiness around online. However, what ultimately gets pinned down in these networked practices of capitalization and community, in these interactions of packets and pockets in everyday life, are the cruel structures, both material and affective, that continue to insist on both precarity and patriarchy.

Notes

1. Sarah Ahmed, *The Promise of Happiness* (Durham, N.C.: Duke University Press, 2010), 21–49.
2. "Press," Pinterest, accessed July 23, 2013, http://about.pinterest.com/press/.
3. "Start-up Pinterest Wins New Funding, $2.5 billion valuation," Reuters, Feb. 20, 2013, accessed July 23, 2013, http://www.reuters.com/article/2013/02/21/net-us-funding-pinterest-idUSBRE91K01R20130221.
4. Wendy Brown, *States of Injury: Power and Freedom in Late Modernity* (Princeton, N.J.: Princeton University Press, 1995), 144.
5. Ibid., 147.

6. Ibid., 144.

7. Mary Beth Haralovich, "Sit-coms and Suburbs: Positioning the 1950s Homemaker," in *Private Screenings*, eds. Lynn Spigel and Denise Mann (Minneapolis: University of Minnesota Press, 1992), 110–139.

8. Lynn Spigel, *Make Room for TV: Television and the Family Ideal in Postwar America* (Chicago: University of Chicago Press, 1992), 85.

9. See for example, Angela McRobbie, "Post-Feminism and Popular Culture," *Feminist Media Studies* 4:3 (2004): 255–264.

10. Susan Sontag, *On Photography* (New York: Farrar, Strauss, and Giroux, 1977), 8.

11. Kathleen Stewart, "Pockets," *Communication and Critical/Cultural Studies* 9:4 (2012): 365.

12. Kathleen Stewart, *Ordinary Affects* (Durham, N.C.: Duke University Press, 2007), 1–2.

13. Ibid., 3.

14. Ibid.

15. Tiziana Terranova, *Network Culture: Politics for the Information Age* (Pluto Press, 2004), 67.

16. Rachel Macy Stafford, "Momastory Series: Guest Post from Rachel, The Hands Free Mama," Momastery, accessed June 1, 2013, http://momastery.com/blog/2013/05/30/momastory-series-guest-post-from-rachel-the-hands-free-mama/.

17. Jennifer Shedd, "Smart Ways to Declutter and Stress Less!" Pinterest, accessed June 5, 2013, http://www.pinterest.com/pin/259097784781728816/.

18. BabyCenter, "Pregnancy and Parenting Tools," accessed June 5, 2013, http://www.babycenter.com/tools.

19. BabyCenter, "Marketing Solutions," accessed June 5, 2013, http://www.babycentersolutions.com/marketing-solutions.html.

20. Ibid.

21. Sam Laird, "The Rise of the Mommy Blogger [Infographic]," Mashable, May 8, 2012, accessed June 4, 2013, http://mashable.com/2012/05/08/mommy-blogger-infographic/.

22. See Lori Kido Lopez, "The Radical Act of 'Mommy Blogging': Redefining Motherhood through the Blogosphere," *New Media and Society* 11:5 (2009): 729–747.

23. Momastery, "The Monkees of Momastery," accessed May 6, 2013, http://momastery.com/blog/who-are-the-monkees-of-the-momastery/.

24. Momastery, "Momastory Series—Meet Jaime and Laura!!!" accessed May 1, 2013, http://momastery.com/blog/2013/04/23/momastory-series-meet-jaime-and-laura/.

25. Terranova, 90–91.

26. Ibid., 94.

27. Jodi Dean, *Blog Theory: Feedback and Capture in the Circuits of Drive* (Cambridge, U.K.: Polity Press, 2010), 95.

28. Ibid.

29. Terranova, 142.

30. Alexander Galloway and Eugene Thacker, *The Exploit: A Theory of Networks* (Minneapolis: University of Minnesota Press, 2007), 107.

31. Ahmed, 21–49.

32. Ibid., 24.

33. Ibid.

34. Ibid.

35. Ibid., 45.

36. Ibid., 59.

37. Modern Parents, Messy Kids, untitled pin, accessed June 10, 2013, http://pinterest
.com/pin/36239971971823206/.

38. Ahmed, 24.

39. Modern Parents Messy Kids Pinterest Board, accessed May 30, 2013, http://pinterest
.com/modrentmessykid/.

40. Ahmed, 37.

41. Modern Parents Messy Kids, "5 Lessons from Great-Playing Dads," accessed May
30, 2013, http://pinterest.com/pin/36239971973012215/.

42. David Harvey, *A Brief History of Neoliberalism* (Oxford: Oxford University Press,
2005). See also Wendy Brown, "Neo-liberalism and the End of Liberal Democracy," *Theory
and Event* 7:1 (2003), accessed May 29, 2013, doi:10.1353/tae.2003.0020.

43. Lauren Berlant, *Cruel Optimism* (Durham, N.C.: Duke University Press, 2011).

CHAPTER 13

Sweet Sisterhood

Cupcakes as Sites of Feminized Consumption and Production

ELIZABETH NATHANSON

In the third season of the HBO television show *Sex and the City*, Carrie (Sarah Jessica Parker) and Miranda (Cynthia Nixon) gossip about men while munching on cupcakes in the New York City sunshine (see Figure 13.1). Having broken up with her on-again/off-again love interest Mr. Big (Chris Noth), Carrie has just met Aidan (John Corbett). With his faded jeans, tousled hair, and hand-made soft leather furniture, Aidan's rugged and warm masculinity sends Carrie into a tailspin, the intimate details of which she shares with Miranda. Sitting outside of Magnolia Bakery with pink frosted cupcakes in hand Carrie declares that she has a "crush." Surprised, Miranda responds that she hasn't had a crush since "Shawn Cassidy," implying that "a crush" is a rarity for adult women who presumably lead more mature lives. And yet, Miranda's response, "At this age, I would have to say I'm crush-proof," is laden with nostalgia for Carrie's experience of fun, carefree sexual desire.

Such "girly" conversation appears to require an equally "girly" treat, one combining soft mounds of pink frosting with palpable sweetness. Unlike the more adult but no less pink Cosmopolitan cocktails for which the *Sex and the City* characters are known, cupcakes match Carrie's PG language of teenage crushes. Cupcakes help facilitate this postfeminist depiction of femininity that valorizes youthfulness over adulthood. Michele Lazar writes that, "The celebration of girlhood is about instant self-gratification and pleasure, but also specifically emphasizes youthfulness as a time of fun."[1] On *Sex and the City*, the

FIGURE 13.1. Carrie and Miranda enjoying the girlish treat of cupcakes and boy talk. *Sex in the City*, "No Ifs, Ands or Butts," season 3, episode 5, HBO.

pink Magnolia Bakery cupcake reinforces such representations of girlishness, for while consuming their treats the two women bond in friendship, sharing thoughts of crushes and the surprising joys of remembering such feminine experiences. The sweet confection has much in common with a crush: Enjoying a crush, like enjoying a cupcake, may not be "good for you" but it sure is fun.

By the early twenty-first century, cupcakes turned up on television, in films, magazines, and websites, and cupcake specialty stores became a global phenomenon. This chapter accounts for the "cupcake craze" by analyzing the distinctly feminized pleasures the confections signify in the postfeminist cultural context. Feminist media scholars have critiqued postfeminist popular culture for producing hegemonic representations that depoliticize feminist ideals. As Angela McRobbie argues, "[T]he idea of feminist content disappeared and was replaced by aggressive individualism, by a hedonistic female phallicisim in the field of sexuality, and by obsession with consumer culture which . . . I see as playing a vital role in the undoing of feminism."[2] In many ways, representations of cupcakes in popular culture participate in such postfeminist disarticulations of feminism. When they appear as objects to be eaten, cupcakes facilitate girly bonding and provide personal pleasures that both expose and uphold dominant ideologies of gender, race, and class. When cupcakes are represented as objects to be made, such as on *Cupcake Wars* (Food Network), *2 Broke Girls* (CBS), the blog *Cupcakes and Cashmere*, or the film *Bridesmaids* (2011), cupcakes promise entrepreneurial freedoms that provide a fantasy work/life balance for women who are expected to "have it all," while ignoring structural inequalities that make balance impossible. While cupcakes may reify postfeminist ideologies that depoliticize feminist aims, they also point toward resistant pleasures; cupcakes invite cultural consumers to take pleasure in depictions of sisterhood that challenge neoliberal individuality by celebrating bonds between women and the liberating potential of difference. By tracing popular representations of cupcakes as items of consumption and production, this chapter finds moments in which viewers are invited to take pleasure in sweet indulgences and feminine friendships that reproduce but also expose the cracks in contemporary gender politics.

Feasting on Frosting

Magnolia Bakery opened in 1996 and following its appearance on *Sex and the City* in 2000 the lines outside grew, the *Sex and the City* bus tour featured the shop on its route, and the "cupcake craze" began.[3] Within a few years cupcake stores appeared in cities from Los Angeles to Philadelphia.[4] In the 2000s, cupcakes became a global phenomenon with stores opening in cities from Dubai to Hong Kong, and cupcakes have been sold from storefronts, websites, and even ATMs. There are cupcake-themed T-shirts and profit-generating blogs like *Cupcakes Take the Cake*.[5] These small confections have had an aura of being recession proof; cupcakes remained a popular business throughout the 2008 global financial crisis, as the press declared it a good business if one could locate "a niche ... among the many cupcake companies ... people are willing to pay for high-end treats."[6] These small personal indulgences have offered consumer joys, promising a temporary break from economic austerity.

While popular discourse makes cupcakes sound well suited to a moment of economic exigency, thus presumably offering gender-neutral pleasures, the treat has been primarily associated with femininity. The press overwhelmingly featured women as the primary consumers of cupcakes. The few articles published about cupcake stores owned by men constantly foreground the manliness of their products. For example, in 2010 the *New York Daily News* profiled David Arrick, founder of butchbakery.com, an online bakery that makes cupcakes like "Beer Run" and "the Campout."[7] Traditional masculine identifiers like beer, camouflage, and the great outdoors differentiate these "macho" products from the domesticated pink pleasures shared by Carrie and Miranda.

As the news media has tried to account for this craze, it has relied on tropes of femininity that in turn have circulated notions about women as the target for cupcake sales and cupcake popular culture. Such discourse draws upon ideas about women as highly emotional and as having desires that can be mobilized by the media and consumer culture. For example, after the premiere of *DC Cupcakes*, a reality TV program about the store Georgetown Cupcakes, the lines at that shop grew, stretching sometimes to 100 people long and resulting in a two-hour wait.[8] The reality television program became an ideal advertising venue, growing an already secure business and providing PR that appeared to easily turn malleable television spectators into shoppers and tourists. Cupcakes seem to drive feminized consumers to extreme ends as they wait to be close to the objects of their affection and fandom: "One sweltering day . . . a young woman was baking in the sun . . . waiting in the long queue to buy some of the bakery's signature sweets, when she fainted on the sidewalk. An ambulance rushed to the scene, but she declined to go to the hospital."[9] The press has painted these cupcake consumers as irrational and sensitive, unable to differentiate between "legitimate" tourism (Washington D.C. as political epicenter) and "illegitimate" tourism (Washington D.C. as consumer metropolis), a distinction that is, of course, also gendered.

Cupcakes have also been coded feminine by their association with fashionable starlets. Magazines like *Cosmo Girl* and *Marie Claire* feature articles in which celebrities like Blake Lively and Katie Holmes declare their cupcake passions while also promoting their favorite cosmetics. For example, in the June 2013 issue of *Marie Claire* Katie Holmes "shared" eleven of her favorite style items that include Bobbi Brown eye shadow, Manolo Blahnik heels, and Georgetown Cupcakes.[10] In such celebrity discourse the confection becomes yet another lifestyle choice that signifies fashionable femininity. Websites like *Cupcakes and Cashmere* have also perpetuated associations between cupcakes and fashion as of the same taste culture; as blogger Emily Schuman explains, she started her blog "as a way to document the things she loved."[11] As such women proclaim the "power" to choose these single-portion, aesthetically appealing desserts, they assert their individuality; when celebrities choose a particular cupcake brand or a flavor they articulate a presumably autonomous sense of self through fashionable consumer items. While cupcakes contain the calories and fat that thin female celebrities must surely battle in order to wear "fashionable" clothing and remain in the public eye, the small indulgence works with, rather than against, contemporary definitions of ideal femininity. They signify one of the qualities of the "postfeminist sensibility" whereby, "Notions of choice, of 'being oneself' and 'pleasing oneself' . . . [suffuse] contemporary western media culture."[12] The contradictions of postfeminist femininity appear in discourses about cupcakes; by embracing such sweet confections celebrities like Holmes or Schuman can demonstrate freedom from the sexist "thin" beauty regimen while their famous, highly visible, willowy bodies uphold it.

Numerous theories have circulated that seek to explain the popularity of cupcakes in this era. Some critics have connected cupcakes to the rise of retrofemininity and the antifeminist backlash such nostalgia seems to invoke:

"Cupcake mania allows a woman to imagine herself in a nostalgic rural idyll, without actually having to look after a cow or deal with its issues. . . . Retro femininity is rising alongside a new social and economic conservatism, in whose frozen embrace women's rights are seriously threatened."[13] Invoking images of bake sales and happy housewives, cupcakes appear to signify family values and women's "natural" place in the home that perpetuate the "new traditionalism" and "retreatism" structuring postfeminist representations.[14] Such conservative associations reached a fever pitch in a post on an evangelical website titled "Hope for Western Civilization" that praised how cupcakes have "become a symbol of rebellion against feminism, materialism and androgyny."[15] As cupcakes appear in popular and consumer culture as feminized treats, they offer an ideal vessel for a postfeminist sensibility that combines feminine and antifeminist discourses, containing feminist power in a neoliberal rhetoric of individual consumer tastes and innate domestic capabilities.

While cupcakes participate in the domestication that has dominated postfeminist popular culture, such claims risk positioning audiences as passively absorbing the antifeminist values circulated by consumer and popular culture. Cupcake culture offers pleasures that complicate these conservative impulses, speaking to feminine desires for connection that exist alongside neoliberal postfeminist discourses. The remainder of this chapter explores how early-twenty-first-century depictions of cupcake production not only contribute to but also push against the "postfeminist sensibility." Representations of and narratives about cupcake production hail audiences who are invited to enjoy portrayals of work that draw on an idealized worker's skills of connection and integration. As small, personalized, easily transported and simply devoured confections, cupcakes signify a labor environment that celebrates mobility, individualism, and consumerism. Rather than view representations of cupcake bakers as merely nostalgic, this chapter argues that cupcake production appears as a pleasurable form of modern feminized labor that blends home and work through depictions of entrepreneurship that reveal fantasies about feminine acts of creativity and collaboration.

Combining Cake and Icing

Since Carrie and Miranda nibbled on pink cupcakes outside Magnolia Bakery, depictions of cupcake production exploded online, on television sets, and even on the big screen. From Kristen Wiig's character in *Bridesmaids*, to reality television programs like *DC Cupcakes* and *Cupcake Wars*, to the blogs dedicated to all things cupcake, women bakers appear throughout the twenty-first-century media landscape. It is no surprise that the color pink also permeates such texts and can be found in a TV program's graphics, a blog's font, or baker's uniform.[16] Cupcake labor is further feminized through the depiction of how cupcake baking is distinguished from labors traditionally associated with masculinity. Annie's love interest in *Bridesmaids* works as a police officer, a physical, heroic career invoking manliness that stands in juxtaposition with her sugary cupcake prowess. Similarly, on *Cupcake Wars*, while the competitors do represent racial and ethnic diversity, many episodes feature only female bakers. Occasionally, a man will enter the competition as the head baker, but these men speak in ways that code themselves as traditionally masculine, such as by calling themselves "pastry chefs," drawing attention to their culinary expertise, or distancing themselves from a cupcake's maternal associations; on one episode, the so-called "pastry chef" from Cups Bakery brags that his product is "not your grandmother's cupcakes." Women competitors on *Cupcake Wars*, by contrast, invoke rather than disavow their maternal baking inspiration. Numerous competitors explain how they use family recipes and were taught to bake by mothers and grandmothers; one African American owner of an online bakery explains that her mother taught her to make cupcakes, and that for her baking is "really close to home." Furthermore, female competitors describe their reactions to the pressures of the competition in personal and emotional language; one competitor states that she cares about each cupcake she makes. In these ways, femininity is depicted in conventional terms that link food to gendered modes of caretaking.

In the early twenty-first century, however, feminized baking is transformed into economic labor by merging traditional notions of femininity with profit-driven workplace strategies, speaking to the unique pressures of the postfeminist context in which women are expected to "have it all." As professional bakers, women on TV are often seen racing to complete their work by a particular deadline, and in this way subject their culinary labor to the rigors of time. As I have argued elsewhere, the focus on time stresses is a defining feature of postfeminist popular culture, representing how domestic spaces have adapted to and incorporated the temporal rhythms of the working world.[17] Time pressures structure programs like *DC Cupcakes* on which episodes are ruled by a plot in which the sisters are hired to create a cupcake sculpture for a particular event. The program derives much of its minimal excitement from this deadline-driven plot that implicitly asks if the sisters will be able to successfully complete the sculpture in time for the party. Similarly, *Cupcake Wars* transforms the kitchen into a time-regulated workspace in which competitors compete with each other as well as the clock. These representations of time-stressed baking speak to feminized audiences; as Diane Negra writes: "Women's lives are . . . simultaneously ever more governed by notions of temporal propriety and conformity but also assessed in relation to women's perceived abilities to defy time pressures and impacts, and the ensuing paradox is one that a variety of forms of female-oriented popular culture seek to manage."[18] Audiences are invited to celebrate successful cupcake bakers who beat their competition and the forward-moving hands of time, demonstrating how they effectively manage their products, and by extension themselves, within the conditions of time-sensitive material labor.

Through depictions of baking that merge home and work, cupcake popular culture offers pleasurable solutions to the tensions that emerge from postfeminist discourses suggesting that feminist goals have been achieved and women can freely pursue personal, familial, and professional ends. The reality is, of course, much more complex, as structural inequities have continued to define gendered experience. In the early 2000s, prominent professional women published highly publicized arguments about the ability of women to be successful in public and private spheres when faced with a system that places competing demands on their time. Anne-Marie Slaughter's article, "Why Women Still Can't Have It All" and Sheryl Sandberg's argument about how women must "lean in" in order to succeed in business illustrate that the route for women to develop careers while raising a family remains both unclear and fraught.[19]

Cupcakes speak to this context, offering fantasy solutions to anxieties about women's work/life balance by offering an opportunity to efficiently combine home and work in the form of a family business. *DC Cupcakes* exemplifies this trend by celebrating feminized entrepreneurialism that is distinctly domestic and as such appears as more ideal than a traditional work environment. As Sophie and Katherine explain in the opening credits in voice-over, "We ditched our corporate jobs to follow our dreams to work together and make the world's best tasting cupcakes." These sisters rejected mainstream corporate careers in favor of a family business grounded in maternal lineage; the sisters learned to bake from their grandmother and work in the store with their mother. Cupcake entrepreneurship underscores how ideal feminized work requires sacrificing financial gain in favor of personal and family rewards. Blogger Stefani Hope Pollack (cupcakeproject.com) efficiently monetized her websites by merging family and career, employing her photographer husband to document her cupcake exploits. As Pollack has explained, "I'm not making as much as I was in the corporate world, so blogging is clearly about the love and not the money."[20] These cupcake entrepreneurs sacrifice traditional financial successes in favor of affective rewards, and in the process demonstrate how women cannot "have it all"; while a family business has its benefits, they come with significant losses that perpetuate and reflect continued gender inequality.

Representations of cupcake entrepreneurialism speak to a larger trend in which women-owned businesses have risen: "Between 1997–2007, the number of women-owned businesses grew by 44 percent, twice as fast as men-owned firms."[21] Since 2008, female entrepreneurs have been celebrated for helping drive postrecessionary economic growth. However, such productive citizenship does not negate the continued inequalities that have impacted women's experiences. Sociologists have argued that as women open their own businesses, they perform both femininity and the masculine qualities associated with entrepreneurship such as initiative and autonomy, resulting in "shuttling between different and dichotomous spaces."[22] Such enactments of gender impact women's identities. As they seek an "authentic entrepreneurial identity" they "draw on antagonistic discourses; that is, a feminine discourse of difference and a masculine discourse of professionalism as a means of linking the internal and external aspects of their sense of self."[23] While it may seem as if women entrepreneurs blend public and private spaces easily, the binary distinctions between home/femininity and work/masculinity remain deeply entrenched in the business (and social) world.

Cupcake businesses promise to help manage tensions implicit in the post-feminist juggling act by bringing feelings of personal, emotional, and familial satisfaction to capitalist enterprises. To this end, early-twenty-first-century cupcake entrepreneurs invest a sense of individual creativity in their product. For example, on *Cupcake Wars*, contestants are not only judged on how well they manage their time, but how well they adapt their cupcakes to the given theme of the episode in both flavor and appearance. On the Matchmaking Party episode, bakers are given the task to "turn up the heat for tonight's singles" by incorporating two "aphrodisiac" ingredients such as oysters, champagne, and strawberries into their cupcakes and then decorate them in a "sexy" way (see Figure 13.2). The program's rhetoric of incorporation, flexibility, and risk represents dynamics of the early-twenty-first-century workplace. Anita Harris argues that the economic and social environment of late modernity is defined by qualities like contingency and individual responsibility and that young women uniquely exemplify such a subject position.[24] On *Cupcake Wars*, women who demonstrate their ability to "choose" the right ingredients and then incorporate those selected ingredients into their own, personal products exemplify Harris's notion of the successful "future girl." They express themselves, and by extension their capabilities in the larger socioeconomic marketplace, through their ability to adapt to the reality TV environment.

FIGURE 13.2. A "sexy cupcake" entry for a Matchmaking Party competition. *Cupcake Wars*, season 1, episode 3, Food Network.

Variety and creative displays of self have been celebrated throughout cupcake culture. The cupcake itself offers a format that can be adjusted, adapted, and arranged in different combinations and thus is uniquely emblematic of the early-twenty-first-century mobile, "flexible" workplace. Blogs like The Cupcake Daily Blog (thecupcakedailyblog.com) offer twists on the standard cupcake ranging from Brown Butter Chocolate Popcorn Cupcakes to Strawberry Balsamic Cupcakes. Such playful work speaks to how Ann Gray argues that women entrepreneurs turn their "natural" consumer skills into marketable skills, founding businesses focused on aesthetics and participating in an economy that values independence and self-regulation.[25] Representations of women's natural adaptability and aesthetic capabilities appear throughout cupcake culture. For example, the sculptures Katherine and Sophie make on *DC Cupcakes* have a base constructed from wood, nails, and Styrofoam and the cupcakes are glued to that base and frosted in colors that shade the structure. There is a predictable gendered division of labor: The masculine employees create the wood and Styrofoam base using workshop tools, while the sisters are in charge of the softer task of decorating with cupcakes and frosting. While Katherine and Sophie appear to use graphs occasionally to create a coherent image out of the cupcakes, their work is largely impressionistic; these women appear to have an innate feel for creating realistic cupcake spectacles. Georgetown Cupcake has been profiled in the press as a successful business because the sisters "learn to adapt as they go."[26] These sisters appear innately responsive to the needs of their business and consumers, and thus are emblematic of "can-do girls" who thrive in the new economy of risk.[27] Watching Katherine and Sophie connect individual cupcakes to each other to construct a whole sculpture depicts them as reassuringly feminine; they may be ambitious entrepreneurs, but their success is contingent upon their "natural" ability to be flexible, feminized subjects who appreciate visual spectacles.

Cupcake culture is thus defined by those who take risks but only with limits, depicting cupcakes and their feminized bakers as creative but only when they conform to strict preestablished confines. For example, contestants on *Cupcake Wars* are judged by experts who evaluate how well the bakers executed their creative choices to suit the theme of the episode. On the "Hawaii Food and Wine Festival" episode, bakers were tasked to use "Hawaiian" ingredients like macadamia nuts, roast pork, and pineapple in cupcakes that also signify Hawaii. Individual ingenuity is prized only when it finds a balance between the personal style of the competitor and the demands of the episode. Bakers like Lily are criticized for making a mango cardamom cupcake that is delicious but only tastes like mango, whereas contestants like Jannelle are praised for incorporating ingredients like absinthe, black currant, and poppy seeds in a cupcake meant to signify a witch from the musical *Wicked*. Similar to the rhetoric of work/life balance, cupcake bakers are expected to manage each part of each cupcake so they add up to a complete, composed whole.

In these ways, cupcake culture dramatizes the feminine pursuit of individual success in the new economy while also exposing the limits set by that economy. Success is found in expressions of a baker's versatility and her ability to create synergy between disparate elements, including herself. Throughout cupcake culture, depictions of "women's work" are made pleasurable by representing baking as an intimate task, inviting viewers to see such businesses and the confections as expressions of feminine selfhood. From the "signature swirl" Katherine and Sophie put on each cupcake to the *Cupcake Wars* contestants' uniforms consisting of headbands, frilly aprons, and pink, purple, or turquoise T-shirts, these women effectively identify with their products. These acts of "self-branding" appear throughout early-twenty-first-century culture, and Sarah Banet-Weiser argues that postfeminist subjects are uniquely encouraged to cultivate a "self-brand."[28] Such self-branding extends beyond women's bodies to the products they make; cupcakes become an extension of the competitor's sense of self; as contestant Tara declares, her cupcakes are "'bangin,' just like me."

By collapsing distinctions between feminized bakers' sense of self and their work, cupcake culture illustrates how women may have increased access to choice and opportunities to articulate their individuality, but their autonomy is constrained by standards that require the baker to sublimate her work and herself to strict standards of acceptability. As one *Cupcake Wars* contestant explains: "I need to win *Cupcake Wars* mostly for myself to verify that my cupcakes are good." Successful, productive femininity is defined by a baker's synergy of self with expectations that lie beyond her. The presentation of self to the public operates as a kind of PR that invites viewers to evaluate along with the judges the degree of cohesion achieved by the cupcakes and feminized labor, and then by potentially patronizing the bakers' businesses as literal cupcake consumers.

Entrepreneurial Sisterhood

Programs like *Cupcake Wars* encourage viewers to enjoy observing how well each contestant innovates and conforms to the changing demands of the marketplace, thus striving to achieve a successful, hegemonic feminized identity. While a winning baker is intimately linked to her cupcakes and her ability to bind work and family together, these sweet treats enable other instances of connections. On programs like *DC Cupcakes* and *2 Broke Girls*, two women team up and become baking entrepreneurs in the urban spaces of Washington D.C. and New York City. Like cupcake consumers Carrie and Miranda, these "sisterhoods" in the city offer a glimpse of feminist ideals, while simultaneously containing those ideals in the safe confines of a traditionally straight, white, middle-class, feminine body. Creative productivity not only perpetuates neoliberal ideals of individual self-sufficiency, but also structures depictions of sisterly bonds and mutual collaboration. Different popular narrative forms offer viewers pleasurable depictions of cupcake careers grounded in feminine cooperation. Rather than merely subjecting women to the postfeminist juggling act, the cupcake stores depicted on TV and film also invite viewers to relish a utopian professional environment where such a boundary does not exist, where distinctions between home/work, sister/colleague are collapsed.

DC Cupcakes presents a world in which women achieve success and can "have it all" when they form bonds between individuals (both between cupcakes and between women). Katherine and Sophie's femininity is constructed not only by their creative labors but also their sisterly relationship, a relationship that participates in the show's larger discourse about "connections." Sisterhood was a rallying cry in second-wave feminism, and as Joanne Hollows summarizes, this concept represented the "common experience of oppression."[29] While Katherine and Sophie may bicker over the details of their cupcake sculptures or who makes the best Halloween cupcake, these are playful encounters; *DC Cupcakes* depicts an image of united sisterhood. As Sophie and Katherine tell a group of girl scouts, "When we were growing up we loved baking and always said we were going to own a bakery together.... When starting your own business, it's not going to be easy, but the one thing that kept us going was that we were sisters and we were in it together and we really wanted to make it work." Girlhood dreams find adult success through the integrating language of "we" as sisterhood is represented as a seamless unit found by rejecting corporate pressures.

Sameness drives both the depiction of sisterhood and *DC Cupcakes'* predictable half-hour narrative structure. The pleasures this reality TV program offers are grounded in an image of sisterhood as reliable and that can be easily achieved by the end of the thirty-minute program. The narrative takes the disparate parts of the catering job—cupcake, the shape of the sculpture, and the sisters' dynamic—and by the end of the episode renders them coherent in a tidy narrative conclusion when the sisters reveal their finished sculpture. In this way, cupcakes catalyze a homogenous fantasy of successful feminine teamwork as bound to a "family" business for viewers' pleasurable visual consumption. Cupcakes are ideal products to generate such success; as small items that can be easily eaten and transported they signify and mobilize the sisters' seamless movement between spaces and identities. The reassuring image of feminine entrepreneurialism is safely contained within this depiction of sisterhood in which no tensions exist between home and work. This brand of sisterhood is distinctly postfeminist; the relatively conflict-free depiction of feminine entrepreneurialism ignores any structural impediments to women's success in business and renders the need for continued critique of gender inequalities unnecessary through its depiction of seamless unity.

While the second-wave call for sisterhood challenged patriarchal domination, second-wave feminists have been critiqued as assuming a notion of "sisterhood" that was white and middle-class, excluding women of color and the working classes and reproducing a biological explanation for gender difference.[30] Other depictions of cupcake-facilitated sisterhood have exposed cracks in homogeneous depictions of feminine unity, and they begin to illustrate how differences *within* sisterhood can strengthen, not undermine, feminist politics in the early twenty-first century. The sitcom *2 Broke Girls* depicts two young women, Max (Kat Denning) and Caroline (Beth Behr), striving to make it on their own by opening a cupcake business. Blonde Caroline was born and raised in Manhattan, received an Ivy League education, and is the daughter of a megarich father. The series begins with Caroline's father convicted for running a Ponzi scheme, and Caroline is rendered penniless. She gets a job at a diner in Brooklyn and meets Max, a sarcastic, buxom, brunette waitress. The two women join forces as roommates, waitresses, and aspiring cupcake entrepreneurs. As is seen on *DC Cupcakes*, the distinctly mobile qualities of a cupcake help this program blur distinctions between home/work, sister/colleague: The first season depicts the roommates baking cupcakes in their apartment to be sold at the diner, effectively vacillating between domestic and workplace environments and identities. From its first season, *2 Broke Girls* was a network hit, and the popularity of the sitcom has partly been attributed to the two lead actors; critics praised these "heroines who are pills and are a pleasure to watch."[31] The sitcom is in the tradition of a recent cycle of female friendship narratives like *Sex and the City*, *Baby Mama* (2008), and *Bride Wars* (2009), which Allison Winch argues place women's friendships at the center of the plot.[32]

Caroline and Max find friendship in a sisterhood that stands in opposition to a world ruled by men. Episodes frequently begin with Caroline and Max arguing with unreasonable, sexist, or demanding customers; for example, Max chides a steampunk customer, "What are you, in the league of extraordinarily pretentious gentlemen?" The show frequently offers Max such moments of comedic social commentary, and such jokes allow the audience to participate in the "girls'" critiques of gendered and economic power, providing present pleasures as viewers wait for Max and Caroline to be free to quit this job in which they are always serving others. Cupcakes mobilize their solidarity and become the dream that promises to create liberated sisterhood; as Caroline says to Max in the premiere episode: "You, cupcakes; me, business background; us, success. What do you think?" This premiere episode launches the series on the premise that if women pool their distinct resources they can achieve entrepreneurial success. Caroline and Max's disagreements drive many of the plots and are the cause of many of the show's comedic situations, as they argue about how to bake kosher cupcakes and the utility of coupons. Each episode concludes with a compromise, though, offering viewers a pleasurable conclusion that appreciates both Max's and Caroline's perspectives.

Brunette and blonde, working-class and upper-class, curvy and thin, sarcastic and cheerful, the two women on *2 Broke Girls* find solidarity in friendship that celebrates their physical and class differences. Caroline teaches Max about luxury spring breaks; Max teaches Caroline how to make fast cash by participating in a drug trial. In the first season finale, they crash the Metropolitan Museum of Art Gala in order to meet Martha Stewart. The episode is structured as a fairy tale in which their friend becomes their fairy godmother and they ride to the Gala on Caroline's horse. In keeping with their characters, the two women consistently solve each other's problems; for example, they are denied entry to the party because of residual bitterness about the crimes committed by Caroline's father on Gala attendees, but Max had been a waitress at the event the previous year and leads them to the service entrance. They change out of their couture and into uniforms, sneak in, and then rush to the bathroom to change into their dresses. There, they encounter Martha Stewart, who admires their "entrepreneurial drive" and agrees to taste the cupcake Caroline smuggled into the Met in her cupcake-shaped Judith Lieber purse (see Figure 13.3). The episode offers viewers the satisfaction of a conclusion in which Caroline and Max become each other's fairy tale princess, supporting each other with skills acquired from their working-class and upper-class experiences.

While 2 Broke Girls follows sitcom form by offering neat resolution at the end of the half hour, a single idea continues to drive the plot forward into the next episode: the promise of the cupcake shop. Each episode of 2 Broke Girls concludes with a black screen on which appears the total dollar amount Max and Caroline earned by the end of the episode. The dollars may increase, decrease, or even stay the same depending upon the action in that episode. Their cupcake earnings create continuity across the seasons and invite viewers to move beyond the current episode and look forward to the next one. This dollar sign reflects their success as sister-entrepreneurs and reveals how cupcakes act like a "happy object." As Sarah Ahmed explains, "Happiness [is] a specific kind of intentionality, which I would describe as 'end oriented.' It is not just that we can be happy *about* something, as a feeling in the present, but some things become happy *for us* if we imagine they will bring happiness *to us*."[33] Happy objects acquire their value over time through social circulation and affect us by orienting us in the direction of happiness not yet realized.

Cupcakes promise women that happiness and the good life are possible but are currently out of reach. The cupcake business transforms 2 Broke Girls from an episodic program into an open-ended series that is secured by the dollar signs at the end of each episode; this invites audiences to return next week to

FIGURE 13.3.
Caroline and Max
show off their cupcake
to their idol, Martha
Stewart. *2 Broke
Girls*, "And Martha
Stewart Have a Ball,"
Part II, season 1,
episode 24, CBS.

see if "the girls" will reach their financial goals and, by extension, achieve happiness. Viewers' pleasure is sutured to Max and Caroline's cupcake aspirations as the serial plot structure offers only partial satisfaction as the "true conclusion" resides in the serial's endlessly receding future. Similarly, in *Bridesmaids*, Annie's deep unhappiness structures the comedy and the film's happy resolution. Her failed bakery is repeatedly referred to as the cause for both the demise of her last relationship and her current financial woes, and her discontent is exacerbated when her best friend Lillian (Maya Rudolph) gets engaged. Annie's sense of self is disturbed until she resolves to start baking again. This return to herself enables her to regain her confidence, stand in solidarity with her fellow bridesmaids, and fearlessly embrace Rhodes, her love interest. In other words, baking brings Annie happiness by reorienting her in the direction of hegemonic sisterhood and heteronormative relationships.

While cupcake culture promises women happiness by facilitating friendships that allow for some class and physical differences, it fundamentally affirms the current status quo. Pleasurable depictions of utopian sisterhood forged in cupcake businesses are predicated on reproducing ideals of straight white femininity. Martha Stewart's elite lifestyle culture is the future promised on *2 Broke Girls*, and it is a future in which the two women will be free from the racially marked world of Brooklyn. Their feminized business and friendship stand in opposition to an urban landscape dominated by men, elite taste cultures, and people of color. Cupcakes offer Caroline and Max happiness by securing white femininity as upwardly mobile, releasing them from the diner operated by men who are marked by racial and ethnic difference. The diner is owned by Han Lee, who is the butt of many jokes about his diminutive height; chef Oleg has a thick eastern European accent and apparently insatiable sexual appetite; and the cashier Earl is an older African American man who embodies suave coolness. These men are defined by their ethnic and racial identities, and while it could be argued that the sitcom uses comedy to call attention to stereotypes, the narrative of the series undermines such an argument, since the goal of the show's heroines is to use their cupcake business to liberate themselves from the diner and the people it contains.

Surprising Cupcake Connections

As early-twenty-first-century cupcake culture circulates stories about the promises of creative, entrepreneurial, sisterly labor we find moments of progressive pleasure as well as of troubling politics. Mainstream narratives about cupcakes have offered an image of sisterhood that celebrates bonds between women while maintaining the white, upwardly mobile, heteronormative status quo. There remain moments, however, in which the hegemonic restraints placed on sisterhood are resisted. For example, rather than neutralizing feminist politics in a nostalgic view of domesticity, blogs like *Cupcake Rehab* demonstrate how domestic labors offer pleasures that generate "sisterhood" through maternal lineage. Marilla Delnick explains how her mother's breast cancer diagnosis in 2006 inspired her to cook, bake, and begin blogging.[34] Here, cupcake production celebrates rather than denigrates the past, rejecting the postfeminist rhetoric that distances itself from feminist politics by rendering generational history no longer relevant to feminine identities. The premiere episode of *Girls* (HBO) also shows how cupcakes can facilitate meaningful connections between women. The main character Hannah (Lena Dunham) consumes a cupcake for breakfast while taking a bath as her roommate/best friend Marnie (Allison Williams) perches on the edge of the tub, shaving her legs and complaining about her dull relationship and how her picture-perfect boyfriend has become so familiar he has begun to feel like "a weird uncle." These women are positioned strangely, as the cupcake is displaced from its correct time and place and heterosexual relationships become incestuous. While *Girls* has been (rightly) critiqued for its focus on the trials of privileged white women, this scene reveals the show's ability to also invite audiences to enjoy depictions of friendship forged through surprising, critical, indulgent moments.[35] Such depictions of cupcake production and consumption speak to a continued need and desire for feminine connections that can reveal the cracks in the moral order.

In the early twenty-first century, women remain challenged by the demand to "have it all" and opportunities for creativity, connections, and surprise seem all too rare. By embodying consumer pleasures in the form of creative variations and through sisterly connections, cupcakes promise temporary release from postfeminist ideals that hold women to unreasonable expectations of seamlessly balancing home, work, and self. Strange representations of feminized objects like cupcakes can encourage viewers to consider what connections may be made and what connections are yet to be created. In the final episode of the self-referential sitcom *30 Rock* (NBC), the writers of a variety TV show enjoy a last lunch on the network dime before their program is canceled. Head writer Liz Lemon (Tina Fey) grabs a cupcake off the table, rips the bottom off the cupcake and flattens it on top of the frosting. With relish, and to the cheers of her writers, she takes a bite from her "cupcake sandwich" (see Figure 13.4). This reconfigured treat enables Lemon to enjoy every component (cake and frosting) all at once, effectively generating her own version of "having it all."

FIGURE 13.4. Liz Lemon relishes biting into her cupcake sandwich. *30 Rock,* "Last Lunch," season 7, episode 12, NBC.

The scene invites viewers to relish such moments of transformation in which women like Lemon resist conforming to normative, proper cupcake consumption and instead celebrate creative, delicious pleasures.

Notes

1. Michele Lazar, "Entitled to Consume: Postfeminist Femininity and a Culture of Post-Critique," *Discourse and Communication* 3, no. 4 (2009): 391.

2. Angela McRobbie, *The Aftermath of Feminism: Gender, Culture and Social Change* (London: Sage Publications, 2009), 5.

3. Jane Black, "Sweet Victory; It Took 8 Weeks, 141 Varieties and Extra Gym Time, but We Found the Best Cupcake in Town," *Washington Post,* Nov. 5, 2008.

4. Carolyn Davis, "Coping, with Cupcakes; They're Comfort in Fluted Liners, a Little Luxury with Fluff on Top. They're More than Fun—They're an Industry," *Philadelphia Inquirer,* Sept. 17, 2009.

5. Marci Alboher, "When the Entrepreneur Has 2 Faces," *New York Times,* May 7, 2007.

6. "Advertising Advice, Revenue Prediction and Other Sweet Stuff," *Washington Post,* Dec. 3, 2012.

7. Nicole Carter, "He's Got a Macho Mix. Cupcake Baker Gives Guys with a Sweet Tooth Their Just Desserts," *New York Daily News,* Feb. 28, 2010.

8. J. Freedom du Lac, "Swooning for the Sugar: Tourists Might Skip the Monuments, but Miss the Cupcake Queue? No Way," *Washington Post,* Aug. 16, 2010.

9. Ibid.

10. Jennifer Goldstein, "Beauty Snoop the Muse Next Door," *Marie Claire,* June 2013, 196.

11. Emily Schuman, "About—*Cupcakes and Cashmere,*" *Cupcakes and Cashmere,* accessed July 27, 2013, http://cupcakesandcashmere.com/about.

12. Rosalind Gill, "Postfeminist Media Culture: Elements of a Sensibility," *European Journal of Cultural Studies* 10, no. 2 (2007): 153.

13. Tanya Gold, "Is Anybody Safe from World War Twee?; Cupcakes, Floral Prints, 'Mad Men,' Bunny Girls . . . What Is It with the Fifties, Wonders Tanya Gold," *Daily Telegraph*, June 24, 2011.

14. See Elspeth Probyn, "New Traditionalism and Post-Feminism: TV Does the Home," *Feminist Television Criticism*, eds. Charlotte Brunsdon, Julie D'Acci, and Lynn Spigel (Oxford: Oxford University Press, 1997), 126–138. Diane Negra, *What a Girl Wants? Fantasizing the Reclamation of Self in Postfeminism* (New York: Routledge, 2009).

15. "A Cultural Return to Femininity and Domesticity: Hope for Western Civilization: Real Clear Religion," *Real Clear Religion: Culture, Christianity, Catholic Dogma and the Death of the West*, Aug. 24, 2008, accessed May 30, 2013, http://www.realclearreligion .com/index_files/71d72dbea66316688ef9d429b1e2c18b-454.php.

16. For a cultural history of the color pink, see Lynn Peril, *Pink Think: Becoming a Woman in Many Uneasy Lessons* (New York: W. W. Norton and Company Inc., 2002).

17. Elizabeth Nathanson, *Television and Postfeminist Housekeeping: No Time for Mother* (New York: Routledge, 2013).

18. Negra, *What a Girl Wants?*, 50.

19. Anne-Marie Slaughter, "Why Women Still Can't Have It All," *Atlantic*, June 13, 2012. Sheryl Sandberg, *Lean In: Women, Work and the Will to Lead* (New York: Knopf, 2013).

20. "About/Cupcake Project," *The Cupcake Project*, accessed Nov. 8, 2013, http://www .cupcakeproject.com/about.

21. U.S. Department of Commerce Economics and Statistics Administration for the White House Council on Women and Girls, *Women-Owned Businesses in the 21st Century* (Oct. 2010), 1. http://www.esa.doc.gov/sites/default/files/reports/documents/women -owned-businesses.pdf.

22. Attila Bruni, Silvia Gherardi, and Barbara Poggio, "Doing Gender, Doing Entrepreneurship: An Ethnographic Account of Intertwined Practices," *Gender, Work and Organization* 11, no. 4 (July 2004): 423.

23. Patricia Lewis, "The Search for an Authentic Entrepreneurial Identity: Difference and Professionalism among Women Business Owners," *Gender, Work and Organization* 20, no. 3 (May 2013): 254.

24. Anita Harris, *Future Girl: Young Women in the Twenty-First Century* (New York: Routledge, 2004).

25. Ann Gray, "Enterprising Femininity: New Mode of Work and Subjectivity," *European Journal of Cultural Studies* 6, no. 4 (2005): 503.

26. Dan Beyers, "It Turns Out the Best Business Plan Might Be to Not Have a Business Plan," *Washington Post*, May 28, 2012.

27. Harris, *Future Girl*.

28. Banet-Weiser writes: "Young women's self-presentation online is a contradictory practice, one that does not demonstrate an unfettered freedom in crafting identity any more than it is completely controlled and determined by the media and cultural industries." Sarah Banet-Weiser, *Authentic: The Politics of Ambivalence in a Brand Culture* (New York: New York University Press, 2012), 62.

29. Joanne Hollows, *Feminism, Femininity and Popular Culture* (Manchester, U.K.: University of Manchester Press, 2000), 5.

30. Ibid., 6–7.

31. Alessandra Stanley, "New Crop of Sitcom Women Can Dish It like the Big Boys," *New York Times*, Sept. 18, 2011.

32. Allison Winch, "We Can Have It All: The Girlfriend Flick," *Feminist Media Studies* 12, no. 1 (2012).

33. Sarah Ahmed, *The Promise of Happiness* (Durham, N.C.: Duke University Press, 2010), 26.

34. "Cupcake Rehab est. 2007," *Cupcake Rehab*, accessed Nov. 19, 2013, http://cupcakerehab .com/about-me/.

35. See, for example, Anna Holmes, "Race in Lena Dunham's *Girls*," *New Yorker*, April 23, 2012.

Contributors

JILLIAN BÁEZ is assistant professor of media culture at the College of Staten Island–CUNY. Specializing in Latina/o media, audience studies, and transnational feminisms, Báez has published her research in *Critical Studies in Media Communication, Women's Studies Quarterly, Journal of Popular Communication, Centro: Journal of the Center for Puerto Rican Studies,* and several anthologies. Báez is currently writing a book on contemporary Latina audiences' engagement with images of the Latina body in film, television, and advertising.

MELISSA A. CLICK is assistant professor of communication at the University of Missouri. She is the coeditor of *Bitten by Twilight* (Peter Lang, 2010). Her work has been published in NYU Press's *Fandom* and in *Popular Communication, Popular Music and Society, Women's Studies in Communication, Transformative Works and Cultures,* and *Environmental Communication.*

SUZANNE FERRISS is professor of English at Nova Southeastern University. She is the coeditor of two volumes on the cultural study of fashion—*On Fashion* (1994) and *Footnotes: On Shoes* (2001)—as well as two companion volumes on contemporary "chick culture": *Chick Lit: The New Woman's Fiction* (Routledge, 2006) and *Chick Flicks: Contemporary Women at the Movies* (Routledge, 2008). Her work on fashion and cultural studies has led her into the emerging area of motorcycle studies.

With Steven Alford, she is the author of the book, *Motorcycle* (Reaktion Books, 2008). She also edits the *International Journal of Motorcycle Studies*.

KYRA HUNTING is assistant professor of media arts and studies at the University of Kentucky. Her research focuses on the intersection of entertainment media and ideologies of cultural marginality and difference, particularly in relationship to feminist theory, queer theory, and the study of religion and media. Her current research focuses on identity and new media spaces, particularly in relationship to fan activity, video games, and transmedia textuality. Her work has appeared in *Communication Review, Quarterly Review of Film and Video, Spectator, Transformative Works and Cultures*, and *Journal of Popular Culture*.

SUZANNE LEONARD is associate professor of English at Simmons College, the author of *Fatal Attraction* (Wiley-Blackwell, 2009) and coeditor of *Fifty Hollywood Directors* (Routledge, 2015). Her specialties include feminist media studies, American film and television studies, and contemporary women's literature, and her articles have appeared in *Signs, Feminist Media Studies, Genders*, and *Women's Studies Quarterly*, as well as in various anthologies.

ALICE LEPPERT is assistant professor of media and communication studies and film studies at Ursinus College. She received her PhD from the University of Minnesota, and her work has appeared in *Cinema Journal, Celebrity Studies, Genders*, and *In Media Res*.

ELANA LEVINE is associate professor in the Department of Journalism, Advertising, and Media Studies at the University of Wisconsin-Milwaukee. She is the author of *Wallowing in Sex: The New Sexual Culture of 1970s American Television* (Duke University Press, 2007), coauthor (with Michael Z. Newman) *of Legitimating Television: Media Convergence and Cultural Status* (Routledge, 2012), and coeditor (with Lisa Parks) of *Undead TV: Essays on* Buffy the Vampire Slayer (Duke University Press, 2007).

BARBARA L. LEY is associate professor in the Departments of Communication and Women and Gender studies at the University of Delaware. She teaches and researches digital technology in the context of gender and culture, health promotion, social advocacy, and citizen science. She is the author *of From Pink to Green: Disease Prevention and the Environmental Breast Cancer Movement* (Rutgers University Press, 2009), and her articles have appeared in journals such as *Journal of*

Computer-Mediated Communication, Science Communication, Public Understanding of Science, and *Medical Anthropology.*

ERIN A. MEYERS is assistant professor in the Communication and Journalism Department at Oakland University. She holds a master's in Women's Studies with a focus on gender representation in popular media from The Ohio State University and a PhD in communication from the University of Massachusetts, Amherst. She has published articles on the intersections of celebrity, new media, and audience cultures in *Celebrity Studies, New Media and Society,* and *Flow.* Her book exploring the rise of celebrity gossip blogs, *Dishing Dirt in the Digital Age: Celebrity Gossip Blogs and Participatory Media Culture,* was published by Peter Lang in 2013.

ELIZABETH NATHANSON is assistant professor of media and communication at Muhlenberg College. Her research examines depictions of femininity and domesticity and definitions of postfeminism in contemporary American popular culture. She is the author of *Television and Postfeminist Housekeeping: No Time for Mother* (Routledge, 2013), and her work has also appeared in *Television and New Media* and *Framework.* Her chapter, "Dressed for Economic Distress: Blogging and the 'New' Pleasures of Fashion," appears in *Gendering the Recession* (eds. Diane Negra and Yvonne Tasker, Duke University Press, 2014).

DIANE NEGRA is professor of film studies and screen culture and head of film studies at University College Dublin. She is the author, editor, or coeditor of eight books, the most recent of which is *Gendering the Recession* (coedited with Yvonne Tasker, Duke University Press, 2014).

BERETTA E. SMITH-SHOMADE is associate professor and chair of the Department of Communication at Tulane University. She is the author of *Shaded Lives: African-American Women and Television* (Rutgers University Press, 2002), *Pimpin' Ain't Easy: Selling Black Entertainment Television* (Routledge, 2007), and most recently, editor of *Watching while Black: Centering the Television of Black Audiences* (Rutgers University Press, 2013). Her research and teaching revolve around television mediation, representation, and industry as well as K–12 media literacy.

KRISTEN J. WARNER is assistant professor in the Department of Telecommunication and Film at the University of Alabama. Her work primarily focuses on production cultures of casting as it relates to race and representation within the Hollywood film and television industry. She has a chapter in *Watching while Black:*

271

Centering the Television of Black Audiences, edited by Beretta E. Smith-Shomade (Rutgers University Press, 2012), and is currently working on a book manuscript about color-blind casting in prime-time network television.

MICHELE WHITE is an associate professor in the Department of Communication at Tulane University. She has published *Buy It Now: Lessons from eBay* (Duke University Press, 2012) and *The Body and the Screen: Theories of Internet Spectatorship* (MIT Press, 2006). *Producing Women: The Internet, Traditional Femininity, Queerness, and Creativity* is forthcoming from Routledge in 2015. Her recent articles on femininity and women's cultures include "Concerns about Being Visible and Expressions of Pleasure: Women's Internet Wedding Forum Considerations of Boudoir Photography Sessions," *Interstitial: A Journal of Modern Culture and Events* 1, 1 (2013) and "Dirty Brides and Internet Settings: The Affective Pleasures and Troubles with Trash the Dress Photography Sessions," *South Atlantic Quarterly* 110, 3 (Summer 2011).

JULIE WILSON is assistant professor of media studies in the Department of Communication Arts and Theatre at Allegheny College in Meadville, Pennsylvania. Wilson's previous work on celebrity and gender has appeared in *Television and New Media, Cultural Studies, Celebrity Studies, Velvet Light Trap,* and *Genders.* Her present research focuses on identity politics in digital media culture, and she is currently working on a book project with Emily Yochim that investigates how digital media is transforming motherhood and women's work.

EMILY CHIVERS YOCHIM is assistant professor in the Department of Communication Arts and Theatre at Allegheny College in Pennsylvania. Yochim's work explores identity at the intersections of media and everyday life. Her first book, *Skate Life: Reimagining White Masculinity* (University of Michigan Press, 2009), is an ethnography that investigates how skateboarders both refigure white masculinity and maintain its power in the practice and portrayal of skateboarding. *Skate Life* won the National Communication Association's Bonnie Ritter Book Award in Feminist/Women Studies in Communication in 2010. Yochim's current book project, with Julie Wilson, explores motherhood and digital media. In between writing and teaching, Yochim is the mother to three young boys, who have taught her much about both masculinity and motherhood.

Index

FEMINIST MEDIA STUDIES